TURN TO GOD
REJOICE IN HOPE

Orthodox Reflections On the Way to Harare

TURN TO GOD
REJOICE IN HOPE

Orthodox Reflections On the Way to Harare

The report of the WCC Orthodox
Pre-Assembly Meeting
and selected resource materials

Edited by Thomas FitzGerald and Peter Bouteneff

World Council of Churches, Geneva
Orthodox Task Force

Layout by Sophie Belopopsky
Cover design by Marie Arnaud Snakkers, from an Ethiopian Cross created by Zoe Hellene

ISBN 2-8254-1278-3

Printed in August 1998 by the Orthdruk Orthodox Printing House, Bialystok, Poland

Contents

Preface

The Orthodox Pre-Assembly meeting was held at St Ephrem Theological Seminary, Ma'arat Saydnaya, near Damascus, Syria 7-13 May 1998. The purpose of this meeting was to reflect upon issues related to the Eighth Assembly of the World Council of Churches which will be held in Harare, Zimbabwe 3-14 December 1998, and upon its theme, Turn to God – Rejoice in Hope.

At the invitation of the WCC, all twenty-one Eastern Orthodox and Oriental Orthodox member churches were asked to send two delegates to the meeting. Sixteen churches sent delegates; these were joined by three Orthodox consultants. All the delegates and the consultants will be among the Orthodox participants in the Harare Assembly.

Our meeting took place during the joyous Paschal season, a time when we celebrate in a special way the Resurrection of Our Lord Jesus Christ. During this period, we recall in our liturgical services the effect of the Resurrection on the lives of many of Christ's followers such as the Apostle Thomas and the Myrrbearing Women. As Bishop Serapion reminded us during his homily, the turning point in the life of the disciples came with their profound discovery of *who Christ is*. After the Resurrection, this group of weak and divided followers came to discover Christ as more that a teacher and wonderworker. They came to know Christ as God and Savior. This was their Turn to God. This was their Rejoicing and their Hope.

Our meeting was hosted by His Holiness Patriarch Ignatius Zakka I Iwas of the Syrian Orthodox Patriarchate of Antioch. The participants benefited greatly from his fatherly care and generous hospitality. His Holiness personally welcomed the participants at the opening prayer service and was available throughout the meeting. His vibrant spirituality, pastoral sensitivity and valuable insights into church relations were greatly appreciated.

Our meeting provided the participants to experience the warm, brotherly relationship which exists between Patriarch Ignatius I Zakka Iwas and Patriarch Ignatuis IV Hazim of the Greek Orthodox Patriarchate of Antioch, as well as the relationship which exits between the two patriarchates. Through our contacts with the patriarchs, bishops, clergy and people, we came to experience firsthand the spirit of cooperation and reconciliation which exists among the two families of Orthodox Churches in this region.

His Beatitude Patriarch Ignatius IV Hazim also was present for the opening prayer service and addressed the gathering. The participants benefited from his thought-provoking contributions to our deliberations. We deeply appreciated his spiritual insights and theological observations which reflected his own rich experience. He also hosted a reception for the participants at his Patriarchate and at the Holy Cross Church in Damascus.

Our deliberations took place within the context of daily services of prayer. These services were conducted according to the various church traditions of the participants. Together with uniting us in the praise of God, these services provided us with the opportunity to experience the rich liturgical traditions of our Orthodox churches. We were especially blessed also to journey to the women's monastery of the Mother of God of Saydnaya. There, we joined the community for vespers and were later warmly received by the abbess and the nuns, who introduced us to their ministry and care for orphaned girls.

The Pre-Assembly meeting took place at a time when many Orthodox were reevaluating Orthodox participation in the World Council of Churches. This topic was discussed at the WCC Central Committee in September, 1997 and at its Executive Committee in February, 1998. Our meeting followed a meeting of representatives of Eastern Orthodox Churches in Thessaloniki, Greece 29 April-2 May 1998 which was called by Ecumenical Patriarch Bartholomew I. While reaffirming Orthodox participation in the ecumenical movement, the Thessaloniki meeting made a number of recommendations regarding Orthodox participation in the Harare Assembly. During the course of our week together, we were informed that the moderator of the WCC Central Committee, Catholicos Aram I of Cilicia, had written to the heads of all Eastern Orthodox and Oriental Orthodox Churches and made a number of proposals to intensify discussions within the Council with regard to Orthodox participation. Naturally, all of these developments had a bearing upon our deliberations.

The WCC Orthodox Task Force had the responsibility for organizing the Pre-Assembly meeting, and set its agenda in accordance with recommendations of the Orthodox members of the Central Committee. This agenda had two major items. Firstly, we reviewed the features of the upcoming Assembly and discussed the Assembly theme, Turn to God – Rejoice in Hope. In order to assist us in reflection on the Assembly theme, presentations were made by Metropolitan Aphrem Karim and Vladimir Shmaliy. Secondly, we reflected upon the broad issue of "Orthodox Participation in the Ecumenical Movement." A presentation was made by Fr. K.M. George. The prepared presentation by Fr. Leonid Kishkovsky was read on his behalf because of his absence due to illness.

The Report of the Pre-Assembly meeting reflects well the thoughtful deliberations which occurred during our time together. It provides a valuable reflection on the Assembly theme. It highlights Orthodox perspectives on the identity of the human person in relationship to God, to others and to the rest of the creation, and the significance of repentance and communion. It also relates these perspectives to the Church's liturgical tradition. The text declares: "The mother Church constantly calls her children to repent and correct their ways personally and in the structures they erect in the material and spiritual realms of life."

The Report also offers insights into some of the issues related to Orthodox participation in the WCC and the ecumenical movement generally. The delegates reaffirm "the importance of Orthodox commitment to and involvement in the quest for Christian reconciliation and visible unity." They declare that "this involvement is rooted in the salutary activity of our Lord and in the teachings of His Gospel." With regard to the coming Assembly, the delegates agree that the Orthodox churches should all be represented by delegates despite the difficulties which Orthodox have encountered. At the same time the delegates recognize that the structures of the Council require a change "which would enable a more effective presence and witness, together with a more constructive and engaged participation from the Orthodox."

A number of persons both in Geneva and in Damascus contributed to making this Pre-Assembly meeting a valuable one and a blessing for the participants. While we cannot mention them all here, we wish especially to express our gratitude to Metropolitan Gregorios Yohanna Ibrahim of Aleppo who oversaw all our local arrangements, assisted by Razek Syriani, Fahima Toro, and the staff and students of St Ephrem Seminary. Likewise, we were greatly assisted in Damascus by Bishop George Abu-Zacham and by Samer Laham.

Finally, we wish to express our appreciation to the other members of the Orthodox Staff Task Force, especially Dr Tarek Mitri, and to Beatrice Bengtsson and Renate Sbeghen who contributed much to the organization of the meeting.

In addition to the official report, the statement on "Orthodox Perspectives from Africa" and the presentations which were made at the meeting, we have also included in this volume a number of other important resource materials which deal with the relationship between the Orthodox Churches and the World Council of Churches in the period leading up to the Harare Assembly. It is hoped that these will be of use in understanding, in all its complexity, this critical time for ecumenism and the Orthodox churches, and thus in helping to prepare for the coming Assembly.

Fr Thomas FitzGerald, Dr. Theol., (Ecumenical Patriarchate)
Moderator, Orthodox Task Force
Peter Bouteneff, D. Phil. (Orthodox Church in America)
Secretary, Orthodox Task Force
Geneva, 6 July 1998

Orthodox Pre-Assembly Meeting

Final Statement of the Orthodox Pre-Assembly Meeting

Introduction

Christ is Risen!

We give thanks to God, Father, Son and Holy Spirit for the opportunity to come together in the Orthodox Pre-Assembly Meeting to prepare for the Eighth Assembly of the World Council of Churches.

At the invitation of the World Council of Churches, the Eastern Orthodox and Oriental Orthodox Churches sent representatives to this meeting, which also included a number of consultants and Orthodox staff members.

We met at the St Ephrem Theological Seminary in Saydnadya near Damascus, Syria, at the gracious invitation of His Holiness Ignatius Zakka I Iwas of the Syrian Orthodox Church of Antioch and All the East. During our stay, we experienced the personal care and hospitality of His Holiness and the members of the Seminary staff who served under the guidance of Metropolitan Mar Gregorios Yohanna Ibrahim of Aleppo.

By convening our meeting in the St Ephrem Theological Seminary, we had the valuable opportunity to experience the brotherhood and common ministry which is shared between His Holiness Patriarch Ignatius Zakka I Iwas and His Beatitude Patriarch Ignatius IV Hazim of the Greek Orthodox Patriarchate.

We attest to their strong desire to restore full communion between the two families of Orthodox Churches and their desire to provide a united witness in this region of the world. We recognize their strong commitment to Christian unity and their willingness to cooperate with their Muslim neighbours for the well-being of the society.

We were very honoured that our meeting was opened with presentations by Patriarch Ignatius Zakka I Iwas and Patriarch Ignatius IV Hazim. In his welcoming address, Patriarch Ignatius Zakka I Iwas recalled the involvement of his Patriarchate in the ecumenical movement and especially in the World Council of Churches and also took note of his own participation in ecumenical theological dialogues, including his participation as an observer at the Second Vatican Council. He affirmed that ecumenical work is not new to his Church and stated that bringing the churches together and promoting cooperation among them in ecclesial and pastoral matters are vital for the continuation of the Christian witness and life".

In his own address, Patriarch Ignatius IV Hazim also affirmed the importance of the ecumenical movement and the World Council of Churches. In speaking about the Pre-Assembly meeting, the Patriarch said that he hoped that "we may arrive at a formula in which we can be with the World Council of Churches – I say *with* the World Council – very seriously and not just present a kind of re-reading of the past."

Our Pre-Assembly meeting took place at a time when many Orthodox are re-evaluating the ecumenical movement in general and the World Council of Churches in particular. His All Holiness Ecumenical Patriarch Bartholomew I convened a meeting of representatives of the fifteen Eastern Orthodox Churches in Thessaloniki, Greece. This meeting was held in response to the request from the Russian Orthodox Church and the Church of Serbia, and to the decision of the Church of Georgia to withdraw from the WCC. (The Church of Bulgaria has in the meantime also announced its intention to withdraw.) While affirming the involvement of the Eastern Orthodox Churches in the ecumenical movement, the Thessaloniki meeting made a number of recommendations to the churches regarding the Eighth Assembly of the WCC.

Through our discussions here in Damascus we were made aware of the fact that the relationship of the Orthodox to the World Council of Churches has become a matter of serious study. At the meeting of the Central Committee in September 1997, His Holiness Catholicos Aram I of the Armenian Apostolic Church of Cilicia, Moderator of the Central Committee, devoted a substantial portion of his report to the issue of Orthodox involvement in the Council. This led to a commitment by the Central Committee and by the subsequent Executive Committee in February 1998 further to discuss Orthodox participation and concerns.

During the course of our meeting, we were also informed that Catholicos Aram I had written on 8 May 1998 to the heads of all the Eastern Orthodox and Oriental Orthodox Churches. In the light of the recent meeting in Thessaloniki, Catholicos Aram I made a number of proposals to intensify as quickly as possible the discussion within the Council of Orthodox participation. Among the proposals, he suggested the immediate establishment of the Mixed Theological Commission proposed by the Thessaloniki meeting, to consist of Orthodox representatives and other representatives from member churches of the WCC.

Our discussions and deliberations took place in a spirit of Christian love, fellowship and mutual understanding, guided by prayer. In our daily prayers we experienced the rich liturgical traditions of our churches. We had the opportunity to participate in the Divine Liturgy at the Church of the Holy Cross and in the chapel of St Ephrem Seminary. We were also blessed with the special opportunity to make a pilgrimage to the Women's Monastery of the Mother of God of Saydnaya. There we were also deeply moved by their ministry and care for young girls.

We gathered in a region rich in Christian history and witness. It is the region where the disciples were first called Christians (Acts 11:26). We always had before us the witness of St Peter and St Paul, of St Ignatius of Antioch, of St Thekla, of St Ephrem of Syria, of St John of Damascus, and many others. Together with them and the Most Holy Theotokos, we are united with the Risen Christ who dwells in our midst and calls us to share in the ministry of reconciliation.

Part I
Turn to God – Rejoice in Hope:
An Orthodox Approach to the Assembly Theme

Introduction

Turning to God is turning to the source of our being and life – the Triune mystery of the Father, the Son and the Holy Spirit. In joyful praise and thanksgiving, together with the whole creation, we affirm that we are created, sustained and redeemed by the infinite love of the Triune God. This is the ground of our hope for the future of our world and the well-being of all creation.

God's Image and Freedom

The Holy Scripture bears witness that created in God's own image, we are endowed with the divine gift of freedom. The Orthodox Tradition teaches us that this freedom is at the heart of humanity and is constitutive of the dignity of human persons everywhere and in every age.

It is, however, by the misuse of the same freedom that humanity turned to sin and alienated itself from the love of God. So turning to God means our return to the source of life in repentance and renewal of heart (Ps. 51:10). It is both an individual and corporate act, a process in which human persons and communities are called by God to enter freely and wholeheartedly throughout their life in the world.

Disease and Healing

The Orthodox tradition places a particular emphasis on the healing dimension of God's call to us to return to him. Our sins are like a disease that eventually leads us to death and corruption. So Jesus Christ, the Incarnate One, has come as the compassionate physician to heal us and restore the integrity of our distorted humanity. Unlike a judge who condemns the guilty to isolation and death, our heavenly physician washes our wounds, anoints us with the balm of the Spirit and leads us back to communion and life with the Triune God. It is this divine therapeutic model of salvation that the Orthodox Church evokes in all her teaching on repentance, conversion and return to God.

Sin is the turning away from God, the breaking of the ontologically vital communion with our Creator. It is indifference to God's goodness. It is missing the mark. The Church distinguishes sin from the sinner with great discernment. In identifying what constitutes sin, the Orthodox Church relies on the teachings of Christ and his apostles as revealed to us in the Holy Scripture and as interpreted by the Tradition. Sin of any kind, as the expression of evil and death, is not justified by the Church under any circumstance. But the sinner, as the sick person whom God never ceases to love, is taken care of with great compassion under the pastoral care and discipline of the Church, with a view to his healing and salvation.

Repentance and Communion

The patristic tradition never ceases to remind us of the scriptural witness of God's infinite compassion for us human beings. God's primordial call "Adam, where are you" is full of that tender love. Using the beautiful image of a mother hen that yearns to gather her chicks under her wings, Jesus reminds us of God's compassionate call to us to return to the Father. Orthodox spirituality is profoundly marked by the theme of *metanoia,* a complete turning around to God in faith, hope and love. Repentance in this sense is not a matter of some occasional feelings. The whole Christian life is conceived as a perpetual movement to God, the source of light and life.

Repentance is for restoring the broken communion between God and humanity, between human beings themselves and between humanity and the rest of God's creation. Every level is connected to the other. So any lack of communion at any level affects the whole.

The Orthodox Church never limits sin simply within the moral realm of an individual's conduct and inner spiritual life. While the Church pays particular attention to the inter-personal relationship of individuals ("loving one's brother who is seen", 1 Jn 4:20), she is equally concerned about the social and economic sins, sins generated by unjust human political structures, sins committed against the poor, the powerless, the little ones of this world and against the harmony of nature. So repentance is required personally and communally, politically and ecologically.

The mother Church constantly calls her children to repent and correct their ways personally and in the structures they erect in the material and spiritual realms of life. As the Apostle Paul teaches, the Church, the Bride of Christ, being constituted by God from among the peoples of this world, is to be presented as holy and glorious, without spot or wrinkle, before her Lord (Eph. 5:27). This is also the pilgrimage of the Church in history. The Church as the Body of Christ suffers in the world because of our sins, as Christ himself suffered on account of the sins of humanity.

As the living Body of Christ, the Church unites in her life the historical and eschatological realities, and as such is not to be identified with any merely human institution. Her calling is to follow Christ in his saving and self-emptying life for the sake of the world. As members of his Body we, as persons and communities, are to manifest this self-emptying and saving mission with utmost love, humility, repentance, and self-correction, but above all with the firm trust in the Holy Spirit of God who perfects everything that is and that is to come.

Growing into the Stature of Christ

The liturgical year of the Church follows the saving events in the incarnate life of Christ. In order to lead us to sanctification and divinization, the Church has laid down a plan for the whole year on the basis of these events. Thus repentance and rejoicing, renewal and restoration are linked to the sacramental life and the eucharistic communion of the Church. Thus the fifty days that precede the Feast of the Resurrection are a period of intense repentance. The Scripture readings and the prayers constantly exhort the faithful to seek justice, forgiveness and reconciliation in their life in the world so that they may genuinely rejoice in the paschal mystery of Christ. As the icon of the Kingdom of God, the Church, takes this period as a figure of her earthly existence and mission, not simply as a socio-political re-ordering of society to be accomplished on an ethical level, but as the gradual fulfilment of the eschatological Kingdom. The Church has to take along with her the whole creation to the resurrection experience of the new heaven and the new earth (Rev. 21). In this period of repentance and renewal, the image of God in us human beings is in the process of growing to the stature of Christ, the perfect image of the invisible God (Eph. 4:13; Col. 1:15).

The Christian "Jubilee"

It is in this context of growth, movement, renewal and transformation of our created world that the Orthodox look at the jubilee tradition of the Old Testament (Lev. 25:10). The Jubilee year, as described in the book of Leviticus, was an inspiring socio-economic utopia which was probably never literally realized in the history of the Jewish people. However, we know that in announcing the Kingdom of God, Christ evoked certain elements of the Jubilee tradition such as "the acceptable year of the Lord" (Lk. 4:19) and the forgiveness of debts (Mt. 6:12, Lk 7:42). Announcing the gospel to the poor, liberating the captives and healing the sick thus became the concrete signs of ushering in the Kingdom of God. The Christian Church developed a spirituality over the centuries in order to respond spiritually and materially to these signs of the Kingdom and to follow up their ethical and eschatological implications.

The patristic tradition, however, seldom appealed to the Old Testament jubilee tradition in their understanding of the Church's social mission. It appealed directly to the philanthropy of God as manifested in Jesus Christ, the Son of God and our Saviour for the healing, reconciling and saving of the world.

Repentance and renewal in freedom, love and hope became the hallmark of true Christian spirituality. No human person or institution is excluded from this process. Since all human institutional structures are liable to be corrupted by sin, the renewal of our lives is necessary for the continuing renewal of institutional structures, in preparation for the coming of the Kingdom.

Sunday and Pentecost

Easter Sunday and Pentecost, the day of the resurrection of Christ and the day of the coming of the Holy Spirit on the apostolic community, represent the foundational event of the Church. They corresponded only externally to the Jewish feasts of Sabbath and Jubilee. The weekly observance of Sabbath was replaced in the early Church by Sunday, the first day of the week, the day of the resurrection of Christ. Sunday was also called the eighth day since, as the symbol of the victory of life over death, it broke in a spiritual sense the ever-repeating cycle of the seven-day week. It thus liberated the whole creation from its subjection to the vicious circle of sin and death and initiated us to the domain of the Spirit. The Pentecost, coming on the fiftieth day (seven times seven weeks) after the resurrection, became the Great Sunday, the day of the indwelling of the Holy Spirit.

Announcing the Kingdom of God, as Jesus did, in the power of the Spirit, thus constitutes the core of Christian "jubilee". It is essentially the work of the Risen One and of the empowering Holy Spirit, the sanctifying and divinizing of the created order. We are called by God's grace to be participants in this mission. All Christian attitude to the created world and all Christian social action have their roots here.

Sunday of Joy and Hope

In today's secularized world Sunday has become a day for lazy rest or a holiday for the gratification of senses even in traditionally Christian societies. It has lost its capacity for spiritual refreshment because it has ceased to be a day of thanksgiving and joyful celebration of the resurrection of Christ. The emptying of Sunday of its spiritual content has made the weekly cycle to return to its monotony and boredom, signs of death in the secular civilization. Rediscovering the Sunday of resurrection as the weekly celebration of joy and hope is central to the Christian jubilee. Without paying sufficient attention to the radical newness of the resurrection experience and its continual spiritual appropriation in liturgy any attempt to revive the jubilee tradition of the Old Testament in our present world will remain only as a social project like any other. Contemporary political-economic ideologies that promise to create earthly paradise of justice and equality by ignoring the sacredness of time and space and the divine dignity of human persons have to be critically evaluated in the light of the "acceptable year of the Lord" announced by Christ.

Part II
Some Observations and Concerns

The Ecumenical Movement

The participants in the Pre-Assembly meeting reaffirmed the importance of Orthodox commitment to and involvement in the quest for Christian reconciliation and visible unity: we believe that this involvement is rooted in the salutary activity of our Lord and in the teachings of His Gospel. He is the one who has given us the ministry of reconciliation (2 Cor. 5:18). Faithful to her Lord, the Church has always sought to proclaim the apostolic faith and to reconcile those who are separated, for the sake of the salvation of all. Every form of division among Christians inhibits the preaching of the Gospel and weakens our witness in the world. Our tragic divisions often lead to divisions within the society. Our unity, on the other hand, strengthens the mission of all those who wish to heal and reconcile in the name of our Lord.

In order to be faithful to the Gospel and to serve the process of authentic reconciliation, Orthodox in some places have had to reassess their involvement in the ecumenical movement. There may be any number of reasons for this. In some places, the Orthodox have become the victims of proselytism. In other places, some ecumenical activities no longer have as their goal the restoration of Christian unity. In other places, Orthodox are deeply troubled by the crisis in values and the moral stances taken by certain Christian groups. To one degree or another, these and similar concerns have contributed to the erosion of the relationships between Orthodox and other Christians.

Because of our commitment to our Lord and the Gospel, we are deeply troubled by these developments, especially as we prepare for the Eighth Assembly of the World Council of Churches.

Participation in the Eighth Assembly

We agreed that the Orthodox churches should all be represented by delegates at the Eight Assembly. Different opinions were heard on the degree of their participation. One opinion was that delegates should attend but as a rule not vote. (Among these, some felt that delegates should vote by abstention only.) Another emphasized the necessity to send delegates with a full mandate to vote. We would like to draw the attention of our churches and of the Mixed Commission to these different opinions.

The WCC and the Process of Change

We appreciate the CUV process as reflecting a careful and painstaking look at the WCC and the ecumenical movement. We have taken note of the proposed constitutional change wherein it is no longer "the Council" calling the churches, but the churches calling one another, through the Council, to unity.

Orthodox Churches have affirmed the WCC since its birth in 1948, and join in celebrating its fiftieth anniversary this year. At the same time, as the CUV process has shown, anniversaries are an opportunity for reflection and reconsideration. We have witnessed again during this meeting fundamental questions being raised with regard to Orthodox participation in the WCC at all levels of its life. These questions are aimed both at ourselves and at the structure of the Council. We affirm the need for change which would enable a more effective presence and witness, together with a more constructive and engaged participation from the Orthodox. In the desire to offer ways forward reference was made to several models, which had in common two broad areas of concern which we would commend to the Mixed Commission for their reflection.

Participation
While numbers and majorities are not the most important factor in participation, they do have a significant bearing in the setting of priorities in the WCC. There is a perception that the fellowship between Orthodox and Protestants in the Council is weakening, and that the Orthodox are finding it more difficult to make a contribution to the Council's agenda. These two inter related problems need to be taken into account in the consideration of all areas of the Council's life, from the staff to the governing bodies and their committees.

Ecclesiology
The CUV policy statement underlined that the WCC as a fellowship of churches poses to its member churches an "ecclesiological challenge", namely to clarify the meaning and the extent of the fellowship member churches experienced in the Council (3.4). Furthermore, the CUV statement strongly confirmed the relationships and the need for further partnership with churches outside WCC membership (4.11-12). Structural changes, tentatively proposed by representatives of some churches, could help the WCC and Orthodox churches to overcome any ecclesiological ambiguities and enable larger participation.

The above concerns were offered with the hopes that Orthodox witness and participation can be improved *qualitatively*, and also that more non-Orthodox churches which are not at present members of the WCC will be able to engage as fully as possible.

Common Prayer
In the history of the modern ecumenical movement, Orthodox Christians have joined in prayer services with non-Orthodox on the basis that our prayer is for the sake of Christian unity, and that we are praying to the same Triune God. Yet the issue of common prayer has increasingly become a topic of discussion.

We take note of the absence in the Eighth Assembly programme of an official "Assembly Eucharist" and that local parishes of different communions will host eucharistic celebrations. This is an accurate reflection of the reality of the ecumenical situation today, in which there are a variety of approaches to the issue of eucharistic communion.

Non-eucharistic common prayer, however, has also become an increasing area of tension in Orthodox discussion. Two *pastoral* factors make common prayer more difficult now than ever before: the increased tension within our churches on this issue, and the changing character of what we experience as "ecumenical worship" in recent years and assemblies. In ecumenical worship services, there is a marked decrease in the sensitivity to the different traditions, their liturgical sensibilities and liturgical ethos.

Christian Morality

As Christians we are concerned with many issues in the moral sphere. We also recognize that on many such issues Christians have not been able to come to a common mind. The WCC can be a useful forum to this end. We recognize for example the need for reflection and study on questions pertaining to marriage and family life, which would include topics such as abortion, human sexuality, drugs and urban crime.

Many of these issues, perhaps in particular those concerning sexual orientation and abortion, are particularly contentious. The treatment of such issues under the banner of "human rights" has both positive and negative potential: on the one hand, it would affirm our common calling to treat all human persons with love and respect in view of their being created in the image of God. On the other hand, we would not want to be prevented, on the basis of "human rights", from stating that certain lifestyles and practices are not God-ordained.

Conclusion

Our Pre-Assembly meeting took place within the context of these significant developments in our churches, the ecumenical movement, and the WCC. Many of the issues and concerns, which have been raised by the Orthodox in recent years, were brought to bear upon our discussions of the Assembly, the Assembly theme, and the role of the Orthodox in the ecumenical movement.

We pray that common Christian reflection on these issues not further divide us, and we encourage the Mixed Commission to take up these issues in order to consider ways of approaching them in the future.

Christ is Risen!

To Him be glory, honour and worship together with the eternal Father and the life-giving Spirit, now and forever and unto the ages of ages. Amen.

This report was received unanimously by the members of the Pre-Assembly Meeting, with some reservations on the part of the delegate from the Russian Orthodox Church.

Address of His Holiness Ignatius Zakka I Iwas
Syrian Orthodox Patriarch of Antioch and All the East

Your Beatitude Ignatius IV, Rum Orthodox Patriarch of Antioch and All the East, Your Eminences, Archbishops and Bishops, Reverend Fathers, Ladies and Gentlemen,

It is my pleasure to greet you in the name of our Lord Jesus Christ and to warmly welcome all of you to our St Ephrem's Theological Seminary, the Patriarchal Foundation in Maarat Saydnaya, Damascus. You have come from different countries, cultures and backgrounds representing the two Families of the Orthodox Church of God.

You are here to prepare for the Eighth Assembly of the World Council of Churches which will be held in Harare, Zimbabwe, in December of this year, whose theme is "Turn to God – Rejoice in Hope".

We hope that during your studies, consultations and discussions you will focus on the role of both Orthodox Families, the Eastern and Oriental Orthodox Churches, in the ecumenical movement. Our Churches have a long history of dialogue, whether at the church level or at the group level. We trust that this meeting will affect the Churches' position positively and actively, especially since we are all part of that ecumenical body and work for its improvement.

When our brother in Christ, His Eminence Archbishop of Aleppo, Mor Gregorios Yohanna Ibrahim asked us if we could host this meeting, we welcomed the idea warmly.

Having you as guests of the Syrian Orthodox Church of Antioch, is a great witness to the unbroken spiritual work with which our Church has engaged herself since the time of the Apostles: seeking the salvation of the souls and spreading the Good News of the Lord. She has continued to bear witness to our Lord Jesus Christ despite the unbearable hardships that she has faced. Our Church has suffered countless persecutions due to political, social and security upheavals. She has presented hundreds of thousands of martyrs through the ages and lately in the beginning of this century, she offered about two hundred thousands martyrs. However, now that the Church is going through times of relative peace, we are directing all our efforts to revive our Church, driven by our strong faith in the legacy which our forefathers have left us. We have inherited their true Orthodox faith, tradition, Syriac Aramaic language spoken by our Lord Jesus Christ and his disciples and an open mind towards all other Christians with their various denominations. This Patriarchal Foundation where you are meeting has been built recently to demonstrate to all generations our hope and eagerness to revive our history, the history of hundreds of monasteries, seminaries and theological schools which were found throughout the Middle East until the thirteenth century. They served as spiritual and intellectual lighthouses, giving the Church great fathers and thinkers who enriched the Christian civilization with their writings. St Ephrem the Syrian is the Patron Saint of this foundation. He is recognized by all churches; thus he is one of the symbols of Christian unity.

We believe that ecumenical work is not new to our Church. Since the division of the fifth century, our forefathers dealt with churches matters in an ecumenical spirit. They believed that bringing the churches together and promoting cooperation among them in ecclesial and pastoral matters are vital for the continuation of the Christian witness and life.

Moreover, after 1950 our Patriarchate played an important role in the ecumenical movement. In 1958, my predecessor, the late Patriarch Mor Yacob III of blessed memory, allowed me, while still a monk and priest, to participate in the theological consultations held in Jerusalem between Theologians of the Oriental Orthodox Churches and the Lutheran Church. It was organized by the Faculty of the University of Kiel, West Germany. In 1962 and 1963, my predecessor appointed me as an official observer to Vatican II. As a Bishop, I started to participate in several unofficial consultations, beginning with the first one which was held between theologians from the two Orthodox families at the University of Aarhus in Denmark These consultations continued in several locations, acquiring official status and yielding fruitful results. I also participated in the unofficial consultations between the Oriental Orthodox Churches and the Roman Catholic Church in Vienna; and last but not least in the consultation of the official representatives of the Eastern and Oriental Orthodox Churches which was held in Balamand, Lebanon in 1975.

We are glad to mention that our Church has been a member of the World Council of Churches since 1960. I was elected as a member of the Central Committee at the Fifth Assembly at Nairobi, Kenya in 1975. After my enthronement as Patriarch, I nominated His Eminence Archbishop Mor Gregorios Yohanna Ibrahim to that post and he was elected later as a member of that Central Committee. And we have recently included ecumenism as a subject to be taught here at the Seminary by H.E. Mor Gregorios Yohanna Ibrahim. We also direct our clergymen and lay people locally, regionally and internationally to be open-minded about ecumenism. For that purpose, our Church is a member of the local ecumenical committees, a founding member of the Near East Council of Churches and a founding member of the Middle East Council of Churches.

Regarding our relations with our sister Orthodox and Catholic Churches, after my enthronement as Patriarch I began to correspond with all their Holinesses and Beatitudes, the Patriarchs and all Heads the Orthodox Churches, His Holiness the Pope of Rome, His Grace the Archbishop of Canterbury and Church Leaders of Protestant denominations. We believe that personal contacts between the heads of the Churches will help much to promote the ecumenical spirit and cooperation. In this regard we are pleased to remind you of the common statement that we were able to sign with our brother in Christ, His Beatitude Patriarch Ignatius IV Hazim, Rum Orthodox Patriarch of Antioch and All the East.

I also find it appropriate to let you know that the last meeting of the Oriental Orthodox Patriarchs in the Middle East which took place in the Monastery of Amba Bishoy, Egypt has opened a new page in our relationship as Oriental Orthodox Churches: Coptic Orthodox-the See of Alexandria, the Syrian Orthodox Church of Antioch and the Armenian Orthodox House of Cilicia, both in regard to our relation with each other's church families. We have stated in our Common Declaration dated 11 March 1998 [cf. pp. 126-129 below] that we would have the same stand in dogma and theology in all the theological dialogues. We shall also have the same understanding in all church matters in the Middle East Council of Churches and the World Council of Churches, and all other ecumenical bodies. This common declaration speaks about having one unified stand and voice as Oriental Orthodox family in the Middle East in any upcoming theological dialogues which will take place with other churches. This, we believe, will enrich those dialogues and ensure their success. Sharing with us this same belief and understanding were the Heads of Oriental Orthodox Churches in the Middle East: H.H. Shenouda III, Pope of the See of Alexandria for the Coptic Orthodox Church, who is also one of the WCC presidents, and H.H. Aram I, Catholicos of the House of Cilicia for the Armenian Orthodox Church, who is also the Moderator of WCC Central Committee.

In this respect we see a remarkable improvement in the dialogue between the two Orthodox Church families. First, we agreed on the theological issues and now the designated Joint Dialogue Committee is studying the pastoral and the liturgical issues. In the last meeting in Damascus where His Beatitude Patriarch Ignatius IV Hazim and my humble self were present, we were assured that the efforts of our theologians have tremendously helped in bringing our points of view closer. We have great hope that full communion will also be re-established in the near future, when all anathemas are lifted and the Synods of the respective churches of the two families will agree on restoring unity between us.

Improvements also are to be noticed in the relationship between our two families of churches on the one hand and the Roman Catholic and Protestant churches on the other hand. We truly trust in the blessings that this wonderful ecumenical dialogue has brought up the church which is guided by the Holy Spirit.

Having said that, I would like to point out to the spirit of love and tolerant co-existence between the different religions and denominations in this safe and secure country, the Syrian Arab Republic. We are honoured and proud to live under the patronage of His Excellency the President Mr Hafez Al-Assad, who looks after all the people of this nation without any discrimination. He also works very hard in order to secure a just and comprehensive peace in this region.

The theme of the Eighth Assembly of the WCC, Turn to God – Rejoice in Hope, is related to us now and provides an agenda for the future of our churches and their role in the ecumenical movement. We pray that God will be with us in all our dialogues as two Orthodox families and bless us to be one. We hope that the other Churches and Christian groups will also cooperate with us for the glory of His name. And as we look forward to more cooperation with the World Council of Churches, we are fully prepared to provide all we can in order to continue this ecumenical endeavour.

We ask God to bless this meeting, to bestow the spirit of renewal and restoration of church unity upon all people involved so that they may be able to see the fruit of all of those years of hard work in the Lord's vineyard.

We welcome you again and wish you a pleasant stay and safe return. May God bless us all. Thank you.

Response of His Beatitude
Patriarch Ignatius IV Hazim
Greek Orthodox Patriarch of Antioch and All the East

Thank you very much, Your Holiness, for accepting to receive all of us. I believe we are so used to meet and even to come to this House that we really feel at home. Many thanks to you for shouldering the burden of having a conference here. It is a well of your achievements in ecumenical life that we experience together in this area.

I hope that this gathering becomes truly meaningful to the Eighth Assembly of the World Council of Churches. For this we need to be clear about our situation and about our attitudes. I am sure of that. Having been an oldtimer in the World Council of Churches, I believe the Orthodox side was not always very, very clear in its own opinion. I remember only one time that we met together in order to have a common attitude and a common opinion on the different subjects of the general meetings. I remember that occurring only once and we do not follow that precedent. I have never understood why we could not follow that precedent.

I have the impression that we are afraid of seeing each other. I have the impression that we fear facing intelligently, deeply and seriously those who have different opinions from our own. I have even the impression that we like divisions – they are very secure. We are happy to be what we are accustomed to, and maybe we think that our major responsibility is to talk to each other in each one of the families because we do not talk to each other, not even in the same family. We have become so foreign to each other even within single Churches, within single countries that we would not like to have concerns and burdens given to us by the presence of the other.

No one can say that the Church, as a living being, can ignore the living situation in which we coexist. People do not understand why we do indeed sit together and meet together here in the Middle East because they do not see that wherever I turn my eyes I see Patriarch Zakka, I see the Roman Catholics, I see everybody here, and I see the Muslim majority in this country. We are asked by some to ignore the other, but we are not allowed to be ignorant so much because we are told that our Lord Jesus Christ is light in the darkness, not more darkness in darkness. We have eyes to see, we have ears to listen and to hear, and therefore we have to reflect: "you are a question posed to me because you are created by God as an authentic human being, somebody who has opinions and to whom I cannot be indifferent."

One has to understand that the Church is a living body, and it is to be questioned – not in its essence, but in the behaviour of its individuals. We have to think. My goodness, we are never told that thinking is a sin! We have to see people, and especially we have to love people. Fear is against love, and maybe it is because we do not love enough that we have fear of each other, not only each other, of those who are here, but any "other", whatever be his religion, whatever be his Church. But how can we place ourselves in any kind of prison cell, ignoring other people, just allowing ourselves to live as if they did not exist? They exist by the will of God, not by our own wisdom. Do we not respect God's will? We say we respect it, but I know that we really do not always respect it. I say this concerning ourselves – this may not be true for everybody else.

I hope that you can profit from this meeting to help the Eighth Assembly to be significant and especially to those who are here representing the Eastern Churches, the Orthodox Churches. I hope also that we correct or redress our attitudes towards the World Council, because we have not done enough in order to make the World Council of Churches more Orthodox than it is now. We are responsible, in my opinion, in that respect. Our collaboration, our contribution was not always very positive or very serious.

I also hope that we contribute more than just ideas. I respect ideas, but sometimes when we hear our theologians we hardly make a distinction between metaphysics as a discipline on the one hand and the theology of the Incarnation on the other hand. It is because the Incarnation needs to be an object of faith. In metaphysics you do not involve faith. You use terms and ways of thinking which are not those used by our Lord nor those used by the Apostles. I believe that we have to take attitudes and express our position for a better collaboration and a better contribution to the World Council of Churches. We have to preach to the World Council of Churches, not only to be concerned about majority.

My hope is that something will emerge from this meeting – for example a small committee to study the different themes of the meeting concerning the Eighth Assembly and to be there to give the opinions of our Churches.

I have this question: without a structure, whatever it may be, opinions may become rather theoretic. We, in the Antiochian Church – I am not speaking about the other Orthodox Churches – are used to saying wonderful things, very correct things, but we behave as if we were *true* "monophysites", ignoring totally our Lord's humanity. We are content with logical discussions, wonderful expressions, wonderful discourses. We are happy with that but we do not interpret that in *reality*. This is why, in my opinion, we can more or less generalise: what we say is wonderful, what we do is practically equal to nothing. We ignore the fact that it is not by chance that we have to deal with an *Incarnate* Lord. We have to deal with a reality, a concrete one, not to simply give a lesson, a verbal lesson, whatever be the verb we use.

I hope that we can interpret our presence in the World Council of Churches in a way which is not against our beliefs. I hope we may arrive at a formula in which we can be with the World Council of Churches – I say *with* the World Council – very seriously and not just present a kind of re-reading the past. In the past we came rather individually. We continue to be there individually because we do not consult. We do not speak to each other in the name of Christ, and for the sake of fraternity of Christ we do not speak to each other. And His Holiness spoke precisely of being together. We need to see each other – how can you love somebody you never see? And we are called to love each other. When the Word of God became God's expression of God's love to us, He came here and became Man. You have men and you are going to ignore them – what a wonderful logic we have in order to justify lazy sense of security in our churches!

I thank you very much, Your Holiness, that you allow me to say just these few words, and I hope hope that this meeting will be a first note, an important note, an important discipline for the Orthodox to be together. We speak of synodality, we are not synodal. We speak of being a community, we are not a community. If I were to say otherwise, I believe that I would be a real liar. And I have to say it in order to really be truthful before God.

I can say that we, in the See of Antioch, we do care about human beings. We do not ignore people because we risk ourselves to be ignored. And if we are ignored, it is God's mission which would be ignored. We would absolutely refuse to be negative to anything which is positive and willed by God. This means the people who are before us. We want to talk to the Muslim, we want to talk to the Protestant, we want to talk to everybody. We want to talk. We are not afraid; we are afraid only of our laziness. Let them stir us and tell us there are a few things that we should read again, say again, formulate again. Why not, my goodness, why? We do not believe that we can in the See of Antioch just retreat into a ghetto. The world will certainly forget all of us. Our world is that of communication. We cannot *not* communicate! Thank you.

His Holiness Ignatius Zakka I Iwas, Syrian Orthodox Patriarch of Antioch and All the East (left) and His Beatitude Ignatius IV (Hazim), Greek Orthodox Patriarch of Antioch and All the East, photographed at the chapel of St Ephrem Theological Seminary, on the opening day of the Orthodox Pre-Assembly Meeting.

The Orthodox Pre-Assembly Meeting:
An Introduction
Fr Thomas FitzGerald

I want to welcome you to this Pre-Assembly Meeting. And I greet you with the words: Christ is Risen!

We have gathered here at the invitation of His Holiness Patriarch Ignatius Zakka Iwas of the Syrian Orthodox Church to have our Pre-Assembly Meeting at St Ephrem Theological Seminary. And, from the beginning, I want to express our deep gratitude to His Holiness for this gracious invitation and for his generosity.

I should also like to thank His Eminence Metropolitan Gregorius Yohanna Ibrahim of Aleppo. Metropolitan Ibrahim is very active in meetings of the World Council of Churches. And once again, we are benefiting from his care and thoughtfulness.

We are also gathered here because of the profound sense of brotherhood and common ministry which is shared between His Holiness Patriarch Ignatius Zakka I Iwas and His Beatitude Patriarch Ignatius IV Hazim of the Patriarchate of Antioch. Both of these Patriarchs are united in their desire for reconciliation and in their desire to give a common witness in this society. There is in this region a profound desire to heal the wounds of the divisions between the two families of Orthodox Churches. And, this desire has expressed itself in a sense of mutual respect, dialogue and cooperation. I hope that in the coming days we have the opportunity to learn more about the powerful witness of these two Patriarchs and their venerable Patriarchates.

We are gathered here as representatives of both the Eastern Orthodox and the Oriental Orthodox family of Churches. I do not need to review the story of the tragic alienation of the churches which took place from the time of the fifth century. This historic division was rooted in differing Christological emphasis. But the discussions were compounded by numerous political and cultural factors.

The very fact that we can come together for this meeting is an expression of the spirit of dialogue and reconciliation which exists between the two families of Orthodox Churches. A number of significant "unofficial theological consultations" between representatives of both families were held in 1964, 1967, 1970 and 1971. These early meetings were facilitated by the World Council of Churches. The statement issued at the first meeting in Aarhus provided a significant foundation for all subsequent discussions. The statement said: "On the essence of Christological dogma, we found ourselves in full agreement. Through the different terminologies used by each side, we saw the same truth expressed... Both sides found themselves fundamentally following the Christological teachings of the one undivided Church as expressed by St Cyrill."

The unofficial consultations provided the basis for the official theological dialogue between the two families of Churches. The Joint Commission for Theological Dialogue between the Orthodox Church and the Oriental Orthodox Churches was inaugurated in 1985. This historic Commission has produced two foundational statements at Anba Bishoi in 1989 and at Chambésy in 1990. Both statements formally affirm that both families have the same faith. This conviction is expressed in the opening words of the Anba Bishoi Statement which says: "We have inherited from our fathers in Christ the one Apostolic Faith and tradition, though as churches we have been separated from each other for centuries. As two families of Orthodox Churches long out of communion with each other, we now pray and trust in God to restore that communion on the basis of the common Apostolic Faith of the undivided Church of the first centuries which we confess in our common creed."

Our gathering here is part of the process of reconciliation between our two families of Churches. The fact that we can meet together is already a sign of the progress that has been made. We are already the fruits of the sacred desire for reconciliation and unity among the families of Orthodox Churches. Yes, we are meant to discuss the coming Assembly of the World Council of Churches. Yes, in our deliberations here together, we can come to know and experience both the rich traditions of our churches and the common faith which unites us. As we prepare for the Assembly of the World Council of Churches, we shall be reminded again and again of our common inheritance. We shall be challenged to give a common witness as believers who profess the Orthodox Faith.

Our Concern for Christian Reconciliation and Visible Unity

We are gathered here because our Churches are committed to the process of Christian reconciliation and unity. This commitment is rooted in the very action of God and in the Gospel of our Lord. We proclaim God as one who reconciles, heals and restores. In so many of the stories of the Gospel, Jesus our Lord is the one who expresses the love of God the Father for all, even those considered by some to be sinners and heretics!

Mindful of this fact, the great Fathers of the Church were concerned both with teaching the true faith and with reconciling those who were alienated from each other. In their understanding, the faith nurtured us in our progress towards God and one another. Distortions of the faith were not beneficial for salvation.

And likewise, the great Fathers were also concerned with the reconciliation and unity of churches. They knew that disunity was a scandal. Disunity compromised the witness of the Gospel in the world. Ultimately, disunity was not from God!

Among the many Father who were concerned about the tragedy of disunity, St Basil spoke strongly to those churches who were tending towards isolation and division. He said:

> ... The Lord himself has cut off the islands from the mainland by sea, but he has united in charity those who live on the islands to those who live on the mainland. We have but one Lord, one faith, one hope; and even if you do consider yourselves to be the head of the universal Church, the head cannot say to the feet, 'I have no need of you'.... So far as we are concerned, in consideration of our own weakness, we are seeking to be united in a living union with you. We realize that even if you are not present in the body, yet the assistance that you obtain for us by means of your prayers will, in these most difficult circumstances, be of the greatest use to us ... For how can we, the sons of those fathers who ensured by a number of small indications that the signs of our relatedness to one another were to be circulated from the end of the world to the other ... how should we now cut ourselves off from the world, how can we possibly fail to be ashamed of keeping ourselves to ourselves, and how indeed can we fail to consider his breach in our unity as nothing less than a disaster. (Epist. 203,3)

The impulse of our Church to seek reconciliation and unity in the faith is at the heart of our scripture and our tradition. It is an impulse which has been present in the life of the Church from the very beginning while it may take different forms and expressions from one period to another.

The World Council of Churches and its Fiftieth Anniversary

We are gathered here at the invitation of the World Council of Churches, and with the blessing of the Primates of the Eastern Orthodox and Oriental Orthodox Churches. This meeting is designed especially to prepare Orthodox delegates for the Eighth Assembly of the World Council of Churches to be held in Harare, Zimbabwe, in December. Most of the members of this meeting are delegates to Harare. Unfortunately, we were not able to invite all Orthodox delegates to this meeting. We have assembled two delegates from most churches – both Eastern Orthodox and Oriental Orthodox.

The World Council of Churches is celebrating its fiftieth anniversary. After much discussion and preparation the Council was formally established in 1948. From the very beginning of its existence, Orthodox Churches have been active in its life. Orthodox theologians have made a profound contribution to the witness and the activities of the Council.

The WCC has brought together the churches for the sake of restoring our visible unity! It has encouraged the churches to engage together in theological dialogue! It has encouraged prayers for reconciliation! It has encouraged the churches to join together where possible in common mission and witness! It has enabled the churches to share together their resources! The work of the Council is a fulfilment of the desires expressed in the historic encyclical of 1920 from the Ecumenical Patriarchate.

Over the past fifty years, the World Council has made a profound impact upon the process of reconciliation and unity among Churches. The relationship among the Churches is very different from what it was fifty years ago. And the Council has contributed to these new relationships in a very dramatic fashion. Ecumenical Patriarch Bartholomew recently spoke of these accomplishments when he said:

> Since the Patriarchal encyclical of 1920, much has been accomplished. We have experienced the truth of the Holy Spirit in our common prayers for reconciliation and unity. Love, joy, peace, and hope have inspired us to strive for greater acts of common experience of the Lord. Prejudice and misunderstanding among Christians from divided Churches has been lessened. We have seen hopeful expressions of theological consensus on certain points among the communions. At times, there is a spirit of cooperation and reconciliation evident between Orthodox, Roman Catholics and Protestants. This must surely be a cause of thanksgiving to God, the source of every good and perfect gift.

During the past few years, serious questions have been raised about the direction and the future of the WCC. Some of these questions reflect the positive changes which have taken place over the past fifty years. For example, in the past few decades there has been an increase of bilateral theological dialogues between the churches. There has been an increase in local and regional ecumenical concerns. Both the Orthodox Church and the Roman Catholic Church have become more active in ecumenical witness.

Issues such as these have led the Council to engage in its own self-study known as the Common Understanding and Vision process. This study began in 1989 and has led to the "CUV" document. Orthodox Churches and Orthodox theologians have made a valuable contribution to this document.

This process of Common Understanding and Vision also revealed that there were some deeper questions which had a bearing upon the future of the WCC. For example, some have asked whether the Council was still concerned with the vision of visible unity. Some have questioned how broad based the Council can be. Others have raised the question of the very meaning of the phrase "ecumenical movement" and the question of the relationship between the Council and the member churches. Some have questioned whether Christ and the Gospel are still at the heart of the Council's life and mission. Others have questioned whether the present structure encourages equitable participation of Orthodox and Protestant member churches.

The CUV document has addressed many of these issues. At the same time, it must be admitted, the discussion process has revealed that there is a great diversity of opinion among those involved in the Council and the ecumenical movement.

The Assembly Theme "Turn to God – Rejoice in Hope"

During our meeting, we will have the opportunity to reflect upon the theme for the Eighth Assembly of the World Council of Churches. Two of our colleagues will present their reflections on the theme: "Turn to God – Rejoice in Hope". The theme of the Assembly is a powerful one. It can be very significant at the present point of the World Council of Churches and the ecumenical movement.

The Assembly theme is first of all a call to repentance. "Turn to God". This is certainly a theme with which we are familiar as Orthodox. It is a theme which is central to the Gospel and to the Tradition of the Church. According to the Gospel of Mark, Jesus began his ministry with a bold call to repentance. He said: "The time is fulfilled, the Kingdom of God is at hand, repent and believe in the Gospel" (Mk 1:15). The Fathers always spoke of repentance as a continuing return to God. It involved turning away from self-centredness and turning away from the idols of power and prestige. And it involved a continuing turning towards the light and life of God.

It is in this re-orientation to God that we see ourselves as His daughters and sons. It is through this re-orientation that we can truly remember the mighty actions of God centered upon the Mystery of the Risen Christ, and accomplished for us and our salvation!

Truly, the reason for our hope and joy is the fact that we have come to know God and have come to know ourselves as his beloved children. We "rejoice in hope" because of the God who has first loved us, and who calls us to be friends and co-workers in the world!

This theme is important not only for us as believers. It is also an important theme for the World Council of Churches and the whole quest for Christian reconciliation and unity. So often, we can become imbued with a "secular" spirit. This secular spirit cuts us off from the living God. This secular spirit emphasizes our contributions and accomplishments. Even though we may claim to be serving God and even struggling for reconciliation, we so easily become self-centered. We can easily create institutions and programmes which seem to relegate God to the periphery. Yes, it is a secular spirit which separates our work from God and his actions.

I hope and pray that we can truly do some theological reflection during these coming days. The Assembly theme lends itself to very rich theological reflection. Can we take this Assembly theme and truly reflect upon it? Can we take this Assembly theme and speak of its relevance for ourselves, for our churches, for the World Council of Churches, and for the quest for reconciliation and unity? Using this Assembly theme, can we uncover the rich theological insights of our Orthodox faith, and offer these insights to the Council and to all the Assembly delegates?

I believe that there is a longing in the Council for good and life-giving theological reflection. There is a longing for faithful words of life rooted in the Scriptures and Tradition. There is a longing for words about the living God which are not only truthful, but which are also healing and life-giving. There is a longing for words about the human person which affirm our relationship to God, as well as our inherent dignity and value! The Orthodox have much to offer! But let us be careful. It is not simply the quantity but the quality!

His All Holiness Patriarch Bartholomew recently spoke about the character of our theological reflections by saying that:

> in order for the theological discussions to bear fruit, they must have a particular character. Above all, our theological reflection must be nurtured by prayer and guided by the Scriptures and Tradition. Our dialogues must be rooted in the life of the Church and sensitive to the needs of the world. Our encounters with one another must be open to the grace and activity of the Holy Spirit in the present. As the Fathers of the Church tell us, theology must be life-giving and must always be centered upon the Source of life. Theological reflection must be done in the presence of God, to the glory of God and for the sake of the salvation of all God's people.

The Orthodox Churches and the Ecumenical Movement

During the second part of our programme, we shall have the opportunity to reflect upon the broad topic of the ecumenical movement and the role of the Orthodox Churches. The present ecumenical movement is multifaceted, and differs from one place to another. In some places, proselytism continues to afflict some Orthodox Churches. In other places, the revival of the Eastern Catholic Churches have created new tensions between Orthodoxy and Roman Catholicism.

An Inter Orthodox meeting on "Evaluation of New Facts in the Relations of Orthodoxy and the Ecumenical Movement" took place in Thessaloniki 29 April – 2 May, 1998 [cf. pp. 136-138 below]. The meeting brought together delegates from the Eastern Orthodox Churches. The delegates denounced the schismatics and extremists groups which use the theme of ecumenism to criticize Church leadership. At the same time, they reaffirmed that Orthodox participation in the ecumenical movement has always been based upon Orthodox Tradition and is in harmony with the decisions of the Synods of the local Orthodox Churches, the Third Pre-Conciliar Conference of 1986, and the meeting of Orthodox Primates in 1992.

With regard to the WCC, the delegates took note of a number of trends in the Council which have troubled the Orthodox. These concerns led them to suggest that the WCC must be "radically restructured in order to allow more adequate Orthodox participation." The delegates also made a number of proposals regarding Orthodox participation in the Harare Assembly. Although the deliberations in Thessaloniki did not involve delegates from the Oriental Orthodox Churches, the results of that meeting are significant because they identify a number of concerns regarding the WCC which are widely expressed by Orthodox in both families of churches.

But we should not easily believe that the ecumenical movement and the relationships between the churches are under pressure everywhere – this is simply not the case. In the days ahead we shall hear of the positive relationships among the Churches here in Syria. We shall hear of a recent ecumenical seminar in Iasi, Romania. I am sure that each of our participants can bear witness to positive ecumenical activities which have contributed to our reconciliation and unity in Christ our Lord.

Our Message is Christ!

The challenge of Orthodox ecumenical witness ultimately leads us back to Christ and His Gospel. Our understanding of the process of reconciliation and visible unity must be firmly rooted in the reality of the Risen Christ and His Gospel. Christ is the one who has reconciled us to the Father through the Spirit. And it is God the Father who has given to us in Christ the ministry of reconciliation.

If we are truly united with Christ through his Body – which is the Church – then we are obliged to be participants in the divine action of reconciliation.

For many of us, the vision of unity in Christ articulated nearly fifty years ago at the Amsterdam Assembly continues to nurture our understanding of the Council and of the quest for reconciliation and visible unity. Listen to these words from Amsterdam:

> Unity arises out of the love of God in Jesus Christ, which, binding the constituent churches to him, binds them to one another. It is the earnest desire of the Council that the churches may be bound closer to Christ and therefore closer to one another. In the bond of his love, they will desire continually to pray for one another and to strengthen one another in worship and in witness, bearing one another's burdens and so fulfilling the law of Christ.

At the first Assembly of the WCC in 1948, George Florovsky was one of the major speakers. Florovsky spoke at Amsterdam at a time when the quest for Christian reconciliation and unity was not a popular subject. A number of Orthodox Churches sent representatives to the Moscow Conference of 1948. This Conference repudiated the Christian unity movement and the upcoming Amsterdam Assembly of the World Council of Churches. Likewise, in the same year, the Roman Catholic Church formally rejected formal ecumenical advances – although a number of their theologians were informally involved in preliminary theological discussions on issues of reconciliation and unity.

George Florovsky could have easily chosen to speak harshly of the ecumenical challenge. This does not mean that he did not have questions and concerns. But, Florovsky centred the movement for Christian reconciliation and unity in the divine action. Listen to his words:

> The judgment begins with the house of the Lord. It is not enough to be moved towards an ecumenical reconciliation by some sort of strategy, be it missionary or evangelistic or social or any other, unless the Christian conscience has already been struck by the greater challenge, by the Divine challenge itself,

We must seek unity or re-union not because it might make us more efficient and better equipped in our historical struggle (and in this case nobody would go far beyond what is strictly required for a victory on the battle field), but because unity is the Divine imperative, the Divine purpose and design, because it belongs to the very *esse* of Christianity. Christian disunity means no less than the failure of Christians to be true Christians. In divided Christendom nobody can be fully Christian, even if one stands in the full truth and is sure of his complete loyalty and obedience to the truth 'once delivered unto the saints' – for no one is permitted freedom from responsibility for the others...

In coming to Damascus, we have undertaken a pilgrimage.

We have left behind us family and friends. We have left behind us the familiar and the routine. And we find ourselves gathered together by Christ in this place at this time. We gather in a region, in a city – rich in Christian history and Christian witness – we come to a region where the disciples were first called Christians!

We will constantly have before us the witness of St Peter and St Paul, of St Ignatius, of St Thekla, of St John of Damascus and of St Ephrem.

What binds them to us is the Risen Christ who dwells among us, and calls us to be participants in the ministry of reconciliation. May the Lord guide us. Christ is Risen!

To Him be glory, honour and worship, now and forever and unto the ages of ages. Amen.

Aphrahat the Persian Sage on Turning to God:
A Reflection on the Assembly Theme
Metropolitan Mor Cyril Aphrem (Karim)

Introduction

It is a privilege and a great honour for me to have the opportunity to share my reflections on the theme of the Eighth Assembly of the World Council of Churches with a distinguished audience of eminent brother archbishops and bishops, reverend fathers and brothers and sisters representing the Orthodox Church of God in the world.

Let me start by expressing my deepest appreciation to the WCC Orthodox staff for organizing this meeting and for inviting me to offer my humble contribution. I wish also to thank the WCC for choosing this theme "Turn to God – Rejoice in Hope".

This theme is a straightforward call for us to turn to God the Abba, source of our being and existence. It invites us to lift up our hearts, minds and thoughts where Christ sits at the right hand of God the Father, as the Syriac Antiochian Liturgy would put it. It requires us to turn to God in our totality with all our thoughts, words and deeds. This act of turning to God is inspired by the hope that promises us a great everlasting joy. This eschatological rejoicing, in turn, encourages us to constantly return to Him, Who is our hope. (1 Tim. 1:1)

Turning to God, therefore, requires a constant change of heart, a real repentance. A true repentance is one that involves a look at the failures of the past and a promise to be more faithful to our calling both now and in the future. This repentance is a personal spiritual exercise, which touches the heart of the believer's relationship with God. But it is also an exercise that concerns communities and institutions. There is a great need for communities and institutions to undergo self-examination from time to time, to recognize their shortcomings and to recommit themselves to be faithful to their calling.

I do not think that this theme of repentance will appeal to any other Church or group of people more than it does to Orthodoxy. This is a topic that is very dear to the hearts of the Orthodox faithful. Several volumes have been written on this issue by the Church Fathers, past and present.

Repentance of the human race is the sole reason for the Incarnation of God the Word. The Lord Himself began His divine Mission by preaching the gospel of repentance. "Repent, for the kingdom of heaven is near" (Mt 4:17). John the Baptist, in preparing the way for the coming of the Saviour, also calls upon his people to repent for the kingdom of God is near. The Apostle Paul makes it even more clear that no one can enter the kingdom of heaven without first repenting and turning to God. He boldly states that there is no communion between light and darkness, between good and evil (2 Cor. 6:14). We cannot embrace God and sin at the same time. We cannot serve two lords (Mt. 6:24).

We Orthodox have much to teach our Protestant partners about turning to God. Our wealth of patristic literature needs to be shared. We ourselves, however, can learn a great deal from the Protestants about rejoicing in hope, giving ecumenism its true meaning, namely giving and receiving. This is not to say that we lack the concept of joy. It is rather a call to give our Orthodoxy a more joyous countenance, one that is in fact part of its nature. To make known that eternal joy, which we strive to achieve, begins in this world. It is very true that our real joy is driven from the mystery of Easter, the Resurrection of our Lord. This joy, although eschatological, can and should be experienced at least partially in this world. We live in a sacred liturgical time that makes the historical events of our salvation present here and now by means of the holy sacraments. These sacraments, as we are aware, will only realize their fullness in heaven when God becomes all in all. Our real and full joy, therefore, will be complete in heaven. Since God has provided us with means to enjoy the blessings and glories of Easter, the joy of the resurrection should be apparent in all aspects of our life.

It is my intention now to share with you some thoughts on one of our great Syriac scholars, Aphrahat, and his views on repentance.

Who is Aphrahat?

Aphrahat is the first Syriac scholar whose writings come to us in full, and the earliest known Christian writer in Persia. He was born a pagan in Persia, as he himself admits, in the second half of the third century. He converted to Christianity and adopted a form of monasticism, most probably that of *Bnai Qiomo*, Sons of the Covenant. He was also known by the name of Jacob. Some suggest that he became a bishop and assumed the name of Jacob on his consecration to the episcopacy. His death occurred after AD 346.

Despite the Orthodoxy of his teachings, Aphrahat was never recognized by the Church as a saint, and was never accepted on the same level as other Church Fathers. One reason for this might be his declaration that the world will last only six thousand years.

His writings came to us in the form of twenty-three sermons, each of which starts with a letter of the Syriac alphabet. As an early Syriac writer, his works are very Semitic in character and content. They are void of almost any foreign influence and tremendously rich in symbolism and scriptural quotations. They were written as a response to a letter sent to him. The sermons cover different subjects such as faith, charity, fasting and prayer. The seventh of these sermons is on penitence. This is the one which I would like to share with you.

All people are sinners; God is the only one without sin

Aphrahat's starting point is the revealed truth of the supremacy of God and His victory over sin. God is the only One Who is not under the susceptibility to sin. Out of all those who were born, only the Incarnate Son of God stands without sin. He not only did not commit a sin, but also gave us victory over sin. Since the fall of Adam, all his descendants were struck by sin. On the Cross, Christ granted us a way of overcoming sin. Through His death we are set free from sin and death.

Aphrahat is very much aware of the strength and skilfulness of our adversary, but he also knows how weak is the devil's armour. Our armour, however, is strong. Our war is with an unseen enemy. Let us, therefore, turn to the One Who sees Satan and is able to save us from him.

God calls us to repentance

God is the One Who takes the initiative and calls us to return to Him. Because of His infinite love, He does not wait for us, but wants us to enjoy an everlasting relationship with Him. He calls us saying: "Return to me and I will return to you." (Mal. 3:7) It is important to notice that God is not calling us to go to Him but rather to return where we ought to be. He is reminding us of what was ours before the fall of Adam. It is we who have departed from our good nature, and now He is calling us to return to the home which we have lost. Does God's call for us to return to Him seem preconditioned? He will return to us only when we return to Him.

In a book entitled *Turn to God*, H.H. Pope Shenouda III comments on this verse saying: "God never abandons us. He never leaves us alone. Even when we are not aware of His presence, He is there watching over us. It is we who run away from Him and hide our faces because of the shame of our sins. God is saying to us: 'My return is guaranteed, though the important thing is for you to return.'"

God is always waiting for us to return. He is standing and knocking at the door of our hearts. If anyone hears His voice and opens the door, He will come in and eat with him. (Rev. 3:20) He is the One Who called Adam for repentance when He said to him "Where are you Adam?" When Adam concealed his sin and blamed Eve for it, the Lord sentenced him and all of his children to death. God did the same with Cain.

The sinner is a sick person

Every illness has a treatment, and repentance is the treatment for sin. The Lord says in the Holy Gospel that "It is not the healthy who need a doctor, but the sick... For I have come to call not the righteous, but sinners" (Mt. 9:12-13). Aphrahat talks extensively about the sinner as a sick person in need of treatment. He sees only one great Physician Who is able to heal the sick. This Physician has the medicine of life to offer to all who ask for healing. This medicine is sufficient to heal all kinds of sicknesses. However, for the sicknesses to be healed, they need to be shown to the Wise Physician. Repentance is the way for us to expose our wounds and be healed.

God wants all people to be healed

It is God's will that all afflicted by sin be healed. He wants all sinners to turn to Him to receive forgiveness. He says in Ezekiel: "Do I take any pleasure in the death of the wicked, declares the Sovereign Lord. Rather am I not pleased when they return from their ways and live?" (Ezek. 18:23). The sins of the people of Nineveh became so great that the Lord decided to destroy their city and all its population. But when they listened to the Prophet Jonah and returned to God, He accepted their repentance, forgave them and saved them. No matter how great is our sin, God is willing and able to accept us, but only if we return to Him. He is calling us, but are we answering His call?

Confession of sins

The one who has been struck by the devil should not be ashamed to confess his foolishness, ask for the medicine of repentance and be rid of his sin. Whoever becomes so ashamed as not to disclose his wounds will be permanently injured. Such a person cannot be healed because he is not willing to disclose his injuries to the Physician, the Good Samaritan who gave two dinars to heal all the afflicted. But anyone who confesses his sins will be forgiven. When David committed his sin, he was rebuked by the Prophet Nathan who told David: "The Lord has removed your sin, but only because you had confessed your sin." Confession, then, is a precondition for forgiveness.

The righteous people, referred to figuratively by Aphrahat as "the fat sheep", should not mock the "thinner" ones in order to be condemned by our Great Shepherd when He comes. The physicians, who are the disciples of our Great Physician, should not prevent healing from whoever is in need of it. They should provide healing to those who ask for it and encourage those who hide their injuries. When the injured people do so, the physicians should not condemn them publicly, but should, with Christian love and compassion, lead them to a sincere repentance and acceptable confession.

God does not ask about our sins, but rejoices in our return

In the parable of the Prodigal Son, the father does not inquire from his son about the possessions he lost, but he receives him with hugs and kisses and declares that his son was dead and now is alive, he was lost and now is found.

H.H. Patriarch Mor Ignatius Zakka I writes in his Lenten encyclical of 1997: "Yet, we are human and are always susceptible to sin, but on the day of judgment, the Lord shall not ask us: 'Why did you sin?' but rather 'Why did you not repent?'."

The Lord's joy in the return of a sinner is too great to be disturbed by the history of that sinner. The Gospel tells us that: "There will be more rejoicing in heaven over one sinner who repents than over ninety-nine righteous persons who do not need to repent" (Lk. 15:7).

Habitual sinners

Whoever confesses his sins and repents of them should not injure the same place for a second time. It is difficult even for the Wise Physician to heal the place that is injured a second time. The one who commits the same sin over and over becomes a habitual sinner. St Paul writes to the Romans: "Or do you despise the riches of His kindness and forbearance and patience? Do you not realize that God's kindness is meant to lead you to repentance?" (Rom. 2:4).

Constant repentance

If a person does good in the eyes of God all his days and does evil at the end of his life, he will die in his evil. Therefore, the just person is advised to be careful not to commit sin and lose his battle. The mercy of God and His compassion should not lead us to laziness. It is better for us not to lose what we have and not to be in need of repentance as there is no comparison between the one who commits sin and repents and the one who is far from sin. He advises us to keep our armour in order to be protected in our struggle. Because the garment that is torn apart, even after repair, will still be noticed by everyone. The wall that has been broken will remain noticeable even after it has been rebuilt with great labour.

What is repentance?

Patriarch Zakka I writes, "Repentance is a return to God and an obedience to His commandments." Pope Shenouda III describes such a return as "forming a real and sincere relationship with God in your heart". He goes on to say, "When I say a relationship, I do not just mean the external signs and practices of religion, but a relationship with God that is one of love."

A return with the whole heart: some final remarks

God says: "Return to Me with all your heart, with fasting and weeping and mourning. Rend your heart and not your garments. Return to the Lord God" (Joel 2:12-13). Pope Shenouda remarks: "It is amazing how many people get caught up in the means to reach God, such as the devotions, the spiritual exercises and the disciplines, but forget the end to which they are directed, which is God."

The return to God should be a firm and lasting return. One in which there is no going back. It should not be a return of convenience. The return to God does not stop there. It should lead to a spiritual growth in the Lord. A growth that should strive to achieve holiness, without which no one can see the Lord.

The chance to repent exists only in this world. A time will come when this age of grace will pass away and the age of justice will begin, an age that is free from repentance and in which only justice will reign.

The Environment
of the Harare Assembly of the WCC:
A Tentative Weather Forecast
Fr K.M. George

As we are meeting in the paschal period between Easter and Pentecost, I am reminded of an interesting experience I had several years ago while on the staff of the World Council of Churches. I was asked to prepare a paper on the Holy Spirit in relation to the theme of the Canberra Assembly. In my little paper I wanted to relate the resurrection of Christ to the coming of the Holy Spirit, and incidentally referred to the fifty days in between Easter and Pentecost. I compared the fifty days of repentance that preceded Easter, a time of intense fasting and innumerable prostrations in my tradition, to the fifty days that followed Easter, a time when prostrations in prayer are not permitted by the Church. The erect standing posture of the human body symbolized the resurrection experience and our transcendent vocation.

To express this idea I wrote in my paper: We are *exhorted* by the Church to *stand up* and pray during these fifty days". I completed the paper and gave the manuscript to be typed at the Secretariat. The well-meaning Protestant colleague, a native English speaker, who typed my paper, struggled with my obscure handwriting and still more obscure Oriental theology and finally brought some enlightenment. The typed paper now read: "We are *exhausted* in the church by standing up and praying during these fifty days".

My western Protestant colleague was probably reflecting in a very honest way her own experience in Orthodox worship services – standing long hours in churches without chairs, listening to unintelligible language and observing archaic rituals...

Well, let us take the fifty days as some sort of a metaphor. Let us now read: fifty years of ecumenical fellowship between Easter and Pentecost. We are *exhorted* by our Lord to stand together as one body in the unity of the Triune mystery. But are we *exhausted* by standing together for fifty years? Has the ecumenical fatigue developed to a breaking point? It seems so.

But there is more to this paschal period of fifty days. The Resurrection has happened and Pentecost has not yet occurred. Peter and his friends have returned to their old boats and nets which they had abandoned in response to the call of Jesus to join his fellowship. Thomas who was willing to go and die with Jesus turned incredulous. It is good to remember that the reactionary relapse in the Apostle's pilgrimage happened after the resurrection of their master. That, however, was not the end of the story.

The ecumenical movement has come out of the ashes of downright hostility, mistrust and mutual ignorance between many of our churches. And we have walked a long way, still on the road to Emmaus, wondering at the great things that have happened so far. Sure, we are still on the way before the joint breaking of the bread and the crucial revelation of the Risen One. The ecumenical movement probably is still monolingual – speaking in only one tongue of one culture, the culture of the dominant partner. The Pentecost of many languages of many nations have yet to come to the ecumenical movement. This is something that clearly bothers the Orthodox who are theoretically and practically used to the diversity of tongues. Even the strictly monological Roman Catholic Church is trying to modify its monolingual-monocultural approach to the question of unity and Christian witness in this world. But let us consider the fifty years as a time of intense prayer and waiting for the coming of the Holy Spirit. It is our common task and calling as local churches of Christ and not simply the business of some leaders and some movements.

Let me now attempt a modest weather forecast of the context of the Harare Assembly as part of the Orthodox preparation for it. Since the parameters available to us now are limited and very vague, we can only make tentative suggestions.

Dreams and Disappointments

By the time the Assembly meets, awareness of the approaching millennium will be heightened. There will be a corresponding expectation in the minds of many people of radical changes happening in society at various levels. Much attention will naturally be focused on the Christian churches. The mounting expectancy will vary from apocalyptic predictions of doom to sober prayers for the advent of a new age – an age of peace, reconciliation and justice to the poor of the earth.

Recent papal encyclicals like *Tertio Millennium Adveniente* and the Catholic Bishops' Synods of all continents being convoked in Rome in the closing years of the century to launch the re-evangelization of the whole world are part of the Roman Catholic attempt to meet the expectations of the people half-way.

Whether we listen to the prophets of doom or not, there will certainly be a lot of anger, frustration and conflict in and around the assembly simply because our churches will not be able to cope with the millennial dreams of our people at the pastoral and spiritual levels. It is more likely they might easily give into reactionary forces from within.

Jubilee of a Roman Calendar

The WCC probably made a wise decision not to follow the early suggestion that it postpones its own fiftieth year jubilee to coincide with the A.D. 2000 jubilee. This is to avoid the Christian triumphalism that might be associated with the millennial celebrations against which the WCC was sternly warned. However, since the jubilee theme is prominent in both, they coincide in the minds of people, and so the assembly cannot totally escape the fireworks of the millennial transition.

There is no conclusive evidence that the Jewish utopia of the Jubilee year was ever practised by the Jews themselves. But the WCC takes it up on the basis that Jesus announced it as "the acceptable year of the Lord" (Lk. 4:19) which centres on preaching the good news to the poor, recovering sight to the blind, setting the oppressed free and forgiving all debts. In the framework of this jubilee year of grace, the WCC wants to address all the social, economic and political issues that haunt the contemporary world from Dalit discrimination in India to international debt of the two-third world.

On the other hand, most Christians would identify the jubilee with the turn of the century. The Roman Catholic Church is preparing its faithful to celebrate the 2000th anniversary of the birth of Jesus – the great Christmas and the new year – by exclusively identifying the birth of Jesus and the origins of Christianity with the birth of a Roman calendar and the great western civilization. Whatever theological legitimation and spiritual sobriety we attach to this jubilee celebrations of the *Anno Domini*, it will essentially be a triumphant celebration of the Roman imperial calendar that measured out time for the whole world at least since the last 500 years or so. We do not know according to what calendar the three wise men from the East recognized and registered the birth of Christ. Most probably it was not by the Roman reckoning of time, since the Eastern cultures had devised innumerable calenders that resonated with the rhythm of nature in their regions and with the pulses of cosmic life as they experienced it. So the coming of "the true light that enlightens every human being" into our world must have been recorded by more than one system of calculating time.

My point is not to minimize the importance of the calendar which was first officially instituted by the Supreme Pontiff of the Pagan Rome, Julius Caesar, and later corrected by the Supreme Pontiff of the Christian Rome, Pope Gregory. The point is, when we exclusively identify the Economy of Salvation in Christ, the Saviour of the whole world with one dominant imperial calendar and then celebrate its jubilee, fundamentalist circles in Islam, Hinduism and Buddhism would get one more handle to identify Christian faith with the west and its civilization. Especially since most populations belonging to these religions had been colonized and exploited by the west, their culture and calendar are recovering their identity in opposition to the cultures and calendars of the west. Calendars are not neutral reckoning of time. When you impose your calendar on me, you are taking a hostage my time, my history, my religion, my relation to nature, my perception of reality, my categories of thinking and imagination and so on. This is nothing other than slavery of the worst kind. The true jubilee is intended to set the captives at liberty. The year 2 000 jubilee instead reinforces the chains of captivity of the two-thirds world by euphemistic mechanisms like economic globalization and global evangelization. Let us hope that the WCC jubilee will be an occasion to set itself free from the hidden chains of a mono-calendar before it proclaims the "year of grace" to the world. But we will have to struggle with this in different ways in the assembly and beyond.

Altering Human Consciousness

Two movements which arose in the closing decades of this century namely the women's movement and the ecological movement, have begun to alter human consciousness in a profound way. Neither of them originated in the Church, but both have produced a powerful resonance in the mainline western churches and through them in the WCC circles. As long as the paradigm of the present global civilization remains, these movements will continue to gather momentum and intensity. Even if the Orthodox churches manage to remain insulated from the infectious contact with the WCC, these elements will seep through because they raise fundamental issues of human nature and human survival. To the ecological issue the Orthodox have begun to respond with some measure of theological and spiritual conviction: for example, in the admirable initiative of the Ecumenical Patriarchate. In responding to the women's movement we need to go deeper than the issues like ordination and inclusive language. These issues probably blocked our finer vision of the essential – the mystery of human nature as manifested in man and woman and which our Lord assumed and transformed. Leave aside all rhetoric and power games of the movement, there is still something which Orthodox Christians both men and women can respond to with joy and thanksgiving to God. This subtle "something" will remind us of God's creation of all out of his love and goodness and God's image in men and women corporately and individually. The spiritual act of mutually discovering the beauty of that image constitutes our human calling on earth. Here begins our participation in the love, freedom and goodness of the Triune God. The Orthodox Tradition has the theological and spiritual resources to go deeper into this matter confidently yet humbly. (Whenever the issue of gender and language confronts me, I gratefully remember St Gregory of Nazianzus, the "Theologian", who called God *anonymous* (having no name) and *panonymous* (having all the names) at the same time. In the Trinitarian controversy, he warned the Orthodox and the heretics alike that human biological terminology should not be applied in an absolute way to the persons of the Holy Trinity though we have borrowed the biological terms like Father and Son in order to speak about the unspeakable mystery. The ambiguity of our expression is that "we are fathers and sons at the same time". In the Trinity, Father does not become the Son nor does the Son Father, yet they are one. The relativization of all human terminology legitimately opens the way for a "panonymous" understanding of God and a polyphonic theology. We in the Orthodox Tradition however remain faithful to the scriptural language about God as a safe principle.) The voice of the feminist movement with all its power equations is likely to reach its highest pitch in the Harare Assembly. The Orthodox will have to exercise a lot of discernment, compassion and confidence.

Neither Scripture nor Preacher

Several years after the 1968 student revolution, one could still see on some walls of the Sorbonne the slogan: *Ni Dieu, ni maître* (neither God nor Master). We are told that the post-modern world erupted decades ago, but we in the Church are terribly late to catch up. Authority is in a shambles. At the beginning of the ecumenical movement things were apparently more clear because there were definite signposts and borderlines. The Bible had authority as the Word of God for Protestants and Orthodox. The ordained pastor had authority not only from men, but also from God. The Church of one's belonging had authority over one's life in the world.

The eclipse of biblical authority and the deconstruction of every name and norm in many Protestant circles in recent years will make the Orthodox-Protestant dialogue in the WCC extremely painful and irrelevant. The most visible signs are in the almost total aversion for any "unity" discourse in the conventional Faith and Order language and total disregard for any scruples regarding eucharistic communion. The Orthodox discourse on these issues will be considered vain rhetoric. This is an area where dialogue and negotiation will not apply because the spirit of the age will reign supreme. Without breaking human fellowship, the Orthodox will have to "stay in the city, until you are clothed with power from above" (Lk. 24:49). In the meantime we can perhaps go back to the norms and practices of communion within our own family and see how true we are to ourselves. Probably we can also make fresh, broad-based proposals for Christian unity to our indifferent brothers and sisters in other traditions.

A host of other trends and issues from globalization to gay rights are on the cards. We cannot list them all hear.

The ecumenical boat is definitely in the doldrums. As Orthodox, should we join the disciples of Christ who were alarmed and threatened by the rising tides of the rough lake of Galilee? Or do we join Jesus to take a little nap in the boat? I think we had better take a little rest with the Lord, but within the boat, gathering strength all the while to talk to the sea and to the wind with the power from above.

The Assembly in Context:
The WCC and the Orthodox Churches
On the Way to Harare
Fr Leonid Kishkovsky

Each of the Assemblies of the World Council of Churches, beginning in Amsterdam fifty years ago, has been a signpost on the ecumenical journey. This image suggests that the journey did not begin with the WCC and its assemblies. The ecumenical journey began long before the Amsterdam Assembly in 1948, and the Orthodox churches have been part of the ecumenical quest for Christian unity from its earliest stages.

Amsterdam was an inspiring sign that many Protestant and Orthodox churches were seeking Christian unity by coming together in an ecumenical organization. Amsterdam, in the well-known words of its message that "we intend to stay together", was not only a signpost on the ecumenical journey, but was a "sign of the times.

The New Delhi Assembly in 1961 became a signpost marking the entry of the Russian Orthodox Church and other East European Orthodox churches into the WCC. Indeed, the WCC became an ecumenical forum and organization in which all the Eastern and Oriental Orthodox churches participated as full members. The WCC was thus not only a forum in which the Orthodox churches engaged in dialogue and common work with Protestant churches; the WCC was the only forum in which all the Eastern and Oriental Orthodox churches could regularly encounter one another and could regularly share the varying Orthodox experiences in the Middle East, Europe (East and West), Africa, Asia, and North America.

As the assemblies followed one another, the profile and inclusiveness of the WCC changed significantly. In 1948 the WCC was a primarily European organization. By the Canberra Assembly in 1991 the strong presence of Protestant churches from Africa, Asia, South America, the Pacific, and the Middle East was obvious.

While the growing breadth and inclusiveness of the WCC from Amsterdam to Canberra is indisputable, it is also quite clear that many conservative evangelical and charismatic churches and movements in the Protestant world have stayed out of the WCC, and have taken a critical stance towards the WCC and the ecumenical movement.

After the Second Vatican Council in the mid-1960s and the consequent opening of the Roman Catholic Church to ecumenism, the WCC and the Roman Catholic Church engaged one another in dialogue and common action. For a time, it even seemed that the membership of the Roman Catholic Church in the WCC could be envisaged. It has become clear, however, that such a development is not a possibility at this time and in the foreseeable future.

The Orthodox member churches, while engaged in the work and activities of the WCC for fifty years, have found their membership in the WCC becoming more rather than less problematic. Just as assemblies have been signs of new ecumenical life and commitment (Amsterdam, 1948), deepening involvement of the Orthodox churches (New Delhi, 1961), painful but necessary engagement with social issues (Uppsala, 1968), and movement towards a deep theological convergence through the Baptism, Eucharist and Ministry process (Vancouver, 1983), so have they provided signs and images of new forms of alienation and estrangement within the WCC and the ecumenical movement.

At Canberra in 1991 some explorations of the role of the Holy Spirit opened new and necessary perspectives for the ecumenical movement and the WCC, perspectives close to the heart of the Orthodox. Other explorations of the role of the Holy Spirit were occasions for controversy and deep division. A plenary presentation on the Holy Spirit blended the spirits of men and women, the spirits of earth, air, and water, and the Holy Spirit. This provoked serious and even angry debates. One of the key issues to emerge from this debate was the question of the "limits of diversity". Everyone accepts and affirms that the quest for Christian unity is not a quest for uniformity. Christian unity presupposes the presence of "legitimate diversity". But is *all* diversity legitimate? Does not "legitimate diversity" imply the existence of "illegitimate diversity"? And what is the ecumenical and theological process to discern which elements of diversity are legitimate and which are not?

Since Canberra, the question of legitimate and illegitimate diversity has grown more acute in the WCC context. An important illustration is the emergence of homosexuality as a point of discussion and debate. It must be stressed that the WCC governing bodies have clearly *not* affirmed homosexuality. Nevertheless, the issue is more and more present both in debates and in publications of the WCC. It is also part of the context of the Eighth Assembly in Harare.

As the Central Committee was selecting Harare as the next Assembly site, and was also beginning a painful engagement with the issue of homosexuality, Zimbabwe entered a major social and political confrontation over homosexuality. President Mugabe took the lead in denunciations of homosexuality. Homosexual groups around the world, and especially in Western Europe and North America, both in society and in some member churches of the WCC, have taken events in Zimbabwe as a challenge to be advocates of a "prophetic justice" on behalf of homosexual persons and homosexuality as a lifestyle. The process of preparation for the Assembly in Harare gave a central place to the Padare, or market-place, concept. The Padare, while not an official part of the WCC Assembly programme, gives an opportunity to raise a wide range of issues of concern to the churches. Among the Padare offerings and events, a certain number are dedicated to the homosexuality issue. In the meantime, as reported by Ecumenical New International in Geneva, at the end of April President Mugabe has once again very harshly addressed the question of homosexuality. He reiterated his view that homosexuality is completely unacceptable and neither African nor Christian. Further, he is quoted as saying that the "World Council of Churches is even coming here to debate homosexuality, even though it is known internationally that Zimbabwe is opposed to it". It is evident that the homosexuality issue may take center stage at Harare, or at least in the media reporting on the Assembly, even though the official agenda of the Assembly is not intended to go in that direction.

The reaction in the Orthodox churches to the above scenario will be profoundly negative. The theological and ethical teaching of the Orthodox, as well as the biblical context in which we understand theology and ethics, do not allow for the affirmation of the homosexual lifestyle. Thus the integrity of the Orthodox perspective requires both a clarity of ethical teaching regarding what is right and what is wrong and a compassionate and healing attitude to every person who falls into what is wrong and sinful.

In addition, the social context in which the vast majority of Orthodox are living will provoke and negative social and cultural reaction to any of the anticipated debates on homosexuality during the Harare Assembly. This is true about Central and Eastern Europe, the Middle East, Africa, and Asia.

It should not be thought that these new and divisive issues in ecumenical life are the fundamental problems for Orthodox participation in the WCC. It has been pointed out long ago by Orthodox theologians deeply engaged in ecumenical life that profound questions of theology, ecclesiology, and ethos make Orthodox participation in the ecumenical movement and its structures an agony. The clearest analysis of this fundamental difficulty was given in 1963 by Father Alexander Schmemann in an essay called "Moment of Truth for Orthodoxy". The ecumenical movement and the WCC, Fr Alexander points out, are built on the presuppositions of Western Christianity and its experience, and the Orthodox theological and ecclesiology perspective is not readily understood in this context.

For many years, the Eastern and Oriental Orthodox churches in the WCC have borne common witness and have made common cause in the articulation of Orthodox concerns and challenges. This has certainly been true in the context of WCC Assemblies, meetings of the Central Committee, and many consultations and conferences. At the last Central Committee meeting in September 1997, His Holiness Aram I, Catholicos of Cilicia and Moderator of the Central Committee, presented a significant assessment of the WCC and its future from an Orthodox perspective [cf. pp. 111-125 below]. He articulated the central concerns of both Orthodox families of churches, and pointed to the need for changes in the WCC.

The recent (29 April-2 May 1998) Inter-Orthodox meeting in Thessaloniki, Greece, convened by the Ecumenical Patriarchate and dedicated to the "Evaluation of New Facts in the Relations of Orthodoxy and the Ecumenical Movement" [cf. pp. 136-138 below], expressed the major concerns of the Eastern Orthodox churches with regard to the forthcoming Assembly and the overall direction of the ecumenical fellowship as expressed in the WCC. The meeting defined the scope of the participation of Eastern Orthodox church delegations to the Assembly in a radical way. While the Eastern Orthodox church delegations are encouraged to be present at the Harare Assembly, they are not to vote or participate in the Assembly in the normal fashion. Rather, they are to raise the central concerns of their churches regarding the direction of the WCC. They are also to insist on necessary changes in the WCC so as to make the participation of the Orthodox churches possible in the future.

While the Oriental Orthodox churches have not taken any similar formal and concerted action, the fundamental concerns and anxieties of churches in both families are similar and parallel, and usually even identical.

The Moderator of the Central Committee, Catholicos Aram I, has issued an invitation to the Eastern and Oriental Orthodox churches to take part in a "mixed thelogical commission" which is to begin its work in Geneva at the end of June.

At this moment of serious crisis in the WCC and the ecumenical movement the Orthodox churches have an opportunity, together with the ecumenical fellowship as it is constituted in the WCC, to redefine the ecumenical quest in a way which is adequate to the serious challenges of today.

As we Orthodox engage in this process, we will need all of our theological and spiritual resources to measure up to the challenge we face. We must, on the one hand, preserve a sense of humility. Our own shortcomings are clearly manifest. It is not an ecumenical secret that we find it difficult, and sometimes impossible, to maintain the unity of the Spirit in the bond of peace within our Eastern and Oriental church families and between the two families. Yet we share a common Christian vision and perspective. Now, more than ever, our common witness is needed in the ecumenical movement.

In conclusion, a word of caution and sobriety. There will be a temptation on the part of many to attribute the present ecumenical anxiety of the Orthodox to the rise of "fundamentalist" or "fanatical" movements and trends in some Orthodox churches. We should resist such simplifications and such reductionism. While it is indeed true that in some churches "fundamentalist" movements have gained strength and sometimes define the public discourse about the role of the Orthodox church, the issues we face in the WCC are not reducible to the influence and impact of "Orthodox fundamentalists". The issues we face in the WCC are much deeper and much more fundamental. They are issues which have been present in the ecumenical movement from the beginning. We must pray for discernment, spiritual maturity, and courage as we seek to face the present challenge through the common witness of the Eastern and Oriental Orthodox churches.

Orthodox Perspectives from Africa

Reflections from Orthodox African participants at the Pre-Assembly Meeting

Zimbabwe, like any other country in Africa (especially black Africa), is a microcosm of the entire continent of Africa. It represents the realities, the hopes and aspirations, as well as the expectations of the peoples of Africa. For this reason, the people of Zimbabwe would quite adequately represent the world-view, the mind-set, the attitudes, the values, even the spirituality of the peoples of Africa.

Perhaps it is even more important to point out that this world-view has often been re-enforced by the traditional teachings of the so-called "foreign" religions that have come to be a part of Africa's reality – Christianity and Islam. And so it is that African views on and attitudes towards sexuality and morality have generally found support both in the Old and New Testaments, and in the traditional teachings of both Christianity and Islam.

President Mugabe's views and attitudes, manifesting themselves in his open hostility towards homosexuality and the gay movement, cannot therefore be viewed or dismissed as the extremist attitude of an isolated leader. On the contrary, it must be seen as a fair representation of the views and attitudes of a vast majority of the leaders and peoples of Africa.

A second point needs to be made. The ecumenical movement in Africa and its main participants are facing a number of challenges. Not least among these are

(a)   the rapid growth and growing influence of Islam resulting from what is now acknowledged as an aggressive systematic effort to islamise Africa,

(b)   a growing "evangelico-pentecostal" movement bringing with it a growing Christian fundamentalism which, though non-militant, is quite aggressive in its attack on what it views as the traditional churches' departure from traditional Christian values.

Finally, it must be pointed out that in the view of the average African, the highest expression of the ecumenical movement is the WCC (local councils of churches are often seen as local expressions of the WCC). For them this "great organization" still has great moral authority and responsibility to speak the "mind" of Christianity ("the Church") on such new and contentious issues as homosexuality.

As the WCC comes to Zimbabwe and to Africa, it is essential that it is sensitive to these realities and local sensitivities. In Africa, the issue of homosexuality is very contentious and potentially explosive. In our considered view, any attempt to introduce it on the agenda of the Assembly, either directly or indirectly, spells potential disaster not only for the WCC but also for the African Churches.

Participants in the Orthodox Pre-Assembly meeting

Church Delegates

AJABAHYAN, V. Rev. Fr Mikael
Armenian Apostolic Church, Holy See of Etchmiadzin

ALEMEZIAN, V. Rev. Nareg
Armenian Apostolic Church, Catholicosate of Cilicia

ALFEYEV, Rev. Dr Hilarion
Russian Orthodox Church

AMLAK, Mr Wosen Seged Gebre
Ethiopian Orthodox Church

APHREM (Karim), H.E. Metropolitan Mor Cyril
Syrian Orthodox Patriarchate of Antioch

APOSTU, Mr Andrei Dan
Orthodox Church of Czech Lands and Slovakia

BOYAJIAN, Ms Manoushag
Armenian Apostolic Church, Catholicosate of Cilicia

CHRISTOS, H.E. Archbishop Merha
Ethiopian Orthodox Church

CHRYSANTHOS, H.E. Metropolitan of Limassol
Church of Cyprus

DAMIAN, H.E. Bishop of Germany
Coptic Orthodox Church of Alexandria

DANIEL, H.E. Metropolitan of Moldavia and Bukovina
Romanian Orthodox Church

DULE, Mr Vangeli
Orthodox Church of Albania

GENNADIOS, H.E. Metropolitan of Sassima
Ecumenical Patriarchate

GEORGE, Rev. Dr K.M.
Malankara Orthodox Syrian Church

GURBUS, H.E. Metropolitan Mor Dionisius Isa
Syrian Orthodox Patriarchate of Antioch

HOVHANNISSIAN, H.E. Nathan
Armenian Apostolic Church, Holy See of Etchmiadzin

IBRAHIM, H.E. Metropolitan Mar Gregorios Yohanna
Syrian Orthodox Patriarchate of Antioch

JIVI, Rev. Prof. Aurel
  Romanian Orthodox Church
KAHILA, Rev. Gabriel
  Greek Orthodox Patriarchate of Antioch
KALLAS, Ms Mouna
  Greek Orthodox Patriarchate of Antioch
KIMYACI, Ms Ioli
  Ecumenical Patriarchate
LABI, Rev. K.J. Ayete
  Greek Orthodox Patriarchate of Alexandria
LAHAM, Mr Samer
  Greek Orthodox Patriarchate of Antioch
PETROS, H.E. Metropolitan of Aksum
  Greek Orthodox Patriarchate of Alexandria
PHILIPOS, H.G. Metropolitan Mar Eusebius
  Malankara Orthodox Syrian Church
SEBOUH (Sarkissian), H.G.
  Armenian Apostolic Church, Catholicosate of Cilica
SERAPION, H.G. Bishop of Los Angeles
  Coptic Orthodox Church of Alexandria
SHMALIY, Mr Vladimir
  Russian Orthodox Church
STARCOVA , Ms Iveta
  Orthodox Church in Czech Lands and Slovakia
STEFANOWSKI, Rev. Pawel
  Orthodox Church of Poland
TARASAR, Dr Constance
  Orthodox Church in America
VASILIOS, H.G. Bishop of Trimithous
  Church of Cyprus
VERONIS, Rev. Luke
  Orthodox Church of Albania

Consultants
DIMITROV, Dr Ivan
  Bulgarian Orthodox Church
FITZGERALD, Dr Kyriaki
  Ecumenical Patriarchate
PATELOS, Dr Constantin
  Greek Orthodox Patriarchate of Alexandria

Members of the Orthodox Task Force of the WCC
    FITZGERALD, Rev. Prof. Thomas, Moderator
    BOUTENEFF, Dr Peter, Secretary
    LEMOPOULOS, Mr Georges
    MORCOS, Ms Salwa
    SAUCA, Rev. Dr Ioan

    Local administrative staff
    SYRIANI, Mr Razek, *MECC, Youth Program Director*

Stewards
    TORO, Ms Fahima
    Students from the Theological Seminary

Conference Secretary
    SBEGHEN, Mrs Renate, *World Council of Churches*

Participants at the Pan-Orthodox Pre-Assembly Meeting

St Ephrem Theological Seminary, Ma'arat Saydnaya, Syria

Selected Resource Materials

Introduction

Participants at the Orthodox Pre-Assembly meeting were provided with several background documents in order to assist their preparation for the WCC's Eighth Assembly, and to orient their reflections on Orthodox-WCC relations. These resource materials, together with several others which were not available at the time of the meeting, are being published here for the first time under one cover, with the hope that their availability to a wider public will be useful.

The first two items are related to the WCC's process of study and consultation "Towards a Common Understanding and Vision" (CUV). Begun in 1989 at the request of the Central Committee, the CUV study has been an occasion for the WCC to reflect upon itself and present a self-definition. Throughout the process the WCC has engaged churches and church organizations in seeking their responses and advice, often through consultations organized on the basis of region or confession. The first document reproduced here is the final statement of an inter-Orthodox meeting on the CUV reflection process.

The CUV process has resulted in a CUV text. A provisional draft was sent out to WCC member churches in the autumn of 1996 with an invitation to respond. Orthodox responses came in several forms, both formal and informal, in person and in correspondence. Published here are three substantial written responses: from the Ecumenical Patriarchate, from the Russian Orthodox Church, and from the Romanian Orthodox Church. These focus primarily on the CUV process, and thus represent reflections on the entire life of the Council. But the responses also address the CUV text, and here it should be noted that the document under review is the penultimate (September 1996) draft, and not the final (September 1997) draft which is being commended to the Harare Assembly for approval.

Following these materials are reports from four recent inter-Orthodox meetings. Two of these are from gatherings primarily of Orthodox women, reflecting on issues touching all aspects of the Church's life. Another two take place within the African context, the first dealing more broadly with issues of how the Gospel interacts with cultures, the second specifically addressing Orthodoxy in Africa, with an added focus on the Church's response to the HIV/AIDS pandemic.

The Report of the Moderator of the WCC Central Committee, H.H. Aram I, Catholicos of Cilicia, is published here in its abridged form, but represents a very substantial and important summary and evaluation of the present situation.

The official statements of five inter-Orthodox meetings, all taking place within a three-month period in 1998, testify to a marked increase in activity in the area of reflection and recommendations on inter-Orthodox relations and church life, on ecumenism, and on the WCC.

The present volume ends with two reports prepared by the Orthodox Staff Task Force of the WCC. The first of these presents a categorized listing of activities reflecting Orthodox-WCC collaborative work in the period since the Seventh Assembly of the WCC in 1991. The second is an attempt on the part of the Task Force to provide a cross-section of current Orthodox concerns, placing them in the context of recent Orthodox statements.

Common Understanding and Vision of the WCC: Preliminary Observations on the Reflection Process

Final Document of the Inter-Orthodox Consultation on the CUV
Chambésy, Switzerland, June 1995

1. At the invitation of the General Secretary of the WCC, delegates of Eastern and Oriental Orthodox Churches, resource persons, and senior WCC staff met in the Orthodox Centre of the Ecumenical Patriarchate, Chambésy, Geneva, from 19 to 24 June 1995. Representatives of the WCC governing bodies, also invited to this meeting in order to ensure a broader dialogical reflection, were not able to attend.

2. This consultation, organized by the WCC's Office on Church and Ecumenical Relations in consultation with the Orthodox Task Force, was convened in relation to the reflection process on the "Common Understanding and Vision of the World Council of Churches", with the aim of pointing the way forward, reviewing the ecumenical commitment of the Orthodox churches and attempting to clarify underlying uncertainties in their relations to the WCC.

3. The following pages constitute the report of this consultation, a "background document" submitted to the attention of our churches in order to facilitate their task in stating their views about the ecumenical movement at the turn of the twentieth century and in formulating their expectations of the WCC. Our reflections, suggestions and questions are also submitted to the leadership of the WCC with the hope that they will facilitate the ongoing dialogue and contribute to the ongoing common reflection process.

A brief account of our consultation

4. The quality of relationship that the Orthodox experience with others within the WCC is a matter of continuing concern for the Orthodox. The new circumstances that constantly arise in our world can affect the ecumenical relations between churches in negative or positive ways. So the Orthodox churches, committed to the visible unity of Christians, seek to improve these relations in such a way as to witness to the Tradition of the one undivided church and to foster all activities in favour of the well- being of God's world. It is with this understanding that the Orthodox churches periodically review the role of the WCC in relation to its member churches and to its goal of visible unity.

5. The consultation thus began with a presentation by Marlin VanElderen on the process of Common Understanding and Vision of the WCC now under way. This process of wide reflection was initiated because of the changes in the world situation at the end of the Cold War era, changes in the global situation of Christianity, such as the rapid growth of "non-ecumenical" groups, the difficulties in the reception of the WCC agenda in the churches and structural problems in the organization of the WCC.

6. In his presentation, Dr Konrad Raiser, General Secretary of the WCC, shared some reflections and proposed some questions for further consideration. He reminded us that, on the ground of earlier discussions about the future and the programmatic orientation of the WCC, it would appear that there are four areas which require close attention in the ongoing process of reflection on "Common Understanding and Vision of the WCC". These include (a) the nature and task of the WCC as a "fellowship of churches"; (b) the role of the WCC in the "one ecumenical movement"; (c) forms of representation, participation and communication within the WCC fellowship, and (d) steps towards an integrating vision of the WCC.

7. Metropolitan John of Pergamon presented the topic of the self-understanding of the Orthodox and their participation in the ecumenical movement. The speaker elaborated this on the basis of the fundamental Orthodox ecclesiological understanding of the Church as a historical, eschatological, relational, and sacramental entity. He pointed out issues involved in the Orthodox self-consciousness vis-à-vis the WCC and called for a creative transformation of the dialectic between West and East. While he clearly affirmed that the Orthodox churches will not be able to identify the WCC as a church body through the marks of the *Una Sancta*, he distinguished between "*being a Church* and *bearing ecclesiological significance*". "Anything that contributes to the building up of the Church", the speaker said, "or to the reception and fulfilment of the churches' life and unity bears ecclesiological significance. In this respect, the ecumenical movement and the WCC are strongly qualified candidates, for they have as their primary object and *raison d'être* the restoration of the unity of the church. This makes it imperative for the WCC to keep the unity of the Church at the centre of its life and concerns. It is this that makes it ecclesiologically significant". The Orthodox self-understanding of the *Una Sancta* will always continue to be the guiding criterion for Orthodox participation in the ecumenical movement.

8. Metropolitan Kyrill of Smolensk made a presentation on the Orthodox expectations from the WCC. In particular he called on the Faith and Order Commission to renew the study of the theme "Holy Tradition", the understanding of which continues to divide Orthodox churches and the churches of the Reformation. This is the reason for which WCC positions very often seem to challenge Orthodox identity. The confrontation is painful and thus it is very difficult to state clearly what we expect from the WCC. In this sense, criticism coming from Orthodox churches has to be answered first by the Orthodox themselves. With regard to the reflection process on the "Common Understanding and Vision of the WCC", the speaker

reminded us that the nature of the WCC should not be understood as an additional stimulus for the ecumenical movement. The "Toronto Statement" not only facilitated but also broadened Orthodox participation. Theological dialogue should help us to grow together. And this very growth will help us to define our position. It is impossible to artificially raise the level of ecumenical awareness. WCC involvement in challenging competition in mission and in enabling the local churches to educate the people of God are two areas of priorities particularly appreciated by the Orthodox. "How do we look at the coming century?" the speaker concluded. We have to be theologically and spiritually prepared, and particularly careful with the new contradictions and conflicts which will emerge. We have to seriously consider questions such as "What is the situation of the Orthodox oikoumene?" and "What will be the place of Christianity as such in the coming years?"

9. In the presentation on the current agenda of the WCC seen from an Orthodox perspective by Fr K.M. George, he pointed out that, in three fundamental areas of worship, interpretation and service to the world, there is still a serious lack of communication between the positions and methodologies of the Orthodox and Protestant partners in the WCC. The Orthodox should continue to view critically' the dominant cultural theological paradigm that guides the WCC. However, the Orthodox by creatively bringing out their own theological and spiritual vision for the guidance of the ecumenical movement can open up new possibilities for the future. The presentation called for stronger Orthodox leadership in the ecumenical movement which can open alternate ways of moving forward to the goal of unity.

10. The first part of the consultation centred around the above mentioned topics raised by the speakers. The discussion took place in a context of dialogue between Orthodox delegates and WCC staff. The discussion on these questions emphasized the following concerns.

Our participation in the ecumenical movement and in the WCC

11. The Orthodox Church is involved in the WCC and other appropriate ecumenical organizations because of its concern for the restoration of Christian unity. Our Lord prayed that his disciples be one so that the world may believe and the Father would be glorified (Jn. 17:21). This prayer of the Lord is reflected in our daily prayer "for the holy churches of God and for the union of all". The saving work of our Lord was directed toward our reconciliation with the Father, with one another, and with creation. Our involvement in the quest of Christian unity is inspired by the Holy Spirit. As St Paul has said: "God was in Christ reconciling the world to himself and he has given to us the ministry of reconciliation" (2 Cor 5:18).

12. We believe that "Orthodox participation in the ecumenical movement does not run contrary to the nature and history of the Orthodox Church. It constitutes the consistent expression of the apostolic faith within new historical conditions in order to respond to new existential demands" (Third Pre-conciliar Pan-Orthodox Conference, 1986).

13. "One of the principal bodies of the contemporary ecumenical movement is the WCC. Despite the fact that it does not include all Christian Churches and Confessions and that other ecumenical organizations are also playing an important role in the promotion of the ecumenical movement at large, the WCC represents today a structured ecumenical body. Some of the Orthodox Churches were among the Council's founding members, and later on all the local Orthodox Churches became its members (...) The Orthodox Church is a full-fledged and equal member of the WCC and with all the means at her disposal, contributes to the progress and success of all WCC activities" (Third Pre-conciliar Pan-Orthodox Conference, 1986).

14. Our Churches participate in the Council with an appreciation of the valuable insights contained in the Toronto Statement of 1950, "The Church, the Churches, and the World Council of Churches". In accordance with this statement, we view the WCC as a Council of Churches whose primary goal is to assist the member churches in the quest for the restoration of full communion. "The WCC is not and must never become a Super-Church". Guided by this affirmation of the Toronto Statement, we do not view the WCC as a "Super-Church", nor do we ascribe any "ecclesial character" to its being. It is presently a valuable instrument for the member churches which serves the churches in their movement towards unity.

15. We wish also to affirm the importance of the constitutional basis of the WCC. In order for the Council to be faithful to its fundamental purpose, it must maintain its identity as a "Council of Churches" composed of member churches who accept its constitutional basis and who are, therefore, committed to the quest for Christian unity. We do not feel that the Council will be served by the inclusion of groups or movements. Likewise, we strongly reject any tendency which would turn the Council away from its fundamental vocation. We affirm that the WCC is "a fellowship of churches which confess the Lord Jesus Christ as God and Saviour according to the Scriptures and therefore seek to fulfill together their common calling to the glory of the one God, Father, Son, and Holy Spirit".

Positive assessment of our participation in the ecumenical movement

16. Orthodox participation in the ecumenical movement in general and in the WCC in particular has proved to be profitable in many ways.

17. The WCC has been a forum for theological dialogue on Christian unity. It has served as a platform for encounter between the Orthodox churches and other churches in different parts of the world. Orthodox churches have been invited to give witness to their spirituality which goes beyond boundaries of East or West, North or South.

18. Participation in the ecumenical movement has allowed Orthodox Churches to transcend all forms of isolation imposed on them by the political developments of the last several decades. The WCC has served as a legitimate facilitator of meetings on the one hand among the Orthodox churches who, otherwise, may have been forced by particular circumstances to remain isolated from each other. On the other

hand, the WCC has offered numerous occasions to Orthodoxy to be introduced to other Christians, religious communities and the world at large. This has helped Orthodox theology to manifest itself in a fuller way.

19. As in this meeting, the Council has always given the opportunity to the Orthodox Churches to discuss together the meaning of their participation in the ecumenical movement as well as the impact of this movement on their lives and local ministries.

20. Moreover, the WCC has began to speak and act on matters of peace, justice and human rights related to particular conditions in which the local Orthodox churches involved were not free to articulate their position or to affect the situation.

21. The WCC has also been able, through its resource-sharing processes, to provide human and material resources needed mainly for the development of the educational and diaconal services of the Orthodox Churches.

The difficulties we face

22. Remembering the past or assessing the present ecumenical situation, we are convinced that any search for a common approach in the future will have to take seriously into consideration a great number of underlying uncertainties. Most of these uncertainties have already been stated in the past (cf. Eastern Orthodox- WCC Consultation in Sofia, 1981; third Pre-conciliar Pan-Orthodox Conference, 1986; Inter-Orthodox Consultation in Chambésy, 1991). The difficulties faced by the Orthodox in the life and decision-making process of the WCC include, among others, dilemmas of theological, cultural and procedural nature.

23. Theological:

(a) We observe that some results of the theological dialogue which have been undertaken to this date by the WCC member churches are not satisfactory.

(b) We note a tendency in some WCC initiatives to address topics without sufficient attention being given to theological perspectives rooted in Scripture and Tradition.

(c) In the ecumenical movement we discern a tendency to accept a certain relativity of Christian faith which seems to minimize the concept of heresy.

(d) In our ecumenical activity we recognize the value of both unity and diversity. We recognize that unity does not mean uniformity but, at the same time, we are concerned about the limits of diversity.

(e) Orthodox churches manifest their life and witness in the context of local ecclesia, as a concrete expression of the one Church. Other member churches of the WCC tend to overlook this concept in the name of a certain universalism which justifies churches or Christian groups anywhere to exercise their missionary outreach or jurisdictional authority regardless of the life, witness and integrity of the local ecclesia. This gives the impression to the Orthodox Churches that while through love, dialogue and mutual respect they are seeking church unity, other member churches of the WCC are exacerbating this attempt by engaging in proselytism among Orthodox Christians, leading to further divisions of the Churches.

(f)   Despite their openness to new biblical insights or interpretations, the Orthodox member churches are clearly hesitant to accept the new radical theologies emerging today in many member churches of the WCC and, consequently, in the ecumenical movement. These theologies are related to inclusive language when referring to God, to women's ordination, to priesthood, to sexual morals, and to abortion.

(g)   We cannot accept any tampering with the language of Scripture or any attempt to re-write it, or any effort to conform it to the beliefs or ideology of any particular culture, denomination or movement.

(h)   Orthodox Churches have demonstrated a genuine openness to other religions. They are also convinced that the encounter with these religions is necessary to promote mutual respect, cooperation in humanitarian service and peace. While affirming the ultimate significance of witnessing to Christ, we enter into a dialogue with other religions without giving in to syncretism but for the sake of mutual understanding and with the awareness that "God's call is a call to live in peace" (1 Cor. 7:15).

(i)   We recognize that in several of our churches, because of inter-Christian tensions, there are questions being raised as to the practice of praying together with non-Orthodox. Orthodox participants in ecumenical events organized by the WCC and other ecumenical bodies can attend common prayers according to the principle of *oikonomia* and under certain circumstances, provided that both the prayers and the shape of worship are consistent with Orthodox teaching and do not contradict Orthodox liturgical ethos or tradition.

(j)   The Orthodox, however, do not participate in ecumenical eucharistic celebrations, for according to our ecclesiology the eucharist is the supreme expression of the unity of the church and not a means towards Christian unity. We reiterate the observation of the Inter-Orthodox Consultation of 1991 that between Christians there is "only eucharistic communion and there cannot be something called 'intercommunion' since that term together with the practice it designates is a contradiction". In that respect we wish to emphasize that the "Lima liturgy" elaborated in relationship with the BEM document, notwithstanding its theological value, cannot be considered as an ecumenical liturgy which enables the participation in it of the entire constituency of the WCC.

24. Cultural:

(a)   In conjunction with their participation in the ecumenical movement, Orthodox Churches have been able to go beyond their traditional cultural boundaries with the belief that their faith, church, and theological expressions are universal. We have the impression, however, that sometimes other member churches of the WCC tend to consider us "of the East" and, therefore, they perceive our theology to be without relevance to the modern, rational, and developed West. We reject this perception and we affirm the catholicity of our faith.

(b) We have the impression that the WCC is succumbing to the pressure of adopting secular values, considering them universal and, therefore, acceptable by all churches or cultural ethos in which these churches live and witness. In this regard it is important to note that the Orthodox participants hesitate to accept any proposed positivistic formula related to these values. Our ethics are person-oriented rather than principle-oriented.

25. Procedural:

(a) Orthodox members of the WCC governing bodies consider themselves a numerical minority. For this reason the WCC is requested to review its constitution with an eye to the distinctive ecclesiological structuring of the Orthodox churches. "An essential Orthodox witness and its specific theological contribution will be weakened, if we cannot find within the WCC the necessary conditions which will enable the Orthodox Churches to act on an equal footing with the other WCC members, on the basis of their own ecclesiological identity and in accordance with their own ways of thinking" (Third Pre-conciliar Pan-Orthodox Conference, 1986). Moreover, the WCC is asked to reconsider the present conditions of membership which seem to allow a continuous increase in the number of member churches.

(b) Orthodox churches appreciate in general the attention given by the WCC to issues of human rights, justice and peace. Nevertheless, the Council should be asked to refrain from taking political positions or actions without sufficient consultation with the local churches concerned. This will help the WCC to avoid attitudes that may be considered discriminatory by the churches involved. The WCC appears to address some ethnic and political conflicts while it appears to avoid others.

(c) The WCC should be asked to review its resource-sharing policy and methodology in order to respect the priorities established by the local churches themselves. This will avoid what is considered in some situations a selective financial assistance based on selected criteria which are foreign to the churches requesting assistance through the WCC.

(d) We commend the Orthodox staff serving today on behalf of our churches the WCC and the ecumenical community. We wish, however, to take note of their numbers in the WCC. Despite the good intentions of the

Council and a certain increase in recent years, the number of Orthodox staff are relatively small compared to the total. At present there are twelve Orthodox executive staff in a total of 102 (cf. Executive Committee, February 1995, Doc. 9.5).

New possibilities or new sources of tension?

26. The interest of non-member churches in the life and work of the WCC has drawn our attention. We welcome this as a sign of hope for the future of the ecumenical movement and the enrichment of the ecumenical vision. We raise the question, however, as to whether such a presence will have a deleterious effect on Orthodox involvement with regard to the issue of balanced participation. We also call for further reflection on the issue of selective involvement in the work of the WCC by non-member churches.

27. An important aspect of the Orthodox contribution to the ecumenical movement is its understanding of the community of women and men in church and society. We welcome the efforts of the WCC to call the churches to inclusive participation. We were reminded by our young participants, for example, of the importance of offering space to Orthodox youth and the need to listen to them. Whether such participation should simply be proposed – and not imposed – on churches is an issue which has to be taken very seriously into consideration.

Looking towards the future

28. "How can we renew our commitment to the ecumenical movement? How can we interpret this movement in a meaningful way? Can we all share a message of hope with the world at the end of this millennium? What should we propose as a basic orientation for the life and work of the Council into the 21st century?" To these questions, raised by the General Secretary, we would like to offer the following observations as a basis for future discussion.

29. We affirm the imperative of placing the confession of the one apostolic faith and the ecclesiology of the one undivided church at the heart of the work of the WCC. It is extremely important to deepen together the understanding of the Church as a historical, eschatological, relational and sacramental entity. We appreciate the contribution of the Faith and Order Commission in this respect

30. In view of the many dilemmas tormenting human existence today, it is essential to deepen together our Christian awareness of social and ethical issues as well as ecology in the light of Christian spirituality rather than on the basis of secular ideology. As stated in the report of the Inter-Orthodox Consultation in Chambésy, 1991, "the Orthodox have had to react against the tendency within the WCC towards a one-sided 'horizontalism' which tends to disconnect social, political, environmental problems from our commitment to the gospel of Jesus Christ. Such one-sided horizontalism suggests an acceptance of the autonomy of secular life. The Orthodox believe that no aspect of life is autonomous or disconnected from the Christian's

confession of the Incarnation and its consequence: the gift of divine life in the image of the Holy Trinity. It is because we believe in the Incarnation and the Trinity that we are committed to problems of justice, peace and the integrity of creation."

31. The issue of contextualization and inculturation of the church needs to receive renewed attention. The experience Orthodoxy has had so far can prove to be valuable in this regard.

32. We commit ourselves to work together to fill the spiritual vacuum created by the secular ideologies and their recent withdrawal. We also need to face the proliferation of sects and the new para-religious and para-church movements. This is yet another priority.

33. Bearing witness to reconciliation in situations of conflict, violence, poverty, and the hardening of attitude of those of one faith community towards another is of paramount importance. In this regard, we may have to pay particular attention to the reality of cultural pluralism and the subsequent threat of future conflicts.

34. We conclude by giving thanks to God for this opportunity to meet together and reflect upon our participation in the WCC. As we look forward to progressing in the quest for Christian reconciliation and unity we recall St Paul: "Bonded and knit together by every constituent joint, the whole frame grows through the due activity of each part, and builds itself up in love" (Eph. 4:16).

Three Orthodox Contributions to the Common Understanding and Vision Process
Responses to the CUV Draft of September 1996

I. Response of the Ecumenical Patriarchate

Introductory remarks

1. The Ecumenical Patriarchate, after having studied with due attention the Working Draft for the Policy Statement "Towards a Common Understanding and Vision of the World Council of Churches", wishes firstly to express satisfaction with the fact that many views formulated in its Memorandum of November 30, 1995, commenting on the first draft, have been taken into consideration and are now reflected in several parts of the present Working Draft.

2. While reiterating some key points of this Memorandum, concerning (a) the nature of the fellowship experienced in the WCC (paragraphs 2-3), (b) the ecclesiastical character of the WCC (paragraph 4), and (c) the meaning and scope of the ecumenical movement (paragraph 8), with the present document we wish to offer some additional observations on a number of crucial points of the Working Draft.

3. In formulating our response, we shall first affirm all those positive elements of the Working Draft which give a new direction and scope to the WCC. Secondly we shall proceed to a wider critique of points of the Working Draft, needing further elaboration. Finally, we shall express some thoughts concerning the institutional implications of the whole exercise on the WCC.

Positive elements of the Document

4. In the Document under study, particularly in paragraph 3.15 which implies constitutional changes, there is strong emphasis on the role the member churches should play from now on in the WCC, which in its institutional expression becomes an instrument of the churches, assisting them in their endeavor to promote Christian unity and serve humanity. This is a positive evolution.

5. We consider that paragraph 3.15 constitutes undoubtedly an important element which positively challenges member churches, inviting them to place themselves at

the epicenter of the WCC. This paragraph attributes a special character and ethos to the WCC, but also gives a more evident role to the churches, which are challenged to fulfill their membership responsibilities vis-à-vis the Council.

6. The policy, throughout the document, to qualify the WCC as a "koinonia" (fellowship) of its member churches, helps us to better conceive the nature of the Council and its acknowledgment as an instrument having a concrete function and mission within the contemporary ecumenical movement. This aspect of the WCC has already been covered satisfactorily, for almost half a century now, by the Toronto Declaration.

7. Yet we consider that the New Testament term "koinonia" (fellowship), used by the contemporary ecumenical terminology either in its full sense as "koinonia", or in its meaning as fellowship, should be deepened further and more systematically by the Council and its instruments. It is necessary to make a theological analysis of this term and further discuss its use by the churches, given the fact that Orthodox and non-Orthodox interpretations vary according to circumstances. We offer some examples of the ways in which this term is interpreted: "Koinonia" could mean theologically "*communio Trinitatis*", namely the communion between the three persons of the Holy Trinity; or the communion, through faith, of human beings with the mystery of the Triune God; a "*communicatio in sacris*" through our participation in the sacraments, particularly the sacrament of the Eucharist. From an ecclesiological perspective, "koinonia" could also mean the simple communication or relationships between churches in dialogue. There is also the more common interpretation of "koinonia" as fellowship, either as a means of communication with each other, or as an instrument of coexistence of parent or homogenous ecclesiastical entities, relating to each other constitutionally and on the basis of common faith, doctrine, and order (i.e. Christian World Communions such as the Anglican Communion). To the above possible interpretations, one should also add the sociological dimension of the term, as it was used by the Ecumenical Patriarchate in 1920, after the example of the "League (koinonia) of Nations" founded also in 1920, to express the wider community or communion of Christian churches called to cooperate and serve together the common endeavor for Christian unity. Such a wide spectrum of meanings should be clarified as precisely as possible, in order to avoid confusion, diverging interpretations, and erroneous use of this term in the churches' ecumenical theology.

8. Once the term "koinonia" (fellowship) is clarified, we shall be able to better understand the shift of the center of gravity described in paragraph 3.15, as well as the redistribution of roles between the Council and its member churches. To our judgement, this redistribution of roles constitutes a triple challenge:

(a) *An ecclesiological challenge*: because it calls the churches not to regard any more the WCC as an instrument which holds, among other things, conferences and consultations to help the search of the visible unity of the churches through theological conversations and agreements, but also as a means which challenges partners in the wider ecumenical movement, calling them to cooperate and reflect theologically, to suffer and witness together, and finally to share a deeper understanding about the church, in order to proceed, God willing, in their unity in faith within the one undivided church, the *Una Sancta*. This is why, as we pointed out in our Memorandum of November 1995, "after fifty years of fruitful cooperation within the World Council of Churches, its members are obliged to clarify the meaning and the extent of the fellowship they experience in it, as well as the ecclesiological significance of 'koinonia', which is, precisely, the purpose and the aim of the World Council of Churches, and not the given reality". This is in fact the ecclesiological challenge about which we spoke in the preceding paragraph 7.

(b) *An ecumenical challenge*: because it compels churches and confessions of a given local situation to live, according to cases, their ecumenical commitment in a concrete way, within a model of ecclesiastical coexistence or a form of ecclesiastical togetherness. At the same time, it invites Protestant churches and denominations of the same ecclesiastical and theological background to fully live this fellowship, particularly in cases where their faithful have in practice overcome denominational barriers.

(c) *An institutional challenge*: because it invites member churches to fulfill in practice their duties deriving from their constitutional rights, through a closer and co-responsible interaction with the Council, and by fulfilling all their moral and material obligations towards it.

9. We note that in paragraph 3.15 the aim of the WCC is stipulated in the following way: "The primary purpose of the fellowship of churches in the WCC is to call one another to the goal of visible unity in one faith and in one eucharistic fellowship, expressed in worship and common life, witness and service to the world, and to advance towards that unity in order that the world may believe". In this way, the paragraph determines the work and the aims of the Council, by giving on the one hand primordial role to the member churches and on the other, by projecting the obvious fact that all the activities of the Council should derive from our unity in Jesus Christ. This is correct and it should never cease to be our final aim.

10. We believe that this last affirmation should not be considered as a subjugation of one ecumenical activity to another one, but rather as a positive step towards assuring a consistent and coherent implementation of the Council's programmatic activities and, at the same time, overcoming the false dilemma between the vertical and horizontal dimensions of its work.

11. We take note of the trend of the Working Document not to present the WCC as the "unique privileged" instrument of the ecumenical movement. As it was stated in the above mentioned Memorandum of the Ecumenical Patriarchate, experience has shown that during the last twenty years the establishment of bilateral relations between churches and the multiplication of ecumenical or inter-Christian organizations and movements, serving also the goal of Christian unity, compel the churches to continue considering the WCC as a positive means and yet not as the unique instrument of ecumenical cooperation. For this reason, we welcome the

emphasis given by the draft document to the obligation of the WCC to be a servant of the "one ecumenical movement", by recognizing the fact that there exists a large spectrum of church related ecumenical partners beyond the member churches and by highlighting the need for increased relationship and cooperation with them.

12. In this conjunction, we consider as positive evolution the willingness of the Council, as expressed in chapter 4, to develop constructive working relationships with the REOs, NCCs, CWCs, and particularly with the Roman Catholic Church.

13. The wish for a closer contact and collaboration of the WCC with the Roman Catholic Church was expressed by the Ecumenical Patriarchate in 1973 on the occasion of the Twenty-fifth anniversary of the WCC. We reiterate this wish today, being convinced that a Roman Catholic presence "would truly enrich the WCC and give to it still wider ecumenical dimensions".

Wider critique

14. Speaking about unity as "gift which is already ours", as paragraph 2.7.1 tries to do, is not entirely accurate. Certainly, in the design of the Divine oikonomia, the Church, as Body of Christ, is one. On the basis of this theological given, many contemporary ecumenical scholars believe that the unity of the Church is a God given gift. Nevertheless the major problem of the ecumenical movement today is the problem of historical and theological divisions, of schisms and heresies. In the course of history the unity of the churches was lost, hence all their efforts to restore this unity both bilaterally and multilaterally, through their direct relationships and also within the framework of the WCC.

15. It is certainly true that in many situations churches and denominations emerged with the Reformation movement, experience various models of unity as a result of "agreements", such as those of Bonn, Leuenberg, Meissen, Porvoo, etc. This is a development to be greeted with satisfaction. The affirmation of paragraph 2.7.6 however that "the unity of the universal church is experienced in the local church and in the communion between local churches", although it is correct as such, does not apply necessarily in regions where co-exist churches of different historical, ecclesiological and theological backgrounds and traditions, given the fact that there is no catholic unity neither between them, nor within the wider framework of the historic as well as the contemporary Christendom.

16. Many times in the past we dealt with the issue of "unity in diversity". Speaking however on the same subject in broader terms (paragraph 2.7.7) we run the danger to give the impression that the WCC considers *diversity in faith* as legitimate. Something in contradiction with the very basis and aims of the WCC which, according to its constitution seeks precisely "*the unity of Churches in one faith and in one eucharistic fellowship*", a unity not realized and not experienced so far. Our readiness to reconcile divided humanity will be credible only when Christians will be truly united and when their churches will be truly sisters.

17. The scope of the *one ecumenical movement* is satisfactorily reflected in paragraph 2.8. We are in favor of contacts and dialogue with other faiths, and in principle we agree with the phrase pleading for "reconciliation... with all who seek the truth within communities of other faiths". We think nevertheless that in doing so we should avoid any religious syncretism which would attribute only a relative value to *the truth* revealed in Jesus Christ, the truth which assures salvation.

18. Having already commented, in the introduction of this response, the principle elements of chapters 3 and 4, we think it is not necessary to develop further thoughts on the self-understanding of the WCC and on its relations with other ecumenical partners of major or lesser ecclesiological identity.

Thoughts on the institutional implications

19. We are aware that chapters 5 and 6 of the Working Draft, dealing with institutional implications, constitute only preliminary suggestions, which after consideration by the member churches and further elaboration will be submitted for study and approval through a separate process.

20. We wish however to underline from now that any structural changes related both to the legislative, governing and consultative bodies of the WCC, as well as to the internal structure of its head-quarters, should be implemented with discernment and sensitivity in order not to alter the main character of the Council. We shall come back on this point after reception of the elaborated version of chapters 5 and 6.

21. For the time being, we wish to offer comments on the following three points:

(a) In principle, we agree with the assertion of paragraph 6.15 that, in the course of the decades, the Assembly became a rather cumbersome instrument which should find a new raison d'être and acquire a more efficacious way of functioning. We note with certain reservation the proposal to abolish the Assembly and, eventually, to replace it by a wider Forum to deal with major ecumenical issues (paragraph 6.15). We also note with even greater reservation the proposal that the heads of member churches meet periodically to get acquainted with each other, to discuss together themes on the agenda of the WCC, and to draw jointly its main orientations. We consider that, for the time being, both suggestions, i.e. the meetings of Heads of member churches and the creation of a major ecumenical Forum, are unachievable, the more so as their relation to the constitutional functions of the WCC are unclear.

(b) We disagree with paragraphs 6.16, 6.17 and 6.18 concerning the representation of member churches and the mode of nomination of their delegates in the governing bodies of the WCC. The proposal foreseeing the election of Central Committee members by "ecumenical electoral groupings" instead of the member churches, underestimates ecclesiological presuppositions and thus, from an ecclesiological perspective, affects the traditional member churches of the WCC, and particularly Orthodoxy as a whole. At the same time, it minimizes the wider character of the ecumenical realities in many parts of the world. And above all, it contradicts the main thrust of the Working Draft which precisely wishes the WCC to remain a "Council of Churches".

(c) Paragraph 6.18 confirms the two-decades old praxis of the WCC to set aside 25% of the Central Committee seats (and consequently of the Assembly and the other governing and consultative bodies of the Council) for the Orthodox, including the Non-Chalcedonian Oriental Churches. We clearly state that this practice was never considered by the Orthodox as satisfactory, for it should not be forgotten that within the Council are represented two out of the three major ecclesiastical traditions of the world, namely, on the one hand, the entire Orthodox world and the Non-Chalcedonian Oriental Churches, and, on the other hand, part of the Protestant world. Yet, both the ecclesiastical and theological ethos of the Council, as well as its way of thinking, acting, and voting remains Protestant, mainly of Anglo-Saxon Presbyterian inspiration. This is why we fear that even if they occupy the 25% of the seats, the Orthodox in the Council will continue to form its *de facto* minority, while the Council will continue moving according to the predominant will of its numerical majority. This is why we think that we should find ways of deciding by consensus, particularly on matters concerning faith, ecclesiastical order, and Christian ethics. We believe that the time has come to seek a qualitative rather than a quantitative presence of the various ecclesiastical traditions present in the World Council of Churches.

(d) The different "quotas" in the WCC (representing gender, age, qualifications, responsibilities and , naturally, geographical belonging) have their specific significance and importance for the Council and should be taken seriously into consideration in the process of building up and strengthening the fellowship which is experienced in the WCC. However, a clear distinction should be made between the nature and character of these categories of representation, in order to avoid comparisons between unequal measures.

22. In anticipation to receiving the final document of the CUV process, which will be worked out by the Central Committee next September *ad referendum* to the forthcoming Eighth Assembly, and which we shall comment in a more definitive way, we wish you every success, praying that the Holy Spirit illumines and guides all those who are entrusted with the implementation of this important undertaking.

At the Phanar, June 1997

II. Response of the Russian Orthodox Church

At the request of the Holy Synod of the Russian Orthodox Church, the Synodal Theological Commission here presents its opinion on the theme "Common understanding and vision the World Council of Churches", together with a response to the draft statement of 27 June 1996 and some editorial amendments to it.

1. A broad and thorough discussion of the theme "Common understanding and vision of the WCC" seems to us quite timely and necessary for several reasons.

Firstly, for the fifty years of its existence the WCC has grown quantitatively, and at present consists of members which had not belonged to it at the time of the Council's foundation. Along with its quantitative growth, the WCC is becoming increasingly heterogeneous, a fact which in some cases complicates dialogue among member churches. There remains a kind of estrangement between Protestant majority and Orthodox minority in the Council. Orthodox participants more often than not find themselves under the necessity of taking a defensive position at large ecumenical gatherings and they do not feel that their voice is properly heard. The correlation of forces in the Council has considerably changed over fifty years, and therefore the common understanding and vision of the WCC is in need of review.

Secondly, some member churches as well as some representatives of WCC leadership are persistently propounding an idea that the Council has grown not only quantitatively but also qualitatively and that it has acquired ecclesiological meaning. Though the term "Super-Church" is not applied to the WCC, sometimes the concepts of the Church and of a "fellowship of Churches" are confused in the Council's documents. Orthodox participants of the WCC think it necessary to give a proper response to these trends and to convey their views on the problem.

Thirdly, public debate on Orthodox participation in the ecumenical movement in general and in the World Council of Churches in particular is growing in some Orthodox Churches, the Russian Orthodox Church among them. The search for doctrinal consensus between the Protestants and the Orthodox which has lasted many years has not yet reached the desired result. At each major ecumenical gathering ideas are suggested which turn out to be unacceptable to the Orthodox, such as "intercommunion", female priesthood, or the inclusive language of the Bible. In this connection we are asked the question: what is the meaning of our participation in the ecumenical movement? In order to answer we must first formulate our present understanding of the WCC.

Fourthly, public dissatisfaction with the World Council of Churches is growing within the Orthodox Church, largely due to various para-ecumenical, youth, feminist and other groups and movements which often use the WCC to express their own interests. Orthodox, Roman Catholics and other catholically minded Christians are deeply concerned at the increasing deviation from the basic norms of Christian morals in such areas as family values, the sacredness of marriage, the right to life, abortions, biotechnology, etc. The problem of our understanding and vision of the WCC becomes even more acute in connection with this process.

Fifthly, the change of political climate in the countries of Eastern Europe has brought about a situation in which a great number of missionaries from abroad are active on many of their territories, and of Russia in particular, where Orthodoxy used to be the traditional confession. Unfortunately, representatives of the WCC member churches are also to be found among them. Though the Council rejects proselytism on the official level, some of its members are engaged in this kind of activity. This makes the problem of the common understanding and vision of the WCC even more acute as there are members of the Council capable of activities which damage the interests of other members.

2. Up to now the WCC's activity has been based on the Toronto Statement of 1950, the major provisions of which reflect the common understanding and vision of the WCC on the part of its Orthodox member churches. It is this Statement that made the Orthodox participation in the Council possible, and any attempt to alter its major provisions brings with it the necessity of revising our own attitude to the Council. The statement of the WCC Eighth Assembly on "Common Understanding and Vision" should deepen and clarify the provisions of the Toronto Declaration, but in no way to disaffirm them.

3. We consider the WCC as a "fellowship of Churches", i.e. as an interreligious forum where every church has a right to uphold its positions and to express its point of view proceeding from its own vision, its tradition and its teaching. The WCC has no right to compel a church to accept a dogmatic statement which to this or that extent contradicts the teaching of this particular church. The WCC has no mechanism, and should not have any in future, to bring influence to bear upon its member churches in doctrinal and other matters. All agreements on dogmatic questions are to be reached between member churches or groups of churches. The Council in this case plays only an auxiliary and coordinating role.

4. The WCC serves the churches on their way to visible unity which should find its expression in the achievement of eucharistic fellowship among them. Until visible unity and eucharistic fellowship are reached, any change of the Council's nature is out of the question.

In this connection any attempt to present the WCC as having qualitatively grown into something more than a "fellowship of churches" should be stopped. It was a "fellowship of churches" at the time of its foundation and remains as such at present. In order to avoid any perplexity and confusion in the WCC documents, the notions of the Church and of a "fellowship of churches" should be clearly differentiated. Traditional ecclesiological terms such as "the body of Christ" should not be applied to the WCC. The term "communion" cannot characterize relationships among the WCC member churches as this term traditionally speaks of the eucharistic fellowship which has not yet been achieved.

5.   Recently one can observe a gradual diminution of theological discussions on key doctrinal themes, and a parallel shift of emphasis towards social programs. The latter are undoubtedly important and conducive to mutual enrichment of member churches as they help them to know one another better. Nevertheless we are convinced that the visible unity we seek can be achieved only on the basis of dialogue on doctrinal questions. In this regard we attach special importance to the work of Unit I and the Commission on Faith and Order which is of primary importance to the major task of the WCC, namely the search for the unity of all Christians.

Discussions of the theme of "Tradition" should be renewed in the framework of this Commission and particularly in the debates on ecumenical hermeneutics, since the different understandings of this theme set up an insurmountable barrier between Orthodox and Protestants. For the Orthodox, Tradition as expressed in the experience of the Early Undivided Church is a norm of faith. Whatever is at variance with this norm is perceived as heresy by the Orthodox, whereas in the Protestant theology a normative and binding perception of Tradition is lacking and therefore the notion of heresy is also lacking. It is evident that until the key notions of the theological language of the Early Undivided Church, such as "Tradition", "dogma", "heresy" and the like are not clearly defined in the vocabulary of the World Council of Churches it will not be possible to achieve visible unity among its member churches.

6.   As far as the role of the WCC in the one ecumenical movement is concerned, we consider it our duty to point out that the term "ecumenical" in our understanding speaks about the movement towards the rapprochement of Christians among themselves for the sake of achieving the unity of the Church. Therefore the ecumenical movement should not become a movement for the rapprochement of Christians with representatives of non-Christian religions. Dialogue between the WCC and non-Christian religions is necessary, but it should not place the inter-Christian dialogue on the periphery. In the course of dialogue with non-Christians a theological syncretism is inadmissible. There must be clear criteria for reasonable dialogue, and it should never become a search for compromise which jeopardizes the major truths of Christianity.

7.   We attach great importance to the studies in the theme "Apostolic Faith" and believe that the acknowledgement of the Nicene-Constantinopolitan Creed by all member churches of the WCC as an adequate expression of the apostolic faith would undoubtedly become a major step towards the doctrinal unity among the churches.

8.   In the course of studies in the theme "Ecclesiology and Ethics" a common criterion should be elaborated for the evaluation of the developments in contemporary life on the basis of moral principles of Christianity. At present many moral values are under attack on the part of the secular society, and some churches are ready to waive moral norms for the sake of retaining their positions in the society. The notion of "sin", which has fallen into disuse in the secularized world, is disappearing also from the vocabulary of some churches. This trend is detrimental not only to these churches which are losing their believers but to the ecumenical movement in general as it sets

up insurmountable barriers between the churches. The voice of Christian churches in the secular world will be prophetic and strong if they learn to speak in the name of the one Tradition, if they come out as a united front preaching one absolute norm of morality which is clearly expressed in the Gospel. Unfortunately, studies in the theme "Ecclesiology and Ethics" are being focused on social subjects while less attention is being paid to personal morality of people. Documents on this theme are addressed to social structures more often than to a person. We see in this loss of personal dimension a digression from moral teaching of our Lord Jesus Christ and of the apostles as expressed in the New Testament. The Gospel message is addressed to a person rather than to social institutions and is aimed first of all at the transfiguration of humans and not at the change of social structures. It is important not to lose the Gospel's vision and not to forget that the change of the world begins with the change of a human person.

9. Cooperation in mission and witness should be a priority in the WCC's activities in future. We are concerned about the growth of proselytism which presents a real danger to the ecumenical movement. Not only sects but some member churches of the WCC are engaged in missionary activities using their financial potential and disregarding traditional local churches. Such activity undermines the authority of the ecumenical movement and is a direct challenge to the World Council of Churches, which stands on a firm position on the matter of proselytism. But until the problem is solved the WCC should not disregard it. Proselytism must not be allowed to destroy the relations which have been formed among member churches over the decades.

10. We are very grateful to the WCC for its diaconal ministry aimed at the assistance to the suffering and the deprived. It is one of the important and inspiring parts of our common work. It is significant that diaconal programs also include assistance to local churches in the matters of catechization and spiritual and moral education of people under difficult circumstances. For instance, the WCC is actively carrying out a program of assistance to the churches of Eastern Europe which experience difficulties caused by economic and political developments in their countries. The sponsoring of educational programs, publishing of theological literature and exchange of students should remain a program priority of the WCC in future.

Comments on the draft statement

11. As far as the proposed draft statement on "Common Understanding and Vision of the WCC" is concerned, its positive aspect lies in its orientation to the Toronto Declaration.

Deserving positive appraisal is the introduction showing a minimalistic common basis which unites member churches in dogmatic aspect, namely, the confession of Jesus Christ as Lord and Savior and an aspiration to fulfill common calling to the glory of the one God, Father, Son and Holy Spirit.

While having no principal objection to the term "visible unity" we consider it necessary to note that this term is understood differently by Protestants and Orthodox.

The former see the Church as fragmented into different confessions and denominations, but as the one church on a deeper, invisible level; and the task of the WCC consists in making this existing unity visible. For the Orthodox, "visible unity" means the reunion with the One, Holy, Catholic and Apostolic Church on the basis of the unity in faith and principles of spiritual life and church order.

1.4.1 is important to us as it reflects the Toronto Declaration.

There is a phrase in 2.1.1 "The thought and action of the church are... ecumenical in so far as they attempt to realize the *Una Sancta,* the fellowship of Christians who acknowledge the one Lord. The term *Una Sancta* traditionally speaks of the One, Holy, Catholic and Apostolic Church and not of a fellowship of churches. Here, as well as in other parts of the document, no confusion of the notions "Church" and "fellowship of churches" should be allowed.

In 2.1.3 the point is the unity of the followers of Christ as an instrument of the healing and wholeness and as a foretaste of the reign of God. Yet, immediately following is an affirmation about "common involvement in the struggles of the human community". Thus an impression is created that the reign of God could be attained through the participation in social struggles. We cannot agree with this.

Some affirmations of 3.2 are written in a woolly style and need considerable polishing up. It is not clear in what way the churches "belong to one another"(3.2.1). The phrase "We may say that the Council has a structure but not that it is a structure" (3.2.2.) is not clear and needs comment. The phrase "membership of the Council may actually damage the ecumenical cause by allowing the churches to live more easily with their continued separation" (3.2.4) sounds as a threat to churches which are not active enough in the ecumenical movement. It is not clear what kind of "renewal" is meant in 3.2.5. The last sentence in 3.2.5 is written in a somewhat aggressive language which should be altered.

In 3.3. we do not agree with an expression "in order that the body of Christ may be built up" in this context as the Body of Christ means the Church which for us, Orthodox, already exists. The point could be in "making growth" of new members to this body (cf. Eph.4:16) and of the "growth" of this body (cf. Col.2:19) and not of a building up of a new Body of Christ out from WCC member churches. The same could be said about 4.2.2.

3.5 speaks of a willingness of the WCC member churches "to pray on a regular basis for other members". Debate is going on in some Orthodox Churches on the admissibility of the participation of Orthodox in the prayers with non-Orthodox. In this context it is necessary to clarify what is meant under the prayer on "a regular basis".

3.7-3.8 speak about a gradual shift in emphasis from the divinity to the humanity of Christ. These points reflect recent developments in many Protestant churches. We consider it necessary to keep the balanced vision of the divine and human natures of Jesus Christ with no shifting of emphasis from one nature to another.

We would like to see in the document an affirmation of the inadmissibility of proselytism and actions of certain WCC members churches to the detriment of other churches. Such an affirmation would be pertinent in 4.2.1.

We consider an invitation to evangelicals and pentecostals to join the WCC (4.3.2) as unnecessary. The Churches should join the Council when they are ready for this.

The expression "carrying with us our God-given differences, but also our human divisions and quarrels" (7.1) seems unfortunate to us. This could give the impression that our divisions and quarrels are also the gift of God. On the other hand, profound doctrinal and other differences which exist among the WCC member churches and which have not been overcome are disregarded. We do not agree with the affirmation that "our churches have become more inclusive communities" (7.1) and that "only together do we become who we are truly meant to be in Christ" (7.2).

12. This is our preliminary understanding of the WCC in its past, present and future. We express our hope that the Council will continue to serve as an important instrument of the ecumenical movement which helps member churches in their search for doctrinal consensus and in their aspiration to restore the unity commanded by God.

6 September 1996

III. Response of the Romanian Orthodox Church

1. The present study represents a point of view of the Romanian Orthodox Church towards the ecumenical movement in general, and towards the World Council of Churches in particular, in the perspective of the anniversary in 1998, of 50 years since the setting up of this ecumenical forum.

This is the result of the initiative of the WCC to propose to the member churches a critical analysis of its activity since its establishment in 1948, in the perspective of the jubilee in 1998, in view of initiating a process of redefining the place and the role of the WCC in the life of the Christian Churches, in the present inter-Christian and inter-religious context.

The Romanian Orthodox Church is attempting, through the present study, to assess the ecumenical activity in the last five decades and to propose some guidelines for the future.

2. The ecumenical movement remains one of the most significant manifestations of the twentieth century. It is for the first time in the course of the second millennium, known as the time of Christian division, that divided Churches began to pass from a policy of confrontation to one of reconciliation in Christ. In spite of all the criticism brought to the ecumenical movement, one must admit that it has allowed various Christian Churches to know each other better and to promote the mutual exchange

of confessional values. Thus, Orthodoxy had the opportunity to contribute to the enrichment of contemporary ecumenism with its own specific values of great importance for the mission of the Churches in the contemporary world. It is enough to remember the theology of the Holy Trinity, of the concept of communion, of grace as energy, of the cosmic dimension of redemption in Christ, to realize the impact which Orthodoxy had on contemporary ecumenism. One must also point out the fact that the Orthodox Churches which, in their great majority are on the territories dominated by the former communist atheist regimes, had great support from the WCC in overcoming the barriers of communication imposed by the totalitarian systems. Thus, due to their participation in the activity of the WCC, the isolation imposed on the Orthodox Churches from these territories was much decreased, both in the relations they entertained with one another and with other Christian confessions. One must also mention the fact that the Orthodox Churches received from the WCC moral and material support before and after the fall of the communist regimes.

3. According to the ecclesiological principles guiding the Orthodox Church through its involvement in the ecumenical movement, it is not the unity "per se" of the Church that is looked for – the mysterious Body of the Lord, as this is already given in Christ whose Body is the Church The Church is one in its being, since unity is a divine gift given in Christ (I Cor. 12:27). The reason for the participation of the Orthodox Church in the ecumenical movement is the achievement of the visible unity of the Church of Christ. This visible unity of the Church is a mission to be achieved by Christians under the unifying influence of the Holy Spirit; it is the Christians' openness to the divine gift of unity.

The purpose of the participation of the Orthodox Church in the ecumenical movement is this very common effort of the persons who believe in Christ and who belong to various confessions to achieve their visible unity in the one Church. This is the stipulation so that the mission of the Church may be credible inside, but especially outside itself: "That all may be one, so that the world may believe" (John 17:21).

4. If one can speak about several positive aspects of the ecumenical movement, some of have been mentioned already, it is also true that ecumenism has been undergoing and continues to undergo obvious periods of crisis. The causes of this situation must be sought in the repeated attempts by the World Council of Churches to propose models of Christian unity made in its own laboratories, with the obvious purpose of retaining the identity of the Christian denominations which make up the Council, rather than to set up a strong foundation to the Christian unity. In other words, one could say that there has always been an attempt to place confessional diversity above the unity of the Church of Christ. This tendency can be seen in the endeavours of certain ecumenical circles to present this diversity, which does not want to know anything about unity as a gift of God. But thus, insurmountable barriers to Christian unity are created, this unity being the main purpose of the World Council of Churches. Thus proselytism is indirectly encouraged, in spite of

all the endeavours of the ecumenical movement to fight against it. One cannot overlook the fact that many Western preachers, who arrived in the Orthodox East in the last few years, belong to member churches of the World Council of Churches.

The problem of the ecumenical movement is not the unity, but the disunity of the Church of Christ. The World Council of Churches is a part of this large movement and not an end in itself, but it could be a valuable instrument for the encounter of the Churches, who alone are able to achieve unity. Yet it is obvious that despite its mission, the World Council of Churches manifests, through some of its representatives, a Super-Church tendency, trying to impose its own theological vision on its member churches.

From the perspective of the Orthodox Church which participates both in the ecumenical movement and in the World Council of Churches according to specific criteria, Christian unity means neither confessional pluralism nor juridical centralization, but unity of life and faith sacramentally and canonically expressed. The restoration of the visible unity of the Church is an issue which aims mainly at the unity in faith, as the disagreements between the various Christian communities can be seen not only at the level of the theological articulations, but especially at that of the content of the teaching of faith. That is why the unity of faith must overcome the present confessional pluralism based on doctrinal diversity. In this sense, there is an organic relationship between the unity of faith in the eucharistic community, due to the fact that the Holy Eucharist is the visible sacramental expression of a local Church which makes the same confession of faith with that of another local Church. Therefore, the communion is the *expression* of unity and not a *means* to unity.

If one always starts from the words of the Saviour "that all may be one" (John 17:21) in order to give new impulses to the ecumenical movement, then one cannot see the reason why the words of the Saviour expressed in the same context are not also mentioned: "Just as You are in Me and I am in You, may they also be in Us so that the world may believe that You sent Me" (John 17,21). This is all the more puzzling since the Basis of the Council has a Trinitarian content. The great difference between the notion of communion circulating with increased intensity in the framework of the ecumenical movement and the Trinitarian communion discovered by the Saviour consists in the fact that while the former is based on the exterior relations among persons, the latter supposes the inner relations among persons, the existence of a person through another person. Therefore one must also underline with all intensity the fact that this Trinitarian communion, thus understood, was at the base of the Christian unity in the first millennium, conceived as a catholic and conciliar unity. Until this deep sense of communion is realized, we appreciate that it is proper to speak of brotherly community rather than of communion in the ecumenical movement. The basis of Christian unity can be only the communion, synodality and catholicity, as it was understood by the undivided Church of the first of millenium of Christian history. This model of unity will always remain valid, as it is not made by a human being, but revealed by God.

In this sense, the World Council of Churches cannot acquire the quality of an organism in which the experience of full communion between the member churches can be achieved. In other words, it cannot claim an ecclesiastical status. It remains a forum in which the member churches find a support in their search of reestablishing full unity and communion. The Churches themselves must present their points of view and discover what is already uniting them and overcome their disagreements. As for the decision-making to achieve communion, the responsibility belongs exclusively to the Churches and not to the World Council of Churches.

5. Two well-known movements are at the root of contemporary ecumenism, "Faith and Order" and "Life and Work". Each of these two movements has made progress both in doctrine and in matters of service. Significant studies were made in the area of Apostolic Faith by focusing on the Nicene-Constantinopolitan Creed, which today is recited by most Christians without the *filioque* clause; great efforts were made in drafting the document known as *BEM*, which attempted for the first time to present a doctrine on Baptism, Eucharist and Ministry to be accepted by the member churches of the World Council of Churches; many other Faith and Order studies have been conducted concerning Tradition and other issues. Many important things have been achieved in the field of service by fighting against social injustice and racism and by initiating actions designed to promote human rights and to overcome ethnic rivalries.

Nevertheless, one must also notice the fact that not even today the separation between the two above mentioned movements has been overcome, the World Council of Churches having been criticized for its more horizontal than vertical preoccupation. There were attempts to correct such excesses and to achieve a more-or-less stable equilibrium between the two dimensions of the ecumenical movement. But nobody has attempted to reveal the deeper causes of this phenomenon which regards not only the relationship between faith and action but also the very notion of Church as a sacrament and historical reality. Moreover, at the origin of such phenomena there is the dissociation between the visible and the invisible Church, typical for the heterodox world. It concerns, on one hand, a spiritual invisible Church, which favours the retirement of the faithful from the world and their isolation in the ivory tower of piety and, on the other hand, a visible Church, separated from the spiritual one, which determines the faithful to engage in social actions and to leave God aside. But the separation between the visible Church and the invisible one decreases and undermines both the sacramental and the historical character of the Church, either when the stress is laid on the invisible Church or when the sacramental character of the Church is stressed to the point of being confused with magic.

From an Orthodox point of view there is no visible or invisible Church, but two aspects of the same Church, a visible one and an invisible one, which do not remain exterior one from another but coincide, as was revealed at Pentecost.

The Church is a concrete, historical, sacramental, relational and eschatological reality. In this light, the role of the Church is neither to favour an escape from the world, nor to immerse the faithful into the world, but to transfigure the world in

Christ. Unless the dissociation between the two Churches is overcome and unless the coincidence and the inner relationship between them are revealed, neither the oscillation between vertical and horizontal – which constitutes a constant element of the contemporary ecumenical movement – will be overcome, nor the sacramental and historical dimension of the Church will be revealed. This seems to be a necessary topic to be discussed within the framework of the World Council of Churches, as it is quite salutary for the progress of the ecumenical movement. The Orthodox can bring an extremely valuable contribution in this field.

The present preoccupation of the World Council of Churches with justice, peace, integrity of creation or inter-religious dialogue, although valuable in its intention, reveals on the one hand a deviation from the initial purpose to achieve Christian unity and, on the other hand, a preference for the horizontal dimension of the Churches.

These are the reasons for which the Romanian Orthodox Church, without being indifferent to the ecumenical movement, manifests a reticence towards some of the present directions of the World Council of Churches.

6. We live in a secularized world which exerts a strong influence over the Christian Churches, both through the attack launched against Christian moral values as found in Holy Scripture, and through the depreciation of the notion of "sin" which has almost disappeared from the vocabulary of certain churches. There are even situations in which certain Christian communities or ecumenical organizations trifle with homosexuality and avoid considering it as being against both nature and Scripture. Holy Scripture is exalted on one hand, and overlooked on the other. The Orthodox Church is open to some new meanings of the word of Holy Scripture discovered in the light of the Tradition. These new senses of the scriptural texts answer the spiritual requirements of the modern human being who looks for salvation in the characteristic terms of our time. But that does not mean that the Orthodox Church can accept to adapt the Scriptures to certain temporary requirements, ideologies, cultures and customs contrary to the full faithfulness towards the holy word in its letter and spirit. A certain relativity in the theological field is also practiced, which replaces the concept of "heresy" with that of the "divine gift of diversity". In this sense, although the Orthodox Church does not insist on the concept of Christian unity as uniformity, it does affirm that there are certain objective limits of a legitimate divergence which one cannot pass over.

All of this springs from a deist conception which subscribes both to the idea of the autonomy of the world and to the loss of its relationship with God. It is claimed sometimes that the meaning of Christianity is to secularize the world, due to the fact that it starts from a wrong theological premise, confusing the transcendence of God with His absence from creation. On the other hand, there is the tendency in the World Council of Churches to emphasize the inestimable value of creation and to relate it to the Spirit of God as it happened at the General Assembly of the WCC in Canberra (1991). This fact is quite remarkable as it was for the first time that the theme of a General Assembly of the WCC had not a Christological content any more, but a pneumatological one. Unfortunately, the starting point was the existence of a Spirit of God separated from Christ which came to confuse the Holy Spirit with some other "spirits of creation, falling thus into an almost "pantheist" conception.

So, in the ecumenical movement we are faced both with a deist conception which favours the secularization of the world and with another conception with pantheist tendencies which would like to make the world sacred. This dilemma can be overcome only if one affirms at the same time both the transcendence of God towards creation from the point of view of the divine nature, and the presence of God in creation through the work of the Spirit, we know from Holy Scripture, and as the Holy Fathers have taught us from the very beginning until today. The Orthodox are called to discuss these themes in the ecumenical forum in order to keep up with the secularization coming from the West and with pantheism threatening us from the East. Unfortunately, it happens rather often that the theological and spiritual perspectives presented by the Orthodox on various issues seem for many members of the WCC as lacking relevance for the "modern", "reasonable" West, based on the humanist values considered as universal.

Unless proper attention is paid to the Orthodox witness, a witness of a Church preserving the truth of faith along the centuries, the present syncretist and secularist tendencies of the World Council of Churches can become so radicalized that the Council could lose its Christian basis. Due to the fact that the disagreements are not only in form but also in content, it is more and more difficult for us to pray together, in spite of the efforts made. It is only if we discuss together, on the basis of Christian faith and spirituality the social, political, ethnic and ecological problems all of us are faced with, that the ecumenical movement can still have a future.

At the same time, the Orthodox Church regrets the fact that its share in the decision-making process within the framework of the WCC is not sufficient when faced with a Protestant and neo-Protestant world which imposes its own point of view due to the majority it enjoys. If progress on the way of Christian unity is desired, this being the main task of the World Council of Churches, the Council needs to stem the tide of illegitimate diversity which is currently surging, and the Orthodox must be given their proper place.

Bucharest, 21 July 1997

Discerning the Signs of the Times:
Women in the Life of the Orthodox Church
WCC Ecumenical Decade of Churches in Solidarity with Women
Final Statements of two meetings

First Meeting
Damascus, Syria, 4 – 10 October 1996

Introduction

We are grateful to God the Father, Son and Holy Spirit for the special opportunity we had to meet together as Orthodox women. The theme of our Conference was "Discerning the 'Signs of the Times' (Mt. 16:3): Women in the Life of the Orthodox Church." We met together in Damascus, Syria from October 4-10, 1996.

Most of the sixty-five participants were official women delegates sent by their churches at the invitation of the World Council of Churches. This meeting took place in the context of the the Ecumenical Decade of Churches in Solidarity with Women. This meeting focused especially upon the concerns of women from the Orthodox churches of the Middle East, Africa and Asia. There was also a small number of lay and ordained Orthodox men who attended the Conference. Their support and encouragement of our efforts were a welcomed resource.

We benefited greatly from the rich hospitality of His Beatitude Ignatius IV, Greek Orthodox Patriarch of Antioch and all the East. He graciously received the participants and opened the Conference with an address. He affirmed that the Church in Syria wanted the event to be an "important one, a significant one so that we can understand more and do more for women."

We were also graciously received by His Beatitude Ignatius Zakka I, Syrian Orthodox Patriarch of Antioch and all the East. He also offered the closing message for the Conference. In his presentation, he affirmed the many important ministries women have had and continue to have in the life of the Church.

The fact that we were so warmly greeted by both patriarchs not only greatly enriched our meeting, but also reminded us of the growing reconciliation between our two families of Orthodox churches. Since our meeting had included participants from both families of churches, we believe that we have also made a contribution to this reconciliation.

We gathered in a land rich in Christian history. In addition to our regular opportunity for worship, we visited: the women's monasteries of Saydnaya and Maalula, the men's monasteries of St George and St Ephraim, as well as the famous site of the Krak des Chevaliers. During our stay here, we were reminded of St Paul's baptism in the city and the witness of so many saints, especially St Thekla and St John of Damascus.

Our Conference focused on a variety of topics about women in the life of the Orthodox Church. Each day had its own theme that was articulated in the presentations and panel discussions. Among our topics, we reflected upon the themes: "The Holy Spirit in the Life of the Church", "Discerning the Tradition Today", and "Reflecting on *Orthopraxia*".

The Good News

We have been richly blessed by our time together. As we prayed, discussed the themes and met together, we recognized that we serve the same Lord and share the same Orthodox faith. It is our common faith which has guided our reflection and which has inspired us to deepen our service to the Orthodox Church and our witness in the world.

We were very happy to learn from each other about the many forms of ministry in which women in our churches are already engaged. We witnessed to a wide range of ministries from the women present at our meeting; some women, for example, were active in monastic life, others were active as single women, wives or mothers, a number were serving within their local parish or diocese, other participants were active in the ecumenical movement, some were involved with the study or teaching of theology, and many were involved in philanthropic, medical and/or educational service in association either with the Church, or a respected regional or national institution.

Undergirding this variety, we observed a high level of competency, intelligence, dynamism, commitment and, most of all, a deep love of the Church and of God. This range of ministries manifested among us was truly inspiring. This variety reminded us how throughout the history of the Church, women have been active in many forms of ministry in response to the same Lord, in the Holy Spirit.

At the same time, we came to see that the Church continues to need the service of faithful women as well as men, who feel called to serve the Lord and His Church. These women, as well as men, deserve the support and encouragement of our Church leaders. These women, as well as men, deserve to receive appropriate theological education and spiritual formation which will assist them in their ministry. These women, as well as men, deserve to have their vocations recognized and blessed.

In our discussions together, we also came to more deeply appreciate the ministry of the wife of the priest. We believe this ministry is tantamount to the ministry of the priest himself. The wives of priests, especially, deserve the recognition of the Church, as well as our encouragement and support. This support is necessary so that the ministry of "priest's wives" may continue to be life-giving to their communities and families.

Concerns

Through the intercession of the Holy Theotokos, who is our role model, we recognize that all Christians are invited to emulate her example as a person of faith. We are all, women and men, called by the Lord, Himself to grow in our relationship with Him and others, so that there is integrity between our faith and our actions.

In our discussions we came to affirm the importance of the witness of the Church in today's world. We also came to sense the challenge of relating more directly our theology with our church practice.

Through our discussions together, we recognize that some of our churches have made a concerted effort to involve women in the different ministries in the Church. Others, have indeed made significant progress in this direction. Yet, there are still some churches who have not yet considered the needs of their women and therefore the whole church itself.

We are concerned that some women have expressed deep disappointment that they have not had the chance to study theology in a formal setting such as a seminary or theological school. This hinders our role and work within the Church. Furthermore, we feel that we must encourage Orthodox women theologians, especially, to study the interpretation of the Scriptures so as to be able to discern their meaning more fully.

We also recognize there are sacramental practices which need study in depth, by both men and women, as they appear to run contrary to our theological affirmations regarding the dignity of women. We specifically call to mind here certain liturgical practices which need immediate attention as we believe they do indeed, diminish the dignity of women. We note, for example, the practice of churching female babies differently from male babies, and the practice of depriving women of the Eucharist during their period of menstruation that continues to exist in some of our churches.

We note as well, with tremendous sadness, how easily it is for the presence of women to be forgotten. From our discussions together, we realize that there are some occasions when the role and presence of women, as well as their work, is not always validated for the value it has in the every day life of the church. Rather, women may be seen by some as more readily dispensable.

Women have also been easily dismissed in other ways as well. We recognize with deep concern how social injustices such as poverty, illiteracy and invisibility may effect both Orthodox women and women in general, in our part of the world. Wherever possible, we must strive to assist them and open our lives and our hearts to them, as our Lord would have us do.

This Conference also recognizes the important ministry of deaconesses as a response to the Holy Spirit for various needs of this present age. Nevertheless, we must emphasize that we still wait for the application of the recommendations from the 1988 Inter-Orthodox Rhodes' Consultation on "The Place of the Woman in the Orthodox Church", to rejuvenate this order of ordained ministry.

Recommendations

In light of the above, we prayerfully recommend to the leadership of our churches:

- that our leaders encourage women's involvement and participation in the every day decision-making process of our local churches; we note this after having recognized the differing practices regarding women among the various Orthodox churches.

- that efforts begin which will raise the theological and spiritual awareness among women concerning their role in the Church, their families and society, through: spiritual retreats, on-going study groups, seminars, lectures and workshops.

- that women receive both spiritual and financial support, in order to pursue studies in theological education; relatedly, that more informal opportunities to study and grow in the theology of the Church be created.

- that more research, presentations and community wide discussions on theTheotokos be encouraged, so that we will grow in authentic relationship and appreciation of her.

- that the sacramental practices which appear to diminish the dignity of women be studied in depth and changed whenever necesary, in order to reflect the more fuller Orthodox understanding regarding women.

- that lay theologians (women and men) be encouraged to direct Bible studies in local parishes, as this form of adult education may help inspire confidence to witness to the Orthodox faith.

- that a space in the life of the Church be provided where Eastern and Oriental Orthodox women may regularly come together, so they we may learn from each other; perhaps they may also be invited to attend some of the suggested activities listed above.

- that our leadership encourage women's informal and formal ministries in pastoral care, so as to reach out to others who may be spiritually isolated, in material need, grieving the loss of a loved one, survivors of abuse or violence, etc. These persons deserve particular attention, as they require the healing presence and assistance of the Church through Her prayer, counseling and support.

- that our leadership develop more ways for the wives of priests to come together for support and opportunities for enrichment.

- that more frequent dialogue take place, both formal and informal, with our surrounding societies, as this will facilitate more focused and appropriate pastoral care and witness; this dialogue also involves taking seriously the presence of Orthodox Christian women who are engaged in various forms of work and service in the world, we desire the ongoing support and encouragement of our leadership in this effort; similarly, as society changes, we recommend that extra care must be paid to understand the concerns of our young people.

— that a qualified woman spiritual advisor and/or canonist be included as an advocate on Spiritual Courts of all our churches.

— that our Church leaders discern prayerfully and courageously the presence of the Holy Spirit in those many places where the ministry of ordained deaconesses, as well as other forms of ministry, are needed.

— that more opportunities for ecumenical dialogue and relationships be encouraged; this would be both beneficial for Orthodox witness and for the strengthening of our relationships with other Christian women in our common work.

— that more clergymen (and male lay leaders) be encouraged to attend these conferences in order to increase their pastoral awareness regarding women's concerns.

— that valuable conferences such as "Discerning the Signs of the Times" be sponsored, making participation open to all women in our churches.

Conclusion

In conclusion, we affirm that holding and participating in this Conference on "Discerning the Signs of the Times" is a direct result of the work of the Holy Spirit and our response to His call. We understand that through baptism and chrismation (confirmation), women also, are called to be a vital part of the Church. Women also, are called to communion with God and that women also, have the vocation of manifesting the presence of the Kingdom even in this life.

The Church is comprised of both men and women called to continue the saving acts of Jesus Christ for the salvation of humanity and the whole of creation. "There is one body and one Spirit... but to each one of us grace was given, according to the measure of Christ's gift. And he himself gave some to be apostles, some prophets, some evangelists, and some pastors and teachers... every part does its share, causes growth of the body for the edifying of itself in love." (Eph. 4:4, 11, 16) Therefore, we believe we have a responsibility to fulfill our calling as disciples and apostles, which is to communicate the Gospel to the whole inhabited earth and strive towards the sanctification and well being of the Body.

Finally, we bear witness to the fact that each member of the Body of Christ is essential for the proper functioning of His Church. We hold fast to the Holy Tradition of our Orthodox Church in which, clergy and laity have constituted an organic whole since the time of the Apostles. Throughout the history of the Church, we have the testimony of countless women saints who responded to Christ in many ways, such as apostles, evangelists, confessors, martyrs, ascetics and nuns, teachers, mothers, spiritual and medical healers and deaconesses. We Orthodox women of today, inspired through the prayers and example of these women saints, now endeavor to continue in their footsteps, as we too, strive to respond to our Lord's call: "follow Me."

Amen.

Discerning the Signs of the Times:
Women in the Life of the Orthodox Church

WCC Ecumenical Decade of Churches in Solidarity with Women

Second Meeting
Istanbul, Turkey, 10 – 17 May 1997

You have destroyed death by your Cross
You have opened Paradise to the thief.
You have changed a lamentation of the
Myrrbearers into joy, and
You have commanded your Apostles to proclaim that you,
O Christ our God,
Have risen and granted the world the great mercy.
(Troparion, Tone 7)

Christ is Risen!

We thank our God, the Life-Giving Trinity, Father, Son and Holy Spirit, for the opportunity to celebrate this joyful season of the Resurrection with our sisters from Europe, North and South America, Australia and the Middle East.

We gathered together in Istanbul, Turkey for this conference on Women in the Life of the Orthodox Church entitled, "Discerning the Signs of the Times." Over fifty women and men from the Orthodox and Oriental Orthodox churches met from 10-17 May, 1997 as participants officially delegated by their churches, as observers and as resource people to represent the concerns of Orthodox women from Eastern and Western Europe and North and South America, coming from Albania, Armenia, Brazil, Bulgaria, Chile, the Czech Republic, Finland, France, the Republic of Georgia, Germany, Great Britain, Greece, Poland, Romania, Russia, Serbia, Switzerland and the United States of America. This meeting took place within the context of the Ecumenical Decade of Churches in Solidarity with Women.

It has been a tremendous blessing to meet and get to know one another, learning more about each other's histories and traditions. We have rejoiced in the commitment to seeking God's will in loving and costly service that has so often been clear in presentations and conversations. While at times we differed in thinking and acting, we have learned that the respect and love which exists among us, which is a gift from Jesus Christ, is one of the most important characteristics of this conference. We have come to realise more deeply the importance of committing ourselves to a community united in diversity.

This is the last of three World Council of Churches' sponsored meetings within the Ecumenical Decade for Orthodox women (the others being Crete 1990 and Damascus 1996). We realize the need to deepen our reflection on many topics and themes, and we are grateful for this conference in that it has helped us to continue this reflection.

We had the opportunity to visit and worship at some of the most historic and ancient Christian sites of this city. We toured Hagia Sophia, the Great Church of Constantinople, the Monastery at Chora where we were inspired by the beautiful iconography of the 11th century, and the Theological School at Halki where we felt as if we had entered a modern-day Garden of Paradise. Also, we had the honor of attending the Divine Liturgy celebrated by His All-Holiness, Bartholomew I, at the monastery of Zoodochos Pege, the burial site of the Ecumenical Patriarchs, and drank from the spring whose water has been known for centuries as a source of healing. We believe Christ, who is the place (*chora*) of Life, revealed himself through the deep spiritual and prayer experiences of our daily worship at Holy Trinity Church, and throughout the entire week. The name of Mother Maria Skobtsova came up repeatedly during the conference and we felt as the week progressed that she was very close to us. Her utter self-giving for the care and salvation of everyone who came her way in World War II France was especially inspiring: Russian students needing a mother, homeless women needing a place to stay, Jews and many others fleeing persecution needing shelter and a hiding place -all came under the wing of her love and compassion. In the end, she gave her life for her friends. She is a holy woman of our day, a model for us, one who lived in our century and in a culture and under conditions that are familiar to us.

Thanksgiving

We thank You, O Lord, our God, for bringing us together in this holy city and granting us the opportunity to worship and partake of Your heavenly blessings. We thank You for bestowing Your divine grace upon us for these few days and ask to keep in our hearts the desire to live for You, our Lord and Benefactor. We thank You for this time together, for being the silent partner in every conversation and the ever-present guest at each meal.

We are exceedingly grateful for the generous hospitality of the Ecumenical Patriarch, His All-Holiness Bartholomew I, Archbishop of Constantinople and New

Rome. In his opening address, the Ecumenical Patriarch spoke of the desire on the part of many people to achieve a more meaningful relationship with the Living God; there is a deep longing for spiritual growth and an even greater longing for holiness, healing and forgiveness which comes from God alone. He blessed not only our conference but our pilgrimage to this holy city, a center of inspiration and spiritual nourishment and asked us to keep the local community in our prayers.

We were also very warmly received at the Armenian Patriarchate of Constantinople by His Beatitude Patriarch Karekin II. We took part in morning prayers and were encouraged to take the initiative in the important ministry work of our church, given the many gifts women offer. His Beatitude mentioned the Armenian Apostolic Orthodox Church has taken the initiative in ordaining women to the order of the diaconate, an order in which both men and women are ordained and perform similar duties.

Both Patriarchs addressed the current official theological dialogue taking place between the Orthodox and Oriental Orthodox Churches and both eagerly anticipate the final reconciliation and restoration of ecclesiastical communion between the two families.

It is equally important to thank the World Council of Churches Women's Program for sponsoring this historic event. This conference and so many that have gone before are of vital importance for Orthodox women, the Orthodox Church and world-wide ecumencial dialogue.

Lastly, we must thank all who have gone before us, women and men, laity and clergy, who have initiated and contributed to the inter-Orthodox dialogue, without whose dedication and love for our Church we would not be here today. Their work, specifically over the last 20 years, has been a source of encouragement and hope for many of us. The consultations of Agapia (1976), Rhodes (1988), Crete (1990) and Damascus (1996) have laid the foundations for the work we are doing here.

Concerns

This consultation studied the statement that emerged from the Damascus consultation and has affirmed many of the concerns there. In addition, we offer the following:
- There is a need to stimulate a desire in our people to take an active role in the life of the church. This may happen with the realization, on the part of Orthodox Christians, of their own royal priesthood.
- There is a need for new workers in the Church, including children and young people, to be nurtured and educated to play a more active role in the various ministries. We must call upon all people to bring their gifts forward, the gifts which have been bestowed upon the laity through the Holy Spirit, for the life and growth of the church. We must stimulate the interest of lay people who feel that they have been excluded in the past and remind them of their individual responsibilities as members of "a chosen race, a royal priesthood, a holy nation." (I Peter 2:9)

– In some of our churches, Orthodox Christians have lost interest and have joined social, cultural and para-church organizations. We are looking for ways to bring Orthodox Christians back to the church.

Recommendations

As members of the church we feel ready to carry out our responsibility to promote the welfare of the Church, particularly by encouraging the various ministries of women.

1. Theological Education

A. Many women seek deeper knowledge of the Church through theological study. In families and schools, women are the primary educators. Women share this task and learn well from one another. Thus, theologically-educated women have a particular ministry in teaching our faithful. For these reasons, Orthodox theological education for women is a priority and should be facilitated on all levels.

B. We recommend that the churches encourage the present efforts of women who are engaged in producing journals, both academic and for the community, in order to inform and educate women and men on the Orthodox faith. There is a real need on the part of women for the creation of a forum where women are able to reflect upon their experiences and engage in theological research. Women need to be notified of publications, theological seminars and other events and materials that are of benefit to them.

C. There is an acute need for resources and materials in the following areas:
1. for Church schools;
2. in multiple languages to address the increasingly multi-national nature of our churches;
3. on how to live one's faith daily;
4. providing up-to-date translations of ancient Christian liturgical and patristic texts specifically dealing with the Theotokos and other women saints.

2. Liturgical Life

A. The perception and interpretation of some of the practices pertaining to liturgical life need to be addressed. We ask for a re-evaluation of certain liturgical customs, for example, the presentation of infants and the forty-day rule for childbirth, the prayer for miscarriages, abortions and post-partum mothers, and expectations pertaining to the reception of communion. Some of us feel these practices and prayers do not properly express the theology of the church regarding the dignity of God's creation of woman and her redemption in Christ Jesus. We realise that the practices in the various local communities may differ.

B. We recommend the incorporation of the lives of the martyrs, both women and men, and the new experiences of the people in this century in the hymnography of the Church. While this may be happening in some churches, we recommend a universal incorporation of the new martyrs of this century in life of our church. Perhaps the best forum for such a recommendation is the upcoming Great and Holy Council.

3. The Diaconate

A. Many of us believe the incorporation of deaconesses in the life of the Church will help contribute to the atmosphere of love and learning in the Church. Deaconesses are able to work as helpers to the priests and counsellors to the people providing an important link and thereby strengthening relationships within the body of the Church.

B. In our discussion we realised we came to this conference with differing assumptions regarding the role of the deaconess. While some see the diaconate for women as a sacramental ministry which takes place by ordination for others the ministry is not sacramental and described as a church ministry. This question has become for some more academic than practical. Therefore while some may affirm the work of our sisters from the previous meetings of Orthodox women regarding the importance of the re-emergence of the order of the deaconess for others there is still work to be done in order to come to a fuller understanding.

C. With the re-emergence of the order of deaconesses, we would not want this ministry in any way to diminish the other ministries of the laity in the Church. Rather, vocations to this ministry may be experienced as another response to the Holy Spirit who fills and guides the Church. We call to mind the words of St. Paul when he says, "it is he who gave apostles, prophets, evangelists, pastors and teachers in roles of service for the faithful to build up the body of Christ, until we become one in faith and in the knowledge of God's Son..."(Eph. 4:11-13).

4. Priests' Wives

A. The ministry of the priest's wife is very specific and unique. We recommend the church offer a special blessing on women who undertake this ministry and provide instruction and guidance for their role.

5. Spiritual Life

A. There is a thirst for spirituality in many of our countries and a rediscovery of the Orthodox living experience. We recommend the development of materials and programmes to help our people grow in their spiritual lives. We feel that the gifts of women may be of service to the churches specifically in this area. Women need concrete teaching in Orthodox spirituality which includes biblical reflection and study.

B. We encourage the development of monastic vocations for women. Historically, Orthodox monastic communities have been a source for theological education and spiritual life. The very presence of the monastics witnesses to the one thing necessary (Lk. 10:42) to which all are called.

C. We recognise that the churches have been helping one another by sending missionary teams and providing materials in local languages. We recommend that the churches incorporate the experiences of women in their teaching materials. These experiences will enrich the spiritual life of the people.

D. Women benefit from sharing spiritual experiences with one another. Opportunities for such sharing should be provided and supported by our churches. This has begun with meetings organised by the WCC for Orthodox women, such as the present one in Istanbul. Networking and sharing should continue on international, national and parish levels. We recommend the appointment of women delegates as representatives of the Orthodox church to the various gatherings and bodies of the ecumenical movement, whether on the international, national or local level.

6. Community Life

A. We feel that women, quite naturally, are peacemakers. Therefore we recommend our churches make a greater commitment to support sister orthodox churches in crisis situations, for example, during natural disasters, and to support refugees and those in war-torn countries. Often, in these situations, women and children suffer most.

B. We recommend our people support, spiritually and materially, the Christians of our churches who are still suffering in various ways, socially, politically and economically. We are also aware of the current climate of increased religous fundamentalism which is affecting the lives of people in all our countries. Some churches need educational materials to help develop programmes for the faithful to combat erroneous teachings.

C. We recommend the issue of sexism be seriously considered. The Church would benefit from theological and soteriological reflection on this issue especially through the medium of consultations, workshops and informal study.

7. Youth

A. We recommend the development of programmes for the spiritual growth of the youth, the hope of our Churches. Because we are one Body, their concerns affect the entire church and their spiritual well-being is vital to the health of our Church.

B. We recommend the development of youth and church school exchange programmes between our churches through national or regional councils of churches.

8. Church Polity

A. As stated in previous meetings of Orthodox women, we recommend the role of the laity in the decision making processes be evaluated. There is a variety of practices in the Orthodox Church regarding this process and this recommendation only pertains to churches in which voting takes place. In those circumstances where there is a need to determine change in Church polity or practice by voting, each man and woman should have an equal opportunity. Women are able to and should be invited to offer guidance to the Church on issues that specifically concern them, for example, family life, social needs, education and charity. Women have unique gifts to offer with regard to these issues.

B. With the advent of a more technologically oriented society, we are finding that our world is changing at a very rapid pace. It is important for our churches to become aware and stay abreast of these changes because, at times, they can contribute to the life of the Church. Women, also, must find a way to become better informed and learn to cope with these changes. We believe this will happen with better educational opportunities.

C. With regard to the various offices within the churches we recommend the churches encourage the participation of women on the local and higher levels.

9. Inter-Orthodox Concerns

A. We recommend our churches continue the theological dialogue regarding the restoration of communion between the Orthodox and Oriental Orthodox Churches.

B. We support and look forward to a resolution to the calendar differences among all Orthodox churches. We realize that the differences which exist are a result of certain historical difficulties. However, we await the day when our churches will celebrate the liturgical year together.

10. And the Future...

A. We ask our churches to consider seriously the request by the World Council of Churches for fifty percent participation by women at the upcoming General Assembly in Harare, Zimbabwe in the fall of 1998. We also ask our churches to bestow their blessings on the women planning to take part in the Ecumenical Decade Festival which takes place a few days prior to the General Assembly.

B. We recommend the establishment of a resource center where theological research and writings by Orthodox women and the reports from conferences such as this will be made available for all.

C. We hope and pray that Orthodox theological institutions which have been closed, such as the Theological School at Halki, will shortly be reopened, and we ask that women be able to participate in theological studies and research at all theological institutions.

D. Some participants at the consultation welcome the idea of organizing an inter-Orthodox conference on the ordination of women to the priesthood. We realize that for some this question is not an issue and will not be discussed.

Any study and examination of the issue in no way presupposes a commitment to move in this direction. This would simply provide the opportunity for women and men to examine this topic in greater depth from both the theological and spiritual perspectives. This conference would include attendance by clergy, laity and monastics.

E. Many recommendations have emerged from previous meetings of Orthodox women. While some recommendations have been addressed others have not. We are concerned about the reception of this document and recommend that our churches make this statement available for women either through general publications or correspondence to parishes.

F. We have gained considerable knowledge and great benefit from the present conference. It is our hope from now on and into the coming millenium our churches will continue to sponsor conferences for women where we can come together to enjoy fellowship, share our concerns and learn from one another.

Conclusion

We began our consultation with the celebration of the Feast of the Holy Myrrhbearers at the Women's Monastery at Balukli. The spirit of these missionary women, which is the same spirit that has inspired the Ecumenical Decade of Churches in Solidarity with Women, comforted us and accompanied us in our prayers and work during this week.

Our spiritual experience was enriched by our visit to the important monuments of the Orthodox heritage, St Sophia and the Monastery at Chora. The mosaic of the Incarnate Word of God, which is the embodiment of living human beings, reassured us of the spiritual reality that salvation is for all.

Finally, the fresco of the Resurrection depicting the Risen Christ pulling both man and woman from the grave shows us, once again, that our common faith and expectation is the central theme of this consultation on "Discerning the Signs of the Times."

Gospel and Cultures:
An Inter-Orthodox Consultation
Final Report
Addis Ababa, Ethiopia, 19 – 27 January 1996

Introduction

The Inter-Orthodox Preparatory Consultation on World Mission and Evangelism gathered in Addis Ababa, Ethiopia, 19-27 January 1996, at the generous invitation of His Holiness Patriarch Paulos and the Holy Synod of the Ethiopian Orthodox Tewahedo Church.

After many years of violent suppression and persecution during which the previous patriarch was jailed, tortured and murdered, and thousands of clergy and laity imprisoned, killed or exiled, the Ethiopian Church has risen in triumph and glory. This Church, so long isolated from the outside world, is an authentic expression, the embodiment of African Orthodoxy.

Participants from twenty nations, representatives of both Eastern and Oriental Orthodox Churches, rejoiced at the three-day Epiphany observances, which included processions and outdoor services attended by hundreds of thousands of jubilant faithful. The vestments and chanting, the processional crosses and arcs-of-the covenant unique to the Ethiopian tradition, revealed to us new dimensions and values of Orthodoxy. The enthusiasm with which over a million and a half believers greeted the patriarch on Sunday, 20 January as well as the lavish and delicious hospitality showered on us these sun-lit days left permanent impressions on all those who witnessed and experienced them. Here, despite the geographic distances and cultural differences, we felt at home.

A week of reflection, even in these near-ideal circumstances, hardly suffices to reflect and articulate an Orthodox Christian response to the issues before us. There is much more to think about, talk about, write about, but this was not the end of the road nor the final word. Our work will resume in Salvador, Bahia, Brazil, and continue for many years thereafter. We only hope this modest contribution to the ecumenical dialogue will enrich and enhance our discussions in Brazil as we continue our common efforts to glorify Christ and proclaim His majestic reign among all peoples.

I. Gospel and Cultures – Biblical, Theological and Patristic Perspectives

The birth of Jesus the Messiah is announced as " *Good news* of a great joy which will come to all the people" (Lk. 2:10). The particularity of that event in the time and space of human history ("for *to you is* born *this day* in the *city of David* a Saviour who is Christ the Lord" Lk. 2:11) soon became the key to the understanding of the cosmic Saviour ("all things are made through him, and without him was not anything made that was made", Jn. 1:3). The Church has always strived to keep in a creative balance the particularity of the incarnation of God in Jesus Christ primarily addressed to one people and the universality of salvation in Christ addressed to all the nations and to the whole creation. In the consciousness of the Church, the incarnate Son of God and the eternal Logos of God are the same person. Since "the Word became flesh and dwelt among us" (Jn. 1:14) there is a radical newness in the good news of incarnation. Since the Word was "the same light that enlightens every human being" (Jn. 1:9) there is an unbroken continuity in the good news prepared "from before the foundation of the world" (Eph. 1:4). For the Christian Church that accepted the Jewish Scriptures as part of her own Holy Scriptures, the truth of continuity was inescapable. The life that is in the eternal Word of God has been the light of all humanity (Jn. 1:4).

In developing the trinitarian doctrine of God, on the basis of the revelation in Christ, the Christian Tradition understood the Holy Spirit in a similar way. The Holy Spirit that was powerfully manifested to the Apostolic Church on the day of Pentecost was the same Spirit of God that hovered over the waters in the beginning of all creation. It is the same Spirit that inspires every creative impulse of humanity and communicates the one Gospel of Christ to diverse nations in their own languages (Acts 2). There is a radical newness and an unbroken continuity in the work of the Holy Spirit with regard to the Church, the new humanity.

Rooted in christological and pneumatological perceptions, the Orthodox Tradition does not set any fundamental polarity between history and eternity, between human creativity and divine intervention. However, it fully recognizes the ambiguity of human freedom that can pervert the course of history and corrupt human creativity. Yet, Orthodox soteriology does not condemn human freedom as such nor stifle human creativity as evil, but discerns them and guides them to the goal of divinization.

In its approach to various human cultures, the patristic tradition took such a positive position. Culture, as the total and living expression of collective human creativity, was taken seriously by the prominent Fathers of the Church. They discerned the presence of the all-pervading Logos of God and the all-inspiring Spirit of God in the noblest spiritual aspirations and socio-political initiatives of human cultures. They also discerned cultural values and practices of their contemporary societies in the light of the life-giving Gospel of Christ and the righteousness of the Kingdom of God.

There was no uncritical identification with any culture as such, nor was there any sweeping condemnation of humanity that carries the image of God.

Following this model, many of the witnesses of the living Orthodox Tradition in our times have developed a critical yet positive approach to human creativity and freedom in different cultural contexts. Their work has demonstrated that the Eastern Christian Tradition has amazing resources to respond creatively to the plurality of human cultures, and religious-spiritual traditions.

The Pentecostal experience of one Spirit speaking to diverse nations in their own tongues profoundly marked the Body of Christ. As the Gospel spread to many places and peoples, this foundational experience became paradigmatic for the Church and her mission.

Patristic exegesis interpreted the Pentecost experience as the reversal of Babel. The diversity of languages was fatal to this unity and common endeavour of the people in the old Babel. In the new Babel, paradoxically, diversity became a gift of the Spirit and constituted the oneness of the Body of Christ.

Every community that celebrated the Eucharist also confessed the one Apostolic Faith. So one faith and one Eucharist in the bond of mutual love became the binding force of diverse communities. However, like the celebrations of the Eucharist, the Apostolic Faith could never be abstracted from the confessing community. Every celebration of this mystery of faith brought afresh the Pentecostal experience of unity to the diverse communities.

From the beginning of God's new covenant in Jesus the Messiah, the various Christian communities produced testimonies to the Apostolic Faith which guarded their unity, identity, integrity, solidarity and continuity in the one Gospel. It is from this unity that the great diversity and variety of expressions of the Gospel emerged. Indeed, it must be said that the greater the unity in faith, life and worship among the various Churches, the greater their variety of expressions, the deeper their oneness, the richer their diversity.

The Church gradually developed the rule of faith not to overrule the constitutive diversity of experiences in the local communities but to test and foster each other in the one Apostolic Faith. By formulating confessions of faiths, like the Nicene-Constantinopolitan Creed, the Church did not claim to capture truth in propositional formulas, but indicated an essential minimum conceptual consensus. The truth of Apostolic Faith was to be experienced in the celebration and practice of Christian faith in daily life in its personal and community dimensions. So, it was the rule of prayer and ethical practice that expressed in each context the content of this one Apostolic Faith.

These testimonies which were developed and continue to be developed and passed on in the various communities from the "deposit" and "rule of faith", the paradosis which preserves the Gospel, the apostolic teaching and the tradition of life in each community, and among them all. They are "what has been entrusted" to the Churches through the laying-on-of hands of the bishops through the ages, and from place to place. They guarantee that each believing community is the Church of Christ, that its Gospel, faith and life are one.

First among the testimonies to the evangelical faith are the canonized writings of the various apostolic communities which are received and shared by each. They demonstrate a communion of faith and life in the Churches who are each "The one Church of Christ." They interpret the scriptures of Israel in the light of the risen Christ who lives in them and whose members they are in the Holy Spirit. Christ opens the minds of the believers in the Church to understand how He is the fulfilment of the law, the psalms and the prophets which speak about him.

II. The Apostolic Faith: Local and Catholic

Instead of developing a concept of universal truth in geographical or cultural terms, the Orthodox Tradition fostered a notion of catholicity or truth "according to the whole" as expressed in each local eucharistic community. This approach was shaped by the work of the Holy Spirit who continually guides us into the fullness of truth. According to this, the catholicity of Apostolic Faith is experienced and expressed by each local community of faith in its own particular context.

But every context is open to change depending on its needs and aspirations and also under the impact of forces from other cultural contexts. If at one time a particular context is in need of liberating forces in sociopolitical terms, at another time, the same context might require healing and reconciling forces. The power of the Gospel through one Apostolic Faith can make us sensitive to the varying needs within the same context or between different contexts.

The catholicity of the Apostolic Faith is neither endangered nor compromised when the Church thus responds to the varying situations. On the contrary, the Church is actually living and fulfilling the Apostolic Faith when she shows compassion and commitment to God's world in different ages and places.

The Orthodox Tradition places great significance on the historic continuity of local Churches that visibly express the communion in one Apostolic Faith and Eucharist. It is this concrete presence of different sociocultural and geographical-political settings that demands their total involvement in their diverse situations.

Living the Apostolic Faith and celebrating the Eucharist have ethical implications for fostering the image of God in humanity, for nurturing human freedom and justice, human dignity and self-sacrificing love. The ethical dimension is integral to the experience of the Apostolic Faith that carries the power of the gospel in our world. The apostolic faith thus becomes our basis for our participation together with others in the process of social transformation in order to bring the world closer to the Kingdom of God. Here the Orthodox Tradition understands the Apostolic Faith not simply as a deposit of faith that belongs to the past, but as the gift of God in view of the realization of the Kingdom of God. No human context lies outside the fulness of God's reign.

Orthodox theology, which constantly draws on such themes as the image of God in humanity, Holy Spirit in creation, new creation in the incarnate Christ, the union of matter and spirit in incarnation, the Pentecost experience, transfiguration of material reality, the communion in the Triune God, and divinization, has the challenging task to bring out the best in our Christian heritage in addressing the multiplicity of cultures in their encounter with the life-giving Gospel of Christ.

III. One Gospel, diverse cultural expressions

The Gospel that shapes the life and the witness of the Church is usually proclaimed in today's world in multi-cultural and conflictual settings. It is a sign of our times that all cultures demand equal recognition of their worth and contribution towards the advancement of human life in the world.

Reflecting upon the theological significance of human cultures, we have come to recognize that *all* cultures have the potential to receive and express the universality of the Gospel which is always communicated as local expression of God's love for the world. Particular Churches whose life is shaped by such local expressions of the faith must be in conversation with each other – being aware of their particularity – and in their communion must search together whether they truly express in an adequate way all that the Holy Spirit has transmitted through the Apostles. The content of the Apostolic Faith must be received, understood and communicated to all peoples. The diversity of its expressions in different cultures becomes necessary for the sake of transmitting the Gospel in its unchanging meaning.

The Gospel is not simply expressed through particular cultures but in its encounter with them contributes to their affirmation and further development. The Gospel affirms in them whatever is compatible with the basic tenets of the Gospel and relativizes whatever ultimately is attributed to them by opening the cultures to the coming reign of God. Furthermore, the Gospel enables the cultures to recognize and reject whatever sinful and destructive forces exist in them.

The eternal truth which is Christ, delivered to the Church in its fulness immediately became incarnate in many languages in Jerusalem on Pentecost. The Gospel is always inculturated, proclaimed, manifest in a particular time and place by a particular people which means in a cultural context. With its reception by a people, their pre-existing culture is fertilized by the Gospel and organically transformed into creative energies towards salvation. There will inevitably be elements, attitudes, values within any culture alien to the Gospel and incompatible with it, which will be purified, transformed or exorcized by the Holy Spirit as the Spirit witnesses to Christ in the continuing life of the local eucharistic community.

There will necessarily and preferably be a plurality of forms and expressions used to convey, proclaim and celebrate the same eternal reality of Christ.

IV. The inclusive nature of the Church

The Church, as the Body of Christ and the temple the Holy Spirit, reveals and actualizes through her life of worship, proclamation and service the love of God for the world. The faithful, through their baptism, are transformed into a new community "For in Christ Jesus you are all sons and daughters of God. For as many of you are baptized into Christ have put on Christ. There is neither Jew nor Greek, there is neither slave nor free, there is neither male nor female, for you are all one in Christ Jesus" (Gal. 3: 26-29).

The unity of the faithful in Jesus Christ transcends all the brokenness and unjust divisions that exist in history. Unity in Christ should not be confused with uniformity. The Spirit of God that constitutes the Church together with Jesus Christ distributes without dividing the ministry of Christ to all the baptized faithful as "He wills" for "the common good" (1 Cor. 12:4-14, 23-24). All the ministries of the Church empowered by the Holy Spirit derive their origins from and lead to Jesus Christ. They enable the Church to be the manifestation of God's transformative presence in the world. Thus the life and the love of Jesus Christ fundamentally conditions the understanding of the Church's diverse ministries and how they must relate to each other. There is an interdependence and interconnectedness within the Church among its diverse members. Those who have been entrusted by the Spirit of God with the ministry of *episkopé* have the responsibility to enable each member of the church to actualize the gifts (ministries) that the Holy Spirit has bestowed upon them for the common witness of the Church. All ministries in the church are related to each other and all of them find their origins and fulfilment in the ministry of Jesus Christ. Acknowledging the equal importance of all the ministries by which the Church lives and witnesses her identity with Jesus Christ, implies that conscious efforts should be made to enable the laity to participate together with the clergy in the church's ministry and witness. In this context, we must remind our churches of the recommendation of the Pan-Orthodox Symposium of Rhodes, Greece (1988), to reinstate the office of deaconess, which is not a novelty but an indispensable element of the Church's Tradition. This report particularly stated:

"The Apostolic order of deaconess should be revived. It was never altogether abandoned in the Orthodox Church though it has tended to fall into disuse. There is ample evidence, from apostolic times, from the patristic, canonical and liturgical tradition, well into the Byzantine period (and even in our own day) that this order was held in high honour... The revival of women deaconesses in the Orthodox Church would emphasize in a special way the dignity of woman and give recognition to her contribution to the work of the Church as a whole" (Gennadios Limouris, ed., *The Place of the Woman in the Orthodox Church and the Question of the Ordination of Women,* Katerina: Tertios Russ, 1992, pp. 31-32).

There is a need to reflect critically why our Churches are reluctant to implement this recommendation. The Gospel as well as the critical spirit of our times demands from the people of God to be true to their calling and to be authentic signs of God's salvific presence in the world.

V. The Gospel, cultures and national identity

Throughout history certain nations have accepted the Christian Gospel as the very focus of their identity, and the entrance of the Gospel into their culture has resulted in its creative transformation. The art, music, architecture, poetry, literature and the language and thought-patterns have, to a large extent, been shaped by the national identity as Christian.

The Gospel has fertilized the creative genius of such peoples, organically and inwardly inspiring their greatest cultural achievements. Monastic life has historically flourished in such nations, giving to the Church some of her greatest saints and a precious heritage of spiritual literature. This inculturation has been one of the Orthodox traditions greatest contributions to world civilization.

No Christian nation or empire, however, can ever fully embody the Kingdom of God, which is ultimately not of this world. In so far as it lives and acts in human history it is subject to the same temptations and sins as all other earthly realities. In so far as even within Christian nations there exist hatred, injustice, economic and social inequalities, greed, selfishness, racial and caste distinctions, etc., it would be inappropriate to identify completely any culture or nation as fully or irreversibly Christian to equate the nation with the Church.

Those who attempt to do so are often guided by political, economic or social principles alien to the Gospel, and in modern times by exclusivist nationalism which violates the very principle of cultural plurality, mutual tolerance and respect, unity in diversity, that is, Christian Love.

In multi-cultural and multi-religious settings, different cultures and religions may compete with each other for predominance. This inevitably leads to violent conflict, exploitation and even persecution and death of the less powerful. In such situations of brokenness and violence, the Church by following the irenic life of Jesus Christ must actively work for the peaceful co-existence of all communities, enabling all to recognize the sanctity of life as a gift of God and the right of all to pursue the quest for human fulfillment not in opposition with the other but in meaningful conversation of enrichment that enhances the understanding of life as God's gift.

Orthodox Witness in Africa Today:
A Pan-African Inter-Orthodox Consultation

Final Report
Kampala, Uganda, 2 – 7 December 1997

Introduction

We, the participants of the First Pan-African Inter-Orthodox Consultation met in Kampala Uganda, 2-7 December 1997. We have gathered as representatives of the Eastern and Oriental Orthodox Churches from Cameroon, the Democratic Republic of Congo, Egypt, Ethiopia, Ghana, Kenya, Madagascar, the Republic of South Africa, Tanzania, Uganda, Zambia, and Zimbabwe. We are happy to have been accompanied by participants and consultants from Orthodox and other Christian confessions from Finland, Greece, Norway, Poland, Romania, Russia, the USA and the World Council of Churches (Switzerland).

With the paternal blessings of His Beatitude Petros VII, the Greek Orthodox Pope and Patriarch of Alexandria and all Africa, we have enjoyed the warm hospitality of our beloved hierarch, His Eminence Metropolitan Jonah and the Holy Orthodox Metropolis of Kampala and all Uganda. *We are grateful for the kind and generous sponsorship of the World Council of Churches* that *has made our gathering possible.*

The atmosphere of our meeting was charged with enthusiasm and high expectation, as this was the first of its kind in recent memory to bring together Eastern and Oriental Orthodox clergy and laity from all over the continent of Africa, accompanied by our own hierarchs as well as hierarchs, theologians and church workers from other Orthodox churches in other parts of the world. As we rejoiced in the fellowship that this meeting afforded us, we were filled with an overwhelming sense of responsibility, being reminded of the glorious years of the great councils of our Church.

As we have prayed, deliberated and enjoyed fellowship together as Eastern and Oriental Orthodox Christians, we have realized how important the search for unity between our two families is to the mission and witness of Orthodoxy in Africa. We pray to God and look forward, with eager anticipation, to the day when full Eucharistic communion will be restored between our two families.

We recognized that participation in the meeting was heavily weighted in favour of the Eastern Orthodox. There were about eighty Eastern Orthodox and ten Oriental

Orthodox participants. We understood that this was inevitable because of the present realities of Orthodox mission in Africa. Therefore it was also inevitable that most of our conclusion and recommendations reflected the aspirations of the Eastern Orthodox participants. We set them forth in the spirit that they will make a humble contribution to the proper growth of all Orthodox mission in Africa.

Our sessions were conducted in an atmosphere of worship, and, in a spirit of love and frankness, we raised pertinent issues affecting our work and mission in Africa.

Our deliberations addressed the following two main concerns:

The incarnation of the Gospel in a local context and its full expression through the cultural patterns of the people in their particular context;

Overcoming the cultural taboos in proclaiming the Gospel of the fulness of life: the role of the Church in confronting the HIV/AIDS pandemic.

A. Orthodox Witness in Africa Today: Challenges, Hopes and Expectations

I. Missionary Renewal

We affirm that mission is the work of God the Father, Son and Holy Spirit. It is the Father who in the power of the Holy Spirit has sent His Son for the salvation of His creation. As members of the Body of Christ, the incarnated Son of God, we participate in God's mission. The Holy Spirit who fills the Church and indwells each one of her members, transforms us into living witnesses, co-workers of Christ, and His ambassadors in the world. Thus, in the power of the Holy Spirit, we are sent by Christ to bring Him to all nations, and all nations through Him to the Father. Mission, therefore, belongs to the very being of the Church and to each of her members.

Orthodoxy in Africa is ancient and yet most of the communities that we represent are neophyte communities needing the nurture of the whole Body of Christ. We believe that the time has come for the renewal of the missionary zeal that enabled the Church to be planted in all parts of the oikumene of the early Church.

We wish to use the opportunity offered us at this meeting to sound an urgent and humble call for:

− an Inter-Orthodox effort to support the work of Orthodox missions here in Africa;

− the secondment of devoted and qualified persons to come as missionaries to support the activities of local Orthodox missions;

− the establishment of a worldwide Inter-Orthodox Commission on Mission to deal with Orthodox mission issues throughout the world;

− the establishment of a permanent centre for the coordination of both Eastern and Oriental Orthodox mission work in Africa.

II. Culture-sensitive Evangelism and Relationships in Mission

We affirm that all cultures are capable of communicating the grace and the love of God. Reception of the Good News of Christ does not destroy culture. Rather, it enables each culture to be transformed. By taking on our human nature and entering into our history, Christ enables our ways of life to be purified so that they can become a means of communion with Himself. We have felt emboldened to use the symbolism of "transfiguration" (metamorphosis) to describe this process, for it is the inner content and meaning of culture that must necessarily undergo this transformation and not its outward forms.

The miraculous stories that we have shared of the origins of most of the communities that we represent, the new and emerging Orthodox communities in Africa, convince us that African culture is ripe for Orthodoxy; that Orthodoxy holds the key to a truly inculturated Christian Gospel in Africa.

Culture-sensitive evangelism is self evident in the Orthodox teaching and practice of mission and evangelism. It is a part of the great tradition and legacy of our Church. However, certain recent developments in the conduct of mission in Africa give us cause to remind ourselves and our partners in the mission fields of Africa of this principle.

We need to remind ourselves that:

— the Church has always done her mission in the language and thought patterns of the people. Her liturgy, catechism, preaching and all aspects of her ministry have been conducted in languages that the people have understood. It is this that has contributed to making this truly universal Church also so truly local.

— All missionaries (both "local" and "foreign") are partners and co-workers in mission. There is need for mutual respect and trust and a mutual recognition of each other's worth in our common task so that love may grow and our witness become credible.

— Our brothers and sisters from other lands and cultures need to be immersed into the culture of the people to better understand their behaviours and practices. African culture, in particular, requires that missionaries, including hierarchs, make themselves available to their people. This requires proper orientation and a certain amount of training for mission work.

— True inculturation cannot be an academic exercise. It is a process that comes from within the very being of the community, involving all its members. It results from the nurture of the people so that all of life, all of culture is transformed from within.

Therefore, we humbly wish to suggest:

— more effort to promote and support the work of translation of liturgical catechetical and theological material into the local languages of our communities;

— vigorous promotion of the use of these local languages in the worship and instruction of these communities;

— the institution of regular Pan-African Inter-Orthodox conferences to deal with the problems and issues of Orthodox mission in Africa. We recommend that these conferences as well as other conferences and seminars devote some attention to the issues of the incarnation of the Gospel in African culture.

— that the official report of the Addis Ababa consultation on Gospel and Culture be studied by all involved in Orthodox mission in Africa.

III. Participation of the Priest and Laity in Decision Making

While it is important to acknowledge the hierarchical nature of the Church, it is equally important to affirm its conciliarity. This conciliarity is applied to all levels of decision making concerning and affecting the life of the Church and the lives of her people. We believe that for the proper governance of the Church, and for true inculturation to take place, all sections of the membership should be involved at various levels and in differing degrees, in making the decisions that affect the life of the Church.

1. The Priests

At the parish, it is the priest who makes the bishop present among his people. The priest is also the eyes, ears and hands of the bishop. It is therefore important that the priests are involved and participate actively in the governance of the Church, at the local, diocesan and patriarchal levels. From this perspective, we humbly make the following suggestions:

— the institution of local councils of priest in each diocese to act as advisory and consultative bodies to the bishops and to assist them in the proper administration of their dioceses;

— that bishops and archbishops consult with their clergy before attending meetings of the Holy Synod;

— that some of the most senior clergymen or those with special skills or responsibilities are allowed to accompany their hierarchs to some sessions of the Holy Synod as consultants and advisors. This would enable and help the Holy Synod to make informed decisions concerning the Church and its mission. We humbly wish to recommend this to the Holy Synod for consideration.

2. Laity

We feel that the time has come to increase the level of lay participation in the governance of the Church and to involve more qualified lay persons in her administration at all levels. This is especially important in the case of the newly emerging Churches that today make up the bulk of the communities that constitute our Patriarchates. Therefore, we humbly suggest:

— that special efforts be made to find and recruit persons from these communities for involvement in local, diocesan and even patriarchal church administration;

— the establishment of councils of clergy and laity in all dioceses to assist our bishops in administering their dioceses.

3. Women

We recognise that women constitute a greater proportion of the membership of all our communities in Africa. This means that they carry the greater portion of the burden for local support of our Churches.

Our women participants have felt especially excluded from many kinds of leadership responsibilities and decision making processes in the Church. We believe that it is time to restore the proper role of women in the Church (including the appropriate leadership roles) and to give more opportunities for women to participate more fully in the daily life of the Church.

We have been informed at this meeting that over the last two decades, a number of consultations have been held by Orthodox women and theologians on the role of women in the Church. These meetings have produced many fruits that could be harvested for the benefit of our Church. However, it is evident that the results of these important meetings have not been available to our women. This is either because the published reports have not reached them or because they do not have the theological capacities to appreciate them. It is also evident that whatever fruits these conferences and consultation have produced have not been harvested.

In order to facilitate the achievement of these desiderata the following suggestions came out of our consultation which we respectfully submit for consideration:

— that special efforts be made in each diocese (and local community) to disseminate the results of these meetings and to solicit the views and responses of African Orthodox women on how these apply to their particular cultural and social circumstances;

— that our Church should make special efforts to study the results of these meetings to determine how their fruits could be harvested for the full benefit of our people.

— the promotion and encouragement of general and theological education of African Orthodox women for a more effective participation of women in the administration and pastoral work of the Church and of their local communities.

4. Youth

We rejoice in the fact that our Church is predominantly youthful. We are also thankful for the fact that, in many places, a growing number of our young are moving into middle level management positions, or are acquiring the skills that will enable them to play increasingly meaningful roles in the affairs of their Church communities.

The youth participants in our meeting have felt that they are able to contribute more, and we hope that the Church would take more advantage of their potential as co-workers in the vineyard of the Lord. Therefore, we humbly propose and submit for consideration:

— that a conscious effort be made to include young people and their organizations in the decision making processes at all levels of local, diocesan and patriarchal administration;

— the institution of appropriate training programmes for the youth to enable them play this role;

— the development and institution of deliberate programmes to address the needs of the youth and their involvement in the planning and implementation of such programmes.

IV. Education and Spiritual Development

Our meeting has identified education as one of the burning issues facing the mission of the Church. Our discussions have clearly showed that we consider education as holding the key to many of the problems confronting the Church and our mission.

It is for this reason that we lament the inadequacy of opportunities for the proper intellectual, spiritual and social development of the faithful, especially the young. This, we feel, has made it difficult for our Church to attain the full measure of its potential for growth.

In general, it seems that our Church is doing her mission among the less privileged of society. Many participants have reported that among the membership of their communities, illiteracy is still rather high and the number of persons with higher education rather low. This is often due to poverty and the inadequacy of the educational systems and/or conditions in the areas where our Churches are located. The result of this is that often, and in many places, the Church lacks the human and personnel resources that she needs to do her work efficiently and effectively.

1. General Education and Development of Skills

We believe that our Church should spare no effort in promoting the general education of her faithful and in improving the educational standards of the coming generations. We must provide our young with good quality education and the skills to survive in these rapidly changing times, and equip them to make more meaningful contributions to the development of their communities.

There is an urgent need for the establishment of educational institutions of academic and vocational excellence in each diocese. Such institutions will not only serve Orthodox faithful, but will be available to all for the overall development of the communities in which we live and do our mission.

Where parochial institutions of general education already exist, efforts should be made to improve and equip them to adequately serve our purposes. We also propose the establishment of local scholarship schemes to cater for the education of our young, especially the less privileged among them. In future, scholarships for studies abroad should not be limited to theological education alone but should include studies in all disciplines of human endeavour and development.

2. Theological Education and Ecclesial Leadership Development

We affirm that proper theological education is one of the essential requirements for the proper growth and development of the Church. It is for this reason that we are thankful for the opportunities that are offered for some of our clergy and laity to acquire theological education and training for service in the Church. We pray that conditions will make it possible for us to continue enjoying these opportunities and privileges. We appreciate the importance of the role that the Patriarchal Seminary at Nairobi has played in the development of our Church. However, we believe that the time has come to upgrade the level of theological education at the seminary and to make efforts to obtain recognition for its diploma. This, we believe, will enable the seminary to better serve the needs of the entire continent of Africa for proper and adequate Orthodox theological formation.

We would appreciate it if our Churches would consider the following:

– that, in addition to their proper spiritual development, any formation of our clergy should have in view the development of their full intellectual capabilities, so that the clergy will be adequately equipped to deal with the needs of their communities in a holistic manner (annual or periodic retreats, seminars and capacity building workshops will be helpful in this direction);

– that due to the urgent needs of the Church for theological formation and maturity, as against the difficulties posed by distances and the lack of adequate resources, the Church should make efforts to make theological education available to all through the methods of Theological Education by Extension;

– that studies in missiology and in African religion and culture be included in the theological formation of our clergy, lay theologians and other church workers.

V. Communication

Our consultation has emphasized the need for improved communication within the Church, recognizing that this is essential for our mission and the growth of the Church.

We humbly suggest:

– that our hierarchs look for ways to improve the existing channels of communicating the meetings of the Holy Synod and its major decisions, so that the faithful will be better informed of its work and join in praying for its success;

– the establishment of a network for sharing information within the Patriarchate and between the churches and dioceses of the Patriarchate in order to promote the sense of the unity of our Patriarchate;

– that our Church should make all efforts to improve the sharing of information about our work and mission in Africa with all other Orthodox Churches;

– that the churches take advantage of the facilities made available by modern technology to achieve this goal. We ask our enablers and partners in mission to support us to acquire the necessary equipment for this;

– that communication and information sharing at the local level be improved;

– that our Church continues improving the channels of communication between clergy and laity and between the leadership and all the people of God;

– that parishes should institute or improve upon their mechanisms for listening to the concerns and aspirations of the people and soliciting their input in meeting the needs of the Church and the faithful.

– that the systems and mechanisms for sharing our faith and making it accessible to all be improved;

– that diocesan and parochial periodicals, newsletters and information bulletin to disseminate information about the Church and our faith be issued;

– that libraries and bookshops that will specialize in Orthodox literature as well as centres for Orthodox information in various places within our Church be established;.

– that effort be made to have media coverage of major events of the Church where and when possible.

VI. Administration and Management

As we have indicated in many parts of this report, we advocate participatory methods of administration in the management of the affairs of the Church.

We recognize that the administrative and management systems that exist within our Church often suffer the lack of adequate human and material resources. Administrators have not always had the adequate managerial skills to administer our communities and manage our resources professionally. Programme and project planning and implementation have more often than not suffered as a result of this.

We humbly suggest:

– the institution of measures to identify persons with adequate administrative and managerial skills for service in the Church, or to equip persons with administrative responsibilities with such skills;

– that capacity building becomes an integral part of our administrative and management systems in order to promote the easier and wider sharing of responsibility;

– increased transparency in the administration of the Church and in the management of resources. This would improve our administrative and management systems even as it improves communication within the Church.

VII. Financial Resource Development

We very much appreciate and are very thankful for the support that our Church has enjoyed and continues to enjoy from our many benefactors and sister Orthodox Churches throughout the world. Some of these are represented at this consultation, and we are grateful for their involvement, support and guidance in these deliberations.

However, we recognize that our Church and its mission continue to be starved of financial and other material resources.

Even as we call for increased support from our traditional partners in mission and the involvement of others for the success of the mission of our Church in Africa, we affirm that the solution to this problem lies in our move from dependence towards increased self reliance.

We humbly propose for consideration:

– that our communities intensify education to increase the level of membership support;

– that communities are also encouraged to increase their support of the dioceses and the activities of the Church;

For local fund raising to be meaningful and effective, however, there is the need to help improve the living conditions and income generation capacities of the members of the communities.

We are, therefore, humbly appealing:

– for the establishment and support of self-improvement progammes for members and groups of members of our communities;

– for the establishment of viable income-generating projects and for these to become a major source of local funding for the Church (our communities should work towards making local income generation through these projects the greatest source of income for our Church);

– for the establishment of a revolving fund in each diocese to support these activities and programmes;

– that our partners give priority to the development of local income generation, through these methods, in their support of our communities.

VIII. Relations between Eastern and Oriental Orthodox Churches

We are most grateful for this opportunity to meet in fellowship and work together as members of the Eastern and Oriental families of the One Holy Catholic and Apostolic Church.

We appreciate the efforts currently being made to restore full Eucharistic union between our two families.

As we have worked and deliberated together, however, it has become clear to us that the issue of Eastern and Oriental Orthodox Church unity affects different Orthodox churches in varying degrees of intensity. We realize that being a mission Church par excellence, and living with each other, thus living daily the experience of the separation, we are among the churches most acutely affected by the continued separation.

We make a passionate appeal to our Holy Synods to make this matter their priority in their relations and dealings with our sister Orthodox churches, and press for the expedited resolution of the remaining obstacles hindering the restoration of full Eucharistic union.

We request our hierarchs here present to take this special appeal to the next meetings of the Holy Synods.

We also humbly request other hierarchs here present and representing their churches at this consultation to carry this message of our concern and our appeal to their respective churches.

Meanwhile, we call for increased cooperation between our two families in all areas where cooperation is possible and feasible, but especially in the area of mission to avoid duplication of efforts and in anticipation of the coming unity of our families.

Conclusion

The Orthodox in Africa, believe and affirm to be the inheritors of the tradition and heritage of the great Apostolic Sea of Alexandria, the Holy Apostle and Evangelist

Mark, Saints Athanasius and Cyril of Alexandria, and a host of great teachers, martyrs and saints of the One Holy Catholic and Apostolic Church.

It is the burden of the witness of this heritage that we find ourselves called to bear. We acknowledge the awesomeness of this call and the enormity of the task ahead. It is a burden that we cannot bear alone, a task for the whole body of Christ

Indeed, the Orthodox Churches in Africa are at a new stage of mission. Once again, they are truly mission Churches. And whilst the history of this new missionary movement clearly demonstrates our affirmation that the Church's mission is the mission of God, we rejoice and are grateful for the support of the many who have accompanied us on this pilgrimage.

B. The Ministry of the Church in Confronting
The HIV/AIDS Pandemic – Concluding Statement

Introduction

We, the participants in the Pan African Inter-Orthodox Consultation in Kampala, 2-7 December 1997 have, with deep concern, discussed issues raised by the AIDS epidemic in our region which the Church has recognized as a problem requiring urgent attention. The Consultation brought together participants from Orthodox Churches in many African countries, dominantly from Sub-Saharan Africa, and with representatives from the Orthodox Churches in Russia, Romania, Greece, USA, Finland and Poland. The Consultation was organized by the World Council of Churches. The second half of the consultation concentrated on discussing AIDS, and resource persons from Uganda and the World Council of Churches were sharing in the process. The participants would like to express their gratitude towards the WCC and the local organizers, the Ugandan Protestant Medical Bureau, for their time, effort and hospitality.

Situation of AIDS in Uganda, Africa and the World

The UNAIDS estimate that more than 30 million people are living with HIV virus world wide, and 5.8 million people are infected only in 1997. More than 10 million people have died from AIDS. About 2/3 of the infected persons live in Sub-Saharan Africa. In Sub-Saharan Africa 50% of the infected persons are women. The large majority of the infected persons are in the age group between 25 and 45 years old, in other words persons in, presumably, their most productive age. In the age group 15-19, there are four to six times as many women as men having AIDS, a figure which clearly demonstrates the increased vulnerability on the part of the women. When they die, many children are left as orphans. It is estimated that there are 7.8 million orphans in Sub-Saharan Africa. From 1994, AIDS has been the leading cause of death among adults in Uganda. Approximately 95% of the adult infections are caused by heterosexual transmission. In Uganda the general awareness about AIDS is higher; despite this people are still infected in large numbers, although rise in numbers is not as steep as it was some years back.

Factors that contribute to this rapid spread include: Multiple sexual partners and unprotected sexual intercourse; the presence of sexually transmitted diseases which increase the transmission; risky cultural beliefs and practices and poverty. The subordinate position of women in many societies is also a contributing factor, as women can often not make decisions regarding their own sexual lives.

Concerns

We, as Orthodox Churches in Africa, recognize that our Churches need to be more involved in addressing the issues this epidemic is raising, and the pain our peoples are facing. We therefore resolve to adopt the World Council of Churches Statement of the Central Committee: "Facing AIDS: The impact of HIV/AIDS and the Churches' response" as a working document upon whose basis our participation in preventing the spread of this pandemic will be made. Programmes, literature, information, activities and other innovations to address the impact of HIV/AIDS will be developed from this document.

The Orthodox Church feels highly responsible about teaching her children how to live the holy life as a holy people of God and gladly accepts into her bosom all people who repent. She emphasizes the Church's teaching on the role and values of the family, that sex within marriage is God's gift, and she does not condone sex before and outside marriage.

The Church thinks that to condemn people is not the solution to fight against HIV/AIDS, but the answer lies in living the Christian life in love and openness according to the Bible and teachings of the Holy Fathers.

From this fundamental principle, we raise the following issues:

1. We firmly believe that the prevalence of poverty and illiteracy among African communities has largely contributed to a wide spread of the scourge of HIV/AIDS.
2. There is inadequate flow of information concerning HIV/AIDS and there is a shortage of counseling personnel, and counseling services.
3. Negative cultural practices and taboos such as wife inheritance, use of unhealthy methods in circumcision, clitoridectomy, and polygamy have been contributing factors in the spread of HIV/AIDS.
4. Marginalisation and alienation of people infected with AIDS.
5. We have realized that women are marginalised and more vulnerable to the risk of infection through sexual exploitation, educational and economic deprivation.
6. The Church has not come out openly to discuss sex-related issues.
7. We acknowledge that the AIDS pandemic creates a magnitude of problems which need varied and collective responses.

Recommendations

We respectfully ask the Orthodox Churches in Africa:

1. To help in literacy education and in eradicating poverty by initiating and

encouraging small scale income generating projects among the various communities.

2. To include HIV/AIDS knowledge and pastoral skills in the training of all clergy and laity. Put in place proper counseling services, encourage debate and dialogue among individuals, groups, and communities to effect behavioral change.

3. To sensitize the community on the risks of following some customs and practices, but at the same time do not destroy the good elements in their cultures.

4. The emphasizes the importance of inclusion, openness and acceptance of all people, made in God's image and the need for people to live a sacramental life based on Christian values. This can be encouraged through pastoral care, giving hope through the Gospel and accepting and supporting people with HIV.

5. To give priority to training programmes and education for women in order to improve their status in society .

6. Together with other churches to address issues related to sexuality and to promote relevant education at all levels. Education needs to be targeted to various age groups.

7. To network and cooperate with other agencies, be they governmental, community-based organisations, non-governmental organisations and other church bodies.

Report of the Moderator*

His Holiness ARAM I, Catholicos of Cilicia
WCC Central Committee,
Geneva, Switzerland, 11 – 19 September 1997

I greet you all in the spirit of Christian love and fellowship. Once more we are gathered here as Central Committee to review the work of the Council, and plan together the coming year in the life of the WCC. This meeting of the Central Committee has a special significance for all of us. First, it is our last meeting as Central Committee and as such it may become, in a sense, an occasion for re-assessing our work for the last six years. Second, the preparations for the next Assembly will be finalized in their important aspects in this meeting. Third, the CUV process will reach its last phase to be forwarded then to the Assembly.

I will outline below my assessment of the present ecumenical situation, and share with you my own reaction to the CUV.

The process of "Common Understanding and Vision of the World Council of Churches" (CUV), which was mandated by the Central Committee in 1989 in Moscow, acquired focused attention last year in all aspects of the life and work of the World Council of Churches. The Executive Committee, the Officers, the General Secretary, various Commissions, staff and a small group appointed by the Executive Committee devoted considerable time to the process, as did the member churches and the ecumenical partners as well. Thus far we have received 135 responses. We are particularly grateful for the substantial and constructive reaction that we received from the Roman Catholic Church; this reaction deserves our deep appreciation and serious attention. The RCC comes to join the process "not just as outsider, but as close collaborator" with a profound sense of "close partnership"[1].

We have reached the penultimate stage of the CUV process. The forthcoming Eighth Assembly (3-14 December 1998, in Harare, Zimbabwe) will say its final

---

* For the purposes of the Orthodox Pre-Assembly meeting and for this volume, the first portion of Catholicos Aram's report, dealing with the business of the Executive Committee, has been omitted.

word. Our common understanding and vision of the WCC will always remain integral to our reflection and growth. Therefore it will, in a sense, continue beyond the Assembly. In fact, the very nature of our fellowship and major changes in the world situation and in the life of our churches will always necessitate a review of the goals, priorities and structures of the Council. We are at a decisive point in the history of the WCC as we move through the CUV process towards the Assembly, the fiftieth Anniversary of the creation of the WCC, and the Millennium. As Moderator I feel that at this last Central Committee, as the final draft of CUV is submitted for the judgment of this body, I must share with you some of my perspectives and concerns.

Towards an Ecumenism that Matters

It is now commonplace to state that the ecumenical movement has entered a most crucial juncture of its history. The impact of a radically changing world with its new moral, political, social and economic values, paradigms and norms on the ecumenical life and witness is strong and far-reaching. Expressions such as "transition" "uncertainty", "paradigm shift", "restlessness", etc., depicting the present state of ecumenism are frequently heard. All these characterizations point, in one way or another, to an ecumenical movement which is in crisis, a crisis which is manifested in different ways and degrees in different regions.

1) Can we talk about the ecumenical movement without talking about the church? Can we draw a line of demarcation between what is now called "ecumenical reality" and "ecclesial reality"? These realities are intimately and inseparably inter-connected; they condition and challenge each other. Ecumenism does not exist outside the church. It is integral to the very existence and vocation of the church, and pertains to the total life of the church. Our ways of life, our patterns of thinking, our self-understanding are deeply affected by the ecumenical movement. The ecumenical crisis is a symptom of the crisis that our churches are experiencing in their own life as they fulfill their missionary task in the world of today. I am absolutely convinced after my almost thirty years of ecumenical service that one of the major roles of the ecumenical movement is to challenge the churches to define what it means *to be a church* in the world of today.

2) The Church of God finds itself in a new world context. Besides the enormous changes that are occurring in practically all spheres of human life, new concerns and tensions are emerging in the life of the churches all over the world. In the North the institutionalized church is facing a growing crisis of identity and relevance and is constantly challenged to find new ways of becoming church. In the South the church is blooming at an unprecedented pace. Evangelical and charismatic movements are attracting many people. These shifts from historical to evangelical churches, from North to South, from institutional church structures to charismatic models, from traditional ecclesiological norms to new patterns of ecclesiological self-understanding are calling the church to a critical self-assessment of its true vocation in the world of today. The emergence of new ecclesial experiences within the churches, often in

contradiction with ecclesiastical institutions, are challenging the churches to come out of their petrified institutionalism which are often a result of historical circumstances. In some regions, especially in the former countries of the Soviet Union, the growing presence of Western secularist values and cultural norms are forcing the churches to re-affirm their ethnic and cultural identity and indigenous traditions. Therefore, the church is called to re-define and to re-affirm its *specific identity* and *vocation* in the power of the Holy Spirit and, in the midst of fragmented and disoriented societies, to act in faithful obedience to the Gospel and to respond to the needs of people by seeking new ways of being church.

3) The church is *the people of God*. This is, in fact, a major emphasis in all our ecclesiologies. We should not define the reality of church only in terms of its dues-paying members. We should not confine the church to its hierarchy, liturgy, doctrine or decision-making processes. The church needs structures to exist and function in society. But we must recognize that institutionalism has drained most of our churches of their vitality, relevance and immediate touch with people. Many people in Northern and Western countries are leaving the church as institution, and are seeking to develop new ways and forms of living out their Christian faith. Recently a bishop of a major European city told me that he has more than two hundred church buildings in his diocese, and almost half of which are empty. But, he added: 90% of the city's population are Christians. I thought to myself: whom should we blame, the people or the church authority? This situation exists in many parts of the world- churches without people, institutions without life! The church is not a "place" where people go, but a reality that should embrace the whole life of people. This is exactly the ecclesiology of my own church. Any ecclesiology that does not touch the concrete and daily life of people at the grass-roots level loses its credibility and reliability.

4) The ecumenical movement reflects what is happening in the churches. The growing ecumenical institutionalism is a symptom of church institutionalism. Ecclesiastical and clerical ecumenism have confined the ecumenical movement to church bureaucracies and to an elite. That is why many people are not even aware that there is an ecumenical movement. Many of the clergy have only a partial and distorted idea about it. There is an increasing antagonism towards the type of ecumenism manifested through offices, programs, structures, reports, etc. People are searching for new forms and expressions by which the ecumenical movement may be given more authenticity, creativity and dynamism within their local contexts. Therefore, ecumenism should become an existential reality within the churches and not an activity outside the life of a church. Some movements and organizations that are part of the WCC network have completely dissociated themselves from the life of the local churches. Ecumenism must be placed within the total life and witness of the church in the modern world. The future of the ecumenical movement lies with the people. We need *people-oriented ecumenism* that touches the life of people, that makes sense and that makes a difference. Therefore the ecumenical formation of people remains a crucial task for our churches.

5) As we move to the end of the 20th century, one may rightly ask whether the ecumenical movement is in growth or in decline. One may even ask whether we are moving to the next phase of the ecumenical movement. For me the fundamental issue is that we need an ecumenism that really matters, an ecumenism that transforms the life of people, that helps the church to have a comprehensive understanding of itself, that brings the churches out of self-centredness and makes them turn to each other with mutual accountability and to the world with a growing sense of missionary engagement. Therefore, we must, first, resist any form of ecumenical dogmatism that confines ecumenism to the institutional church, and any expression of ecumenical liberalism that does not recognize any boundaries to the ecumenical movement; second, we must resist any type of ecumenism that reacts only to world concerns and problems; we must also develop a *pro-active ecumenism*, a *prophetic ecumenism* that also challenges and leads.

We need a World Council of Churches

The CUV helps us to see ourselves in the right perspective in the present context of the ecumenical movement, and to look forward together with greater hope and faith. Hence, the CUV is not an isolated process pertaining exclusively to the internal restructuring of the WCC. It transcends, in a sense, the boundaries of the Council and has a broader significance and wider implications. The main intention of CUV is to challenge the churches to clarify their common understanding of the WCC, and to re-affirm their ecumenical commitment. In my judgment the following factors and perspectives should constitute our criteria as we attempt to assess and appropriate the CUV.

1) The CUV does not deal with the structures and programs of the Council as such, but essentially with the churches' understanding of themselves within the fellowship of the WCC. This is the main focus of CUV; this is also the way it has to be treated. Sometimes we tend to speak about the WCC as if it is a reality outside the life of the churches. Yet what is happening in the WCC is, directly or indirectly, the projection of the internal life of our churches. In fact, the WCC is the churches together in Council. As such the Council does not take any decisions nor does it advocate issues apart from the churches. Therefore the CUV is intended to become essentially the *churches' process*, and not an intra-Council affair. Its basic concern is how to redefine and restrengthen the togetherness of the churches in the Council. CUV urges the Council to listen carefully to the churches, and respond seriously to the changing conditions and expectations of the churches. It also calls the churches to re-assess and re-appropriate the meaning and implication of their life together in the Council.

2) One of the merits of CUV is that it spells out clearly the *fellowship* character of the Council, and develops a "relational" understanding of the Council. The Council is not a global and self-sufficient organization that has constitutionally established "basis", "purposes" and "functions". It is a shared life, a shared witness, a shared

vision. Its very identity and vocation is to promote and deepen the sense of inter-connectedness between the churches committed to grow together. All structures, organizational forms, programmatic priorities and working styles of the Council must be determined by this fundamental fact. The WCC as a "fellowship" raises some basic questions:

a) Is the WCC a global "forum" where the churches express their views on issues, defend their rights and pursue their interests or is it a fellowship of churches determined not just to co-exist peacefully, but to grow together towards visible unity "in one faith and one eucharistic fellowship"? The WCC has been understood differently by various churches according to their ecclesiologies. Some member churches, including the Orthodox, refer to it as a fellowship of divided churches called to collaborate with each other in the area of diakonia, mission and evangelism and to work for unity. Thus the Orthodox Churches have always maintained the "instrumental" understanding of the fellowship i.e. the WCC as an *instrument for working together*. Other churches think that by *being in fellowship* the churches experience *Koinonia*. The Koinonia the churches experience in the WCC is broken and incomplete. When they meet, pray and work together in the WCC, they discover and experience their inter-relatedness and thus grow together towards fuller Koinonia. By re-affirming this fundamental self-understanding of the Council as a "fellowship" of churches, the CUV also reminds us that the goal the WCC seeks transcends the present fellowship. After fifty years in fellowship, it looks as though the churches still need further clarity on the nature of their "fellowship".

b) There has always been an inclination to open the WCC to non-church related movements and organizations. In the last few years this inclination has again come to the fore of our discussion. Some of us consider movements, action groups and other ecumenical networks as being *integral* to the reality of church; therefore the Council should provide a space for them. For others however they are *extra-ecclesial* realities; therefore they should not be directly related to the Council. In the light of these various tendencies and different approaches, what then is the identity of the WCC? The WCC has to make a choice: either it will remain a council of churches or it will move towards inclusive ecumenism. I am of those who consider the WCC as a council of *churches*, but never a frozen, closed, self-centered fellowship of institutional churches. The WCC as a council is related to member churches; but as an instrument of the ecumenical movement it is open to all ecumenical partners. It is therefore decisively important for the life and witness of the Council and for the future of the ecumenical movement that the WCC collaborate closely with agencies, groups and movements (which are themselves part of the churches). However, *the nature and scope of this partnership* must be spelled out; otherwise the Council may lose its specificity. The two-fold vocation of the WCC as fellowship of churches and as an instrument of the ecumenical movement are, as CUV points out, intimately and dynamically inter-connected. We cannot make the Council an open arena where everything is introduced and discussed.

3) Concern for *coherence and integrity* has been a permanent consideration in the ecumenical movement in general, and the WCC in particular. We have been able to develop plurality and diversity, but we have failed to create coherence and integrity. One may easily identify many discrepancies in our ecumenical life on local, regional and global levels.

a) For various reasons many of the churches are attracted more and more to the national and regional councils. These councils consume much of the human and financial resources of our churches. The integration of global, regional and local concerns and expressions of ecumenism are lose, even non-existent. This condition creates confusion, leaving the church to define its commitment and set its priorities for each of the levels of ecumenical relations. The WCC should encourage the churches to respond properly to the local and regional priorities. It should at the same time help the churches to give a global expression to shared priorities and concerns. The CUV strongly challenges us to move from interaction to integration, from co-existence to coherence on these multiple levels and diversified contexts and expressions of the ecumenical movement.

b) The CUV states emphatically that coherence and integrity must permeate the entire life of the Council as well. We must get rid of prevailing dichotomies: unity and mission, ecclesiology and ethics, local and global etc. A comparative approach to many documents and studies in the Council and the ecumenical movement at large highlights a continuing tension between the so-called Faith and Order agenda and JPIC agenda. These two agendas and perspectives must be integrated. We must by all means avoid new polarization and fragmentization that potentially exist in all aspects of our ecumenical life. This is a major task before us. Structures and programmatic priorities are provisional; more important is a common vision that affirms and sustains the coherence of our work and the integrity of our fellowship.

4) The WCC is increasingly threatened by *institutional paralysis*. We have identified the Council too much with structures and programs. For some churches the WCC is Faith and Order, for others it is Mission and Evangelism, and for many it is Inter-Church Aid or common action for justice, peace and human rights. These institutionalized structures and traditional models cannot be sacralized. Over-institutionalism made the Council lose much of its creative dynamism and vision. Meetings, paper work, computers, and travel have heavily dominated the life of this house. We have spent a great deal of money, energy and time dealing with structures and methodologies. We have developed an ecumenism of reports and statements. The WCC's *raison d'être* is a vision that goes beyond the Council. Therefore we must restructure the Council in a way that is *flexible, adaptable and responsive* to changing realities. We must establish the kind of programmatic priorities that enhance our common vision and engage the churches beyond their institutional and confessional interests in a continuous process of deeper commitment to their basic calling.

5) The common denominator of all the reactions to CUV is that the existence of the WCC is a necessity. The churches are grateful that the Council brought them together out of their isolation. During the period of the Cold war the churches have

been able, through the WCC, to build bridges across geographical, ideological, racial and cultural divisions. Now it looks as though the churches of the former countries of the Soviet Union, and the Orthodox Churches in particular, are becoming less and less enthusiastic about the Council. Some are even strongly critical of it. This situation is due on the one hand, to the growing conservatism of these churches resulting from the increasing presence of religious movements and sects in their regions, and, on the other hand, to some of the emerging trends in the life of the Council which are not in line with their ecclesiological and ethical perceptions and church traditions. These churches are reminding us, out of their painful experience, that *ecumenism and proselytism cannot co-exist.* They are telling us that they remain faithful to the ecumenical fellowship, but are against the kind of Council which provides an open space to all sorts of tendencies and movements (which are often the projection of the internal life of member churches) that may, in their judgment, jeopardize the identity of their Christian faith and the integrity of ecumenical fellowship. We must listen to these churches with utmost care and sensitivity.

Humility to recognize our limitations and short comings
If the role of the Council is to build relationship and deepen Koinonia between the churches, its internal structure and programmatic framework must be reshaped accordingly. The nature of fellowship establishes well-defined boundaries which the Council cannot trespass. Yet, as a privileged instrument of the ecumenical movement the Council is called to go beyond itself. This is, in fact, both the strength and weakness of the WCC. Sometimes these two dimensions of the Council are in creative inter-action and sometimes in tension. It is in this context that I want to identify some limitations and shortcomings that we are facing in the Council:

1) We repeatedly remind ourselves that *the ecumenical movement is one.* I wonder whether ecumenism is the same in Geneva, in Rome, in other regions and in the life of our churches. We have different perceptions and convictions about the ecumenical movement, and we participate in it with different motivations and expectations. How then is the ecumenical movement one? What constitutes its oneness? Is it a reality or a vision? How is it maintained and manifested in the midst of diversities? It is a common conviction that the oneness of the ecumenical movement is grounded in the vision it holds. What is the vision: obedience to the Gospel of Jesus Christ? The ecumenical movement is called first, to explain more clearly and articulate more visibly its oneness, affirming at the same time its contextual specificities and expressions; second, it is called to redefine more sharply its identity and vision in the pluralistic societies of today. Unless this is done, confusion and ambiguity will always surround us. The CUV raises this question without pretending to have found the full answer. Therefore this matter requires further and deeper reflection, together with our ecumenical partners and particularly with the Roman Catholic Church.

2) The WCC has grown quantitatively over fifty years. Its structure has enlarged and its programmatic priorities have multiplied. The WCC has become a centralized

bureaucracy acting for the churches. I wonder whether we need any more multiple levels of governing and advising bodies; a presidium that in spite of its purely ceremonial role has become (we should not forget our bitter experiences in Vancouver and Canberra Assemblies) and will become more and more, a source of tension between the confessions, regions and categories; an assembly with heavy agendas, complicated procedures and more than two thousand participants. The churches are expecting the WCC to come with a *simpler, efficient and transparent* structure; a Council which plays the role of "co-ordinator" and "facilitator", as well as "initiator", particularly on the global level. I believe that these are legitimate concerns which must be seriously considered.

3) Visible unity must remain the major goal of the Council. CUV has placed a particular emphasis on visible unity. However there are two questions that must be dealt with realistically:

a) In recent years it has often been asked whether priority should be given to unity or JPIC? Any kind of prioritization or drawing a line of demarcation between unity and issues of justice and peace is an ecumenical heresy. I have already made a strong statement to this effect at the Fifth Conference on Faith and Order.[2] They have to be taken in their dynamic inter-relatedness as one whole. This is not a question of methodology, but an ontological one related to the very nature of our faith and the vocation of the church. The Message of the Fifth World Conference on Faith and Order is straightforward on this question: "No turning back, either from the goal of visible unity or from the single ecumenical movement that unites concerns for the unity of the church and concern for engagement in the struggle of the world."[3] The Faith and Order study on ecclesiology and ethics is a significant step forward in this respect. I should however warn you that many Orthodox discern a potential danger in such an inter-related and integrated approach. They fear that unity may be marginalized in view of the growing pragmatism and activism in the ecumenical movement.

b) After so many years of theological debate and dialogue, we are still far from reaching unity based on theological and doctrinal consensus. Are we at an impasse? In our common search for visible unity we have learned that unity is not merely a theological agreement; it is the full Koinonia in the Triune God, manifested in one faith and one eucharistic fellowship. Therefore unity must be placed in an eschatological perspective. We are "on the way". Unity must be conceived as a vision and not an immediate goal. And, as such, it must be attained by growing together, praying and working together. An unrealistic pragmatism and exaggerated enthusiasm will create disillusion and we will be caught up in a dilemma.

4) The WCC came into existence mainly as a Council of European-Protestant Churches and then it became a *World* Council through the participation of Orthodox Churches and other regions. Fifty years of Orthodox-Protestant ecumenical partnership within the fellowship of the WCC did not change the Western and

Protestant character of the Council. Nearly two-thirds of the churches that formed the Council were European and North American. Today, almost two-thirds of the member churches come from the South. The Council's *ethos* however remains the same. This fact is not due so much to Protestant intention to dominate the Council, but, rather to Orthodox reluctance to become fully involved in the total life and work of the Council and to identify with it. In fact, the Orthodox Churches have always kept some distance from the Council and conceived their role as one of "contribution".Again, it looks as thought we are in some kind of dichotomy: on the one hand, the Orthodox rightly claim a change of the Council's ethos, and on the other hand, they still maintain distance from the Council. I believe that the Orthodox must move from mere contribution to a real partnership. In our ecumenical growth the Orthodox have gone through many difficulties. They have experienced frustration. They still feel uneasy and uncertain in the Council. But if the Orthodox are seriously committed to transforming the ethos of the Council, which is the source of some prevailing concerns and tensions, they have to replace their growing alienation, resignation or indifference by a *critical approach* and *constructive participation*. The Orthodox should also be prepared to learn from the others by engaging themselves in creative dialogical relations with others. I cannot imagine the WCC without the Orthodox presence. It is not enough to have an Orthodox Moderator or even an Orthodox General Secretary. For the Orthodox Churches it is important to fully and seriously participate in the life and work of the Council, and for the Protestant Churches it is important to recognize the specificity and quality of Orthodox participation. Hence, the structure, methodology and working style of the Council must be reshaped in order to provide more space to Orthodox participation and interaction.

5) The end of this "ecumenical century" marks the predominance of confessionalism over multi-confessionalism and bilateralism over multilateralism. In spite of emerging dead-ends in many bilateral theological dialogues, churches are still attracted by bilateral ecumenism. In view of new developments and emerging trends in global multi-confessional ecumenism, a great number of churches are looking for a "safer" and a more "practical" ecumenism within their own confessional boundaries. Thus confessions are spending large sums of money for themselves, while multi-lateral ecumenism is suffering from lack of financial support. Confessions are more concerned about their own confessional priorities than about the priorities of multi-confessional ecumenism. This new ecumenical situation has direct and concrete implications for the life and witness of the WCC in its various aspects and dimensions. The purpose of the ecumenical movement is to defuse, not to refocus confessionalism, preparing the way for a *multi-confessional conciliar fellowship*. Undoubtedly confessions have an important role to play in ecumenical fellowship. Their role must be defined, otherwise the growing confessionalism may disintegrate and eventually destroy the ecumenical movement.

6) Particular attention has been given to the concept of *multi-centered ecumenism* in recent years. In fact, the growing pace of regional ecumenism, with a strong

participation of Catholic and Evangelical churches, has created new "centers" of ecumenism. There is an increasing tendency to decentralize the work of the Council, leaving more space and initiative to the regional bodies. CUV speaks of a "co-operative" style of work which will imply "decentralization" and "regionalization". What do we mean by these concepts? What are the limits and limitations of such a methodology?

a) Most member churches of the WCC are also active in several other ecumenical bodies. This situation may disorient or even destroy ecumenical commitment, priorities and resources if the WCC does not take more seriously and existentially the concept of "partnership" by developing new patterns of working together with the churches and ecumenical partners. "Partnership", an old ecumenical concern, returns with new force and importance. *Real partnership* is established by *mutual trust, mutual accountability and by sharing resources.* In fact, multi-centeredness means multi-partnership. Coherence and integrity are secured only through a profound sense of partnership reflected in all aspects of the life and work of the Council and the ecumenical movement. The WCC ought to conceive of itself as an integral part of a wider partnership and network, and provide space for global networking.

b) The WCC should constantly work to relate itself to regional and local ecumenism, identifying what should be done regionally and what should be done globally. It must however avoid two possible temptations: to simply relocate some of its activities to the regions, and to create new competition or tension among the partners. Regionalization does not necessarily mean relocation; it means a full partnership which could be manifested in different ways and forms. If regionalization and decentralization are not done properly they may lead to disintegration and fragmentation. Therefore, before we take any concrete steps, we must first initiate a *process of confidence-building* with REO's by establishing a close working relationship with them. Second, we must establish well-defined criteria and guidelines where the identity, mandate and vocation of the WCC within the global ecumenical movement are explicitly articulated and affirmed.

The courage to live with our differences

Ecumenism is the courage to be together and to grow together. Our obedience to the command of our Lord and our faithfulness to our missionary vocation have given us the courage to come together in the power of the Holy Spirit. We have brought with us in this Council our differences, our problems, our experiences, our hopes and our dreams to the service of a common ecumenical cause.

1) The CUV says only that we can say together, and proposes to do only that which we are able to do together at this point of our ecumenical growth. In other words, CUV does recognize the limits that the churches cannot go beyond. But it also challenges the churches to explore new ways of being and acting together and walking together "on the way" towards full and visible unity. We should realize that the credibility of the ecumenical movement is in question in some regions. Expressions such as "ecumenism is heresy" or "ecumenism is betrayal of Orthodoxy" that we hear

now in the Orthodox world should not be simply ignored. The growth of the Council is conditioned by the committed and active participation of the member churches. We always remind our churches, as the CUV does, what they can do for the Council. I believe that the churches' commitment to the Council has a great deal to do with the Council's readiness to *listen to the churches, to promote ecumenical education, to help the churches* to deal efficiently with their own problems. There may be times when a church could help the Council significantly. There may also be times when the same church may need the support of the Council. The concept of *mutual help* should be given a focal attention in the new structure. How to reach the churches? How to incorporate the expectations and concerns of the churches into the total life of the Council? It is my hope that the CUV, with its strong emphasis on the "relational" aspect of the Council, will give due consideration to these questions.

2) In such a fellowship of wide diversities it is crucial that the churches listen to each other carefully, responsibly and sensitively. If we have been able in the last fifty years to enter into dialogical inter-action with each other and grow together after centuries of isolation, estrangement and controversies, it was the Holy Spirit who gave us the courage and humility to listen to each other. Apart from formal consultations or meetings, we must initiate the kind of informal encounters and open dialogue which can really contribute to confidence-building. The Antelias (Lebanon) meeting[4] could be considered a concrete example in this respect. We must learn to be "more humble listeners to one another"[5].

3) The ecumenical movement also taught us how to *tolerate our divergences* and even to live with tensions. It seems to me that the patience and humility to accommodate each others' differences are steadily decreasing. The Council sometimes is used by certain groups to express their own interests. Some churches are pressing certain issues to reach the agenda of the Council. Others feel uncomfortable when these issues are raised, and are not prepared to discuss them. Therefore, dialogue between the churches on potentially divisive issues is an urgent ecumenical priority to prevent the ecumenical fellowship from being transformed into a platform of power games between the churches or the regions. The WCC will never become a homogenous fellowship. It is destined to grow in the midst of diversities and even tensions. How can we prevent our differences from dividing us and estranging us from one another? The Council cannot be a platform where churches, pressure groups or movements project their own agendas. Such an approach to the Council will distort its very nature and vocation. The problem is not with the ecumenical movement as such but with the churches themselves as they redefine their identity and mission in the contemporary societies. For instance, Orthodoxy today is caught up in a conflict between Western secular culture with its stress on materialism and consumerism, and ethnic cultures with their concern for identity and security. How could the WCC transform such conflicts into mutually enriching and challenging experiences through a process of creative interaction? Almost daily the churches in the West are facing ethical issues that are shaking and challenging the life and witness of their

churches in the context of their own societies. How can we help these churches to discover the authentic way of being church in full obedience to the Gospel? How can we help each other to solve problems which are, in a sense, *our* problems as a fellowship of churches?

4) We should not pretend to teach to each other; we should rather be ready to *learn from each other*. The ecumenical movement engaged the churches in a learning process. This has, indeed, been one of the most significant contributions of the ecumenical movement. We now have a greater understanding of each other. Mutual listening has become a source of mutual learning. But we still need to deepen and enlarge the scope of our mutual knowledge. We still have to accept each other. Knowledge generates confidence. It also implies responsibility. We are responsible towards each other. We should have the courage to accept each other as we are. Let us not claim that we can or must change each other. The WCC has made us cling more firmly and faithfully to our respective teachings and traditions. It has also led us to enter into a process of mutual learning, sharing and challenging. Ecumenical learning is not only learning about each other, but also rediscovering our own history and identity in a broader Christian context, in inter-action with the others. Someone recently said to me: either the Orthodox Churches are moving slowly or others are moving rapidly. I responded that both are true. We have to accept that in all churches there are trends opposed, for one reason or other, to the ecumenical movement. In some churches ecumenism is becoming more and more an "underground", marginalized movement. Hence, we need each other, we need to strengthen each other if we are to be committed to a common vision.

5) The reality of the *Protestant majority and Orthodox minority*, if one may use this expression, imposed by Western democracy will always remain with us. CUV does not offer any solution for it, and the decision-making continues to remain a lobby exposed to different kinds of influences. We have already been convinced out of our bitter experiences in the past, that *we cannot settle controversial issues by vote*. In the name of democracy we should never try to force a majority solution by vote particularly on delicate and decisive questions. Such a practice could be disastrous for the future of our fellowship. The minority feeling has become a serious concern for the Orthodox, affecting all aspects of Orthodox presence and role in the Council. All attempts, including the "twenty-five per cent" arrangement, have simply failed. Whenever applied, they have produced cosmetic changes only. The Orthodox Churches still feel that their voice is not properly heard in the Council. This situation must be addressed. In my view more radical steps must be taken in order to secure a qualitative and full Orthodox participation in the life of the Council. The model of "families of churches" adopted by the Middle East Council of Churches, could be regarded one of those models that the WCC might envisage in the future.

6) The ecumenical movement should no more aim for *consensus*. This strategy has failed. The "reception" processes aimed at convergence, that the Council initiated on

a number of controversial issues, did not bring about any change in the theological teachings and doctrinal positions of the churches. On the contrary, it created more problems. The Council should provide a context where different views inter-act. We are not in the WCC because we agree. We are here precisely because we disagree. We are here to enter together in a learning and sharing process. We are in this fellowship to struggle together for visible unity and common witness. The CUV does not call us simply to explore together the nature of our fellowship, but also the meaning and concrete implications of our "common calling". We have to know and respect the limits and limitations imposed by our theological convictions and the contexts we come from. But at the same time we must fully and responsibly engage ourselves to grow together towards full Koinonia, transcending our differences. This should become the central concern and the primary goal of our fellowship.

7) Therefore, we should address the frustrations of those churches that remain in a situation of indifference or which plan to withdraw from the WCC. No church should feel *defeated, ignored or marginalized* in this fellowship. We all are equal partners in this Council which is ours. We have a responsibility towards each other. We should know how to accept each other and live with our differences. In fact, honest recognition of our differences is a source of strength, confidence and growth. As Visser 't Hooft has rightly said: "the originality and *raison d'être* of the World Council lie precisely in this respect for differences".[6] We have to know how to live with risks and hopes. This is the mystery and challenge of the ecumenical movement. But the recognition of our differences should not lead us to stagnation; it has to challenge us to transcend them and to grow together towards full Koinonia in faith and life.

Let us then recommit ourselves to a fellowship of risks and hopes

In 1974 Visser 't Hooft raised a crucial question: has the ecumenical movement a future?[7] Now the question is: what kind of future does the ecumenical movement have? From here to where? In which direction is the ecumenical movement moving? The CUV comes as a hopeful sign in the midst of uncertainties. Of course it does not, it can not, solve all our problems; it can not satisfy all our expectations. It has its deficiencies and limitations. Yet, it provides us with a clear direction to follow by articulating a common understanding and vision that the member churches can appropriate and recognize themselves. The CUV comes to assure the churches that whatever structure the WCC may take in the future, its central mandate and core functions will never be compromised. I believe that this is the greatest merit of the CUV.

"Emotional ecumenism" played its significant part by generating great enthusiasm. We are bound now to become more and more realistic as we are called through the CUV to recommit ourselves to this fellowship of risks and hopes. The road of ecumenism will always remain thorny. The Council may continue to face more challenges and problems. Our divisions may deepen further and acquire new acuteness as we confront the issues of the present world in all their complexities and implications for the life and mission of our churches. But we need the WCC since we need each other. The WCC remains the unique place where our churches can come together on a global level for common reflection and witness. Our common understanding of the Council may be changed as we grow together. Yet our common vision should remain the same; it is our common faithfulness to God's call to be one; it is our common commitment to our God-given vocation to be a missionary people to build together the household of God in the perspective of the Kingdom of God. We must constantly discern the changing *ecumenical reality* and respond to it realistically and responsibly by sustaining it with, and orienting it towards the *ecumenical vision*. At the same time we must re-affirm our full commitment to the ecumenical vision by making it relevant to the changing ecumenical reality.

The Pilgrimage towards full Koinonia in the Triune God implies fears and risks. It also generates hope and joy. Our "common calling" obliges us to wrestle courageously with fears and risks and grow together in hope and joy, in mutual love and trust. This is the nature and meaning of our fellowship. This is the mystery of the Holy Spirit. Some churches may hesitate and even resist taking full part in this risky journey. Let us always remember that the ecumenical movement is the movement of the Holy Spirit. He brought us together; He bound us towards a common vision. Therefore He will protect and sustain us in our fears and anxieties, and will take us towards God's future. Half a century ago churches from different confessional, ethnic and cultural backgrounds made a firm commitment "to stay together" within the fellowship of the WCC. As they move towards the twenty-first century, the churches are called to redefine the way they want to stay and grow together, and re-commit themselves to the common vision which sustains this fellowship. The CUV helps us to move to the next century more confidently.

Some of us think that the ecumenical movement is in winter. There is no spring without winter. As we move towards the end of the century, the coming Assembly, the fiftieth anniversary of the WCC and the Millennium will become important steps on the way towards ecumenical spring. Let us always remember that the ecumenical pilgrimage is a costly one. We should have the courage to pay the price if we are committed to one faith, one eucharistic fellowship and a common witness to the world.

Notes

[1] Cf. the letter of Cardinal E. Cassidy, the President of the Pontifical Council for Promoting Christian Unity (Vatican) addressed to Dr. Konrad Raiser, the General Secretary of the WCC, 26 April 1997.

[2] *On the Way to Fuller Koinonia – The Report of the Fifth Conference on Faith and Order held at Santiago de Compostela,* 1993 Geneva, T. F. Best and G. Gassman eds., p. 225.

[3] Ibid. p. 225.

[4] Cf. Minutes of the Executive Committee Meeting, 12-15 February 1997, Cyprus, pp. 32-35.

[5] Minutes of the Central Committee Meeting, Utrecht 1972, p. 67.
[6] Visser 't Hooft, *The Genesis and Formation of the WCC*, Geneva, 1982, p. 175.
[7] Visser 't Hooft, *Has the Ecumenical Movement a Future?*, Geneva, 1974.

Meeting of Patriarchs of the Middle East Oriental Orthodox Churches

Common Declaration
St Bishoy Monastery, Egypt, 10 – 11 March 1998

In the Name of the Father, the Son, and the Holy Spirit.

We, Pope Shenouda III, Pope of Alexandria and Patriarch of the See of Saint Mark, Patriarch Mar Ignatius Zakka I, Patriarch of Antioch and all the East and Catholicos Aram I, Catholicos of the Armenians of the Great House of Cilicia, and the members of the preparatory committee of this meeting who are with us, give thanks to God for bringing us together at the Monastery of the great Saint Bishoy in Wadi El Natroon, Egypt, on Tuesday and Wednesday, 10 and 11 March 1998. We have gathered together as Heads of the Oriental Orthodox Churches in the Middle East to re-affirm our unity of faith and our common ministry in the life of our people in the Middle East and all over the world, and explore together the most efficient ways and means to strengthen our common presence and witness in the region.

On the basis of our Joint Agreed Statement issued on 14 June 1996 at the Armenian Catholicosate of Cilicia, in Antelias, Lebanon, we studied a number of issues and questions of common concern. Hereunder we mention briefly some of the issues and perspectives which acquired an important place in our deliberations:

First: In our common witness to our faith in the Only-Begotten Son, the Incarnate Logos, our Saviour Jesus Christ, we hold firmly to the Apostolic Faith handed down to us from the Apostolic Fathers through the Holy Scriptures of both the Old and New Testaments, from the three Ecumenical Councils of Nicea (325AD), Constantinople (381 AD) and Ephesus (431AD); and through the teachings of the saintly fathers of our three churches who have struggled in keeping the doctrines of our churches and the teachings of these Councils. In fact, our Churches have strived throughout their history and at the cost of the blood of their martyrs to keep intact the teachings of the Council of Ephesus concerning the incarnation of the Logos based on the teachings of Saint Cyril the Great (444AD) as well as the decision of the said Council. We want to mention here from among our Holy Fathers, especially Saint Gregory the Illuminator, Saint Dioscorus of Alexandria, Mar Philoxenus of

Mabbugh, Mar Jacob Baradeus and Saint Nerses the Gracious who have kept firm the Apostolic Faith and strongly defended the orthodoxy of the teachings of the first three Ecumenical Councils.

Second: The teachings of Saint Cyril the Great constitute the foundation of the Christology of our Churches. It was on the basis of these teachings that the Committee of the Joint Official Theological Dialogue between the Oriental and Eastern Orthodox Churches was able to formulate a joint agreement which is now under study by the Holy Synods of both families. In fact, the following statement was mentioned at the beginning of this agreement: "We have found our common ground (i.e. in the Apostolic faith) in the formula of our common father Saint Cyril of Alexandria: "Mia Physis tou Theou Logou sesarkomeni" One Incarnate Nature of God the Logos and in his dictum that "it is sufficient for the confession of our true and irreproachable faith to say and confess that the Holy Virgin Mary is the Mother of God, the Theotokos".

Third: In accordance with and in faithful obedience to the faith, doctrine and teachings of our Holy Fathers, we firmly restate our common rejection of all the heretical teachings of Arius, Sabellius, Apollinarius, Macedonius, Paul of Samosata, Diodore of Tarsus, Theodore of Mopsuestia, Nestorius, Eutyches and of all those who follow these and other heretics and propagate their erroneous and heretical teachings.

Fourth: We believe that our Lord Jesus Christ the Logos, Son of God, came in His own person. He did not assume a human person, but He Himself by hypostatic union took full and perfect human nature; rational soul and body, without sin, from the Holy Virgin Mary through the Holy Spirit. He made His own humanity one incarnate nature and one incarnate hypostasis with His divinity in the very moment of incarnation through a true natural and hypostatic union. His divinity did not separate from His humanity even for a moment or a twinkling of an eye. This union is superior to description and perception. When we speak of "One incarnate nature of the Word of God", we do not mean His divinity alone or His humanity alone, i.e. a single nature, but we speak of one united divine-human nature in Christ without change, without mixture, without confusion, without division and without separation. The properties of each nature are not changed and destroyed because of the union; the natures being distinguished from each other in thought alone (τῇ θεωρίᾳ μόνῃ).

Fifth: We agreed on the necessity of maintaining a common position of faith in all theological dialogues. Thus, henceforth, we will engage as a family of Oriental Orthodox Churches in the Middle East in any theological dialogue with other churches and Christian world communions. We hope that this basic principle will also be accepted by other beloved churches of our family, as is happening now in many theological dialogues.

Sixth: We re-affirm the vital importance of establishing more organized and close collaboration between our churches to ensure the oneness of our faith, our full communion in the ecclesial and liturgical life, and our partnership in evangelism, diakonia and in witnessing Christ the Lord in the Christian world and to the entire humanity. We believe that this goal could be achieved by several means, some of which are:

1. To meet periodically and regularly every year.
2. To have a common doctrinal and theological attitude in all theological dialogues.
3. To have a common position on issues of vital concern for our churches in the Middle East Council of Churches, the World Council of Churches, Pro Oriente and other ecumenical organizations.
4. To exchange teachers and students among the seminaries and theological institutes of our churches.
5. To exchange pastoral letters dealing with matters of faith and issues related to the witness, mission, evangelism and diakonia.
6. To exchange books, periodicals, and publications pertaining to Christian education, theological formation and moral teachings of our churches.
7. To exchange information related to the various activities of our churches.
8. To take a common stand on issues of justice, peace and human rights.
9. To encourage our clergy and people to establish close collaboration on the diocesan and parish levels in the Middle East and everywhere.

Seventh: We hope that through our common efforts the scope of our meetings will be widened in the near future to include other beloved churches of the Oriental Orthodox family, in continuation with the historic meeting of Addis Ababa, Ethiopia in 1965.

Eighth: We wish to meet periodically with the Heads of Eastern Orthodox family to enhance our theological dialogue and strengthen further our ecumenical collaboration on local, regional and global levels.

Ninth: We discussed the celebration of the 2000th anniversary of the birth of Christ our Lord, and gave a special responsibility to the Standing Commission (ref. N. 11) to organize properly this important event.

Tenth: We discussed the prevailing situation in the Middle East. The difficulties that the peace process is facing actually are due to Israel's uncompromising and hard-line policy. We shall together exert strong and continuous efforts through the worldwide ecumenical fellowship and in international community so that the people of the Arab world may regain their violated rights in Jerusalem, Palestine, Golan, and South Lebanon. It is also our demand that the embargo and sanctions imposed on the people of Iraq be lifted immediately. We pray that peace with justice prevails throughout the world.

Eleventh: A Standing Committee was appointed by us to implement the decisions of this meeting. This committee shall meet twice a year. The members of the Standing Committee are: H.E. Metropolitan Bishoy and H.G. Bishop Moussa from the Coptic Orthodox Church of Alexandria; H.E. Metropolitan Mar Gregorios Yohanna Ibrahim and H.E. Metropolitan Mar Theophilus George Saliba from the Syrian Orthodox Church of Antioch; H.G. Bishop Sebouh Sarkissian and Archimandrite Nareg

Alemezian from the Armenian Orthodox Church (the Armenian Catholicosate of Cilicia). At the conclusion of our meeting we joyfully present our thanks to Almighty God who has promoted and sustained our endeavours. We ask Him to always assist our efforts for the well-being of our churches, for the unity of all churches and the salvation of the world.

We thank the Church of Alexandria for its love and kind hospitality. We also thank all who prayed and worked for the success of this meeting. Glory be to God the Father, the Son and the Holy Spirit, forever. Amen.

Pope Shenouda III   Mar Ignatius Zakka I   Catholicos Aram I

The Ecumenical Movement in the TwentiethCentury: The Role of Theology in Ecumenical Thought and Life in Romania

Final Statement

Iasi, Romania, 27 – 30 April 1998

Introduction

From 27-30 April 1998, fifty years after the world-wide ecumenical movement took concrete institutional form in the World Council of Churches, a seminar entitled *The Ecumenical Movement in the Twentieth Century: The Role of Theology in Ecumenical Thought and Life in Romania* was held in the city of Iasi. This Seminar, held on the occasion of the Jubilee Anniversary of the World Council of Churches, began a process of critically evaluating the dynamics presently operating within ecumenical relations, while at the same time considering the implications for the future. We used this opportunity to explore both the progress made and the hopes unrealized in the ecumenical dialogue.

Both aspects of the general theme were dealt with during the three days of the Seminar divided into five sub-themes:

i) A theological evaluation of local ecumenism in Romania (1948-1989);

ii) The place of ecumenical theology in the post-modern context: issues, methodologies, ecumenical formation, models of culture and society;

iii) New ecumenical approaches to and practices in support of national reconciliation, common Christian witness, European integration, and participation in the ecumenical movement;

iv) Common Christian witness in contemporary society; Orthodox ecclesial identity in an ecumenical perspective;

v) An analysis of the Common Understanding and Vision (CUV) document.

The Seminar was organized by Unit I – Unity and Renewal of the WCC and the Metropolia of Moldova and Bucovina through the St. Nicholas Ecumenical Institute. The meetings took place at the Orthodox Theological Faculty of Iasi.

Participants included representatives of the World Council of Churches, the Conference of European Churches, AIDRom, the Orthodox Church, the Roman Catholic Church, the Reformed Church, the Lutheran Church, Hierarchs, professors from the theological faculties from throughout Romania, as well as students from the Orthodox Theological Faculty of Iasi.

I. The Ecumenical Movement – Christian Imperative and Vocation

A. The Historical Beginnings of the World Council of Churches

Before His crucifixion and resurrection our Lord Jesus Christ prayed for his disciples "that all may be one" (John 17:21). At Pentecost, by the descent of the Holy Spirit, this prayer was fulfilled for the first time in human history with the founding of the first Christian community in Jerusalem. The Church then began to grow and develop, founding new local Christian communities, and expanding to the ends of the earth (*oikoumene*). Down through the centuries, the Church – One, Holy, Catholic, and Apostolic, of which the ecumenical Creed of 381 bears witness – has been confronted by different tensions and even conflicts that arose both internally and externally. And if in the first Christian millenium the local Christian churches were able to maintain visible unity around the canon of the Christian Scriptures and a common Apostolic Tradition, through a concillar discipline, in the second millenium the One Church has been confronted with divisions, schisms, and doctrinal errors, all of which created a mutual distancing becoming concretized in the rupture of eucharistic communion.

At the end of the Second World War, the world was divided into military and political camps as well as competing and antagonistic economic systems. The Churches understood that at this moment they had a responsibility to address this tragedy of the Cold War. And so the idea emerged of giving an institutional form to the ecumenical movements that already existed under the name the World Council of Churches (WCC). It had as its main purpose the restoration of the visible unity of Christians as a ministry to divided humanity.

The founding of the Council is due to many reasons:

– Among these are missionary reasons: the Gospel that was being presented to new converts was being interpreted differently – according to the particular confession of the missionary – and because of this they realized that only a common witness could give credibility to the proclamation of the Good News. A divided Church could not help but give a contradictory witness;

– In spite of confessional differences, the churches were able to recognize together a common witness to a Trinitarian, Christological, and Pneumatological faith expressed in the very theological *Basis* of the World Council of Churches;

– All of the member churches of the World Council confess a belief in the "One Holy" Church, and are committed to the process of restoring the visible unity, that has always been threatened by the shortcomings of its members something which is inherent in the history of humanity;

– The recovery of the visible unity of Christians was conceived from the beginning as a necessary precondition of restoring human unity and solidarity, especially given the social context encountered at the time of the establishment of the World Council of Churches.

B. The Ecumenical Movement in the context of contemporary society

Over the last fifty years of its activities, the World Council of Churches has contributed to:

– The achievement of a number of major theological convergences. For example, in the area of doctrine: the Baptism, Eucharist, and Ministry (BEM) Document, The Symbol of Faith of Nicea-Constantinople, etc., and in the area of Mission and Evangelism: An Ecumenical Affirmation of Common Witness, and the rejection of proselytism, etc.;

– A great rapprochement of churches and people, including mutual recognition by confessions separated for centuries;

– Inter-church solidarity and humanitarian aid in general.

Even given all of this, the ecumenical movement is going through a crisis that has multiple aspects and consequences. On the one hand, this crisis reflects the crisis of values which all of contemporary society is going through, a crisis which shapes attitudes toward the Church and Christian teaching: individualism, syncretism, subjectivism, and the lessening of authority. On the other hand, the over-emphasis of diversity at the expense of unity and theological consensus has brought on a relativism in substance both in doctrine and Christian ethics. Moreover, the fear of loosing confessional, cultural and national identity in an ecumenical context of the type that might be characterized as "organic unity", universalist and with egalitarian tendencies, has brought on a growth in confessionalism and a diminution of active participation in ecumenical life.

As a response to this crisis the WCC has put into motion a process of seeking out a new profile and vision, elaborated in the document: *"Towards a Common Understanding and Vision of the World Council of Churches"*.

The participants took up this complex situation, as well as the CUV document, in their discussions and reaffirmed both the ecumenical vocations of their churches as well as the necessity of their remaining loyal to their ecumenical commitment, co-sanctified by their predecessors.

II. A Critical Look at Past and Present Ecumenism in Romania

Ecumenism represents a call to Christians to respond to Christ's prayer "that they all be one, so that the world might believe" (John 17:21). It, in fact, represents a major duty to go beyond the sin and tragedy of division. This obligation represents a cross which all Christians are called to carry, with the hope that in it they will find the power of the resurrection which manifests itself in reconciliation and the restoration of the communion of love.

It is in this way that new relations between peoples and confessions can be established, inspired by a Christian ethos. Christian teaching is addressed to all so that they may be transfigured by the power of renewal and reconciliation in the Risen Christ.

A few decades ago, the question of the relationship between Christianity (the Church) and the nation was put into such sharp relief that one could come to the place where there was a total identification between a given nation and a religious confession. After 1989, this question of Church-nation relationship was again taken up. Today, in an ecumenical context, we find that the existence and worth of ethnicities (peoples) is confirmed at Pentecost, not one against the other, but within the universal communion of Churches who are one in Christ. The words of the Holy Apostle Paul are particularly applicable here: "There is neither Jew nor Greek, slave nor free, male nor female, for you are all one in Christ Jesus" (Galatians 3:28). Within the bosom of a nation there may be found a majority church as well as one or many minority churches. The relationship between them should be based on Christian love, on understanding, service and tolerance. Christians in Romania have understood ecumenism not as a "fatum" (tragic fate) but as a "datum" (a given or gift) by God, as a cross which brings blessings. Some characteristics of this kind of ecumenism can be described as follows.

In the period between 1948-1989, although ecumenism was somehow forced reality given the political context in which the churches and confessions of Romania lived, God often changed evil into good (cf. Gen. 50:20) with some beneficial effects in deepening fraternal relations, understanding, and mutual assistance. Inter-confessional theological conferences constituted remarkable moments in local Romanian ecumenism. During the years of communist dictatorship many significant representatives of Romanian churches and confessions: priests, theologians, hierarchs and lay people were thrown into prison, who in this oppressive regime, gave a Christian ecumenical witness by their common suffering. This kind of witness has been called, significantly, "ecumenism behind bars" or "ecumenism under the cross".

After 1989, we can speak of an ecumenism in freedom, which means an extra responsibility for the Christian churches and confessions. Relations between Christians have become more sincere and open – not modified by the inhibited behavior obligatory given the restrictions of the totalitarian ideology of the former period – which now permits an intensified effort at the national, regional and local level toward the vision of reconciliation and Christian unity. In this sense, then, we can recall some concrete projects of AIDRom, which has as a mission the stimulation of ecumenical efforts. In addition we can mention the exchange of professors and students, the organization of ecumenical camps, prayers for Christian unity, social and philanthropic projects which taken all together give a personal dimension to ecumenism, as direct relationships between Christians, precious, open, and friendly.

III. Educating for Ecumenism

During the plenary discussions the participants emphasized the fact that the difficulties that have arisen since 1989 within the ecumenical dialogue have been due to, on the one hand, a lack of information, and on the other, the absence of an educational strategy for the formation of a realistic and responsible ecumenical consciousness.

In order to move beyond these difficulties (inherent in a society having been profoundly marked by militant, aggressive and ideological atheism), the participants proposed that all of the local churches should commit themselves to an ecumenical education project for the faithful which would be concretized on three essential levels:

– the establishment of chairs of ecumenism at all schools of theology, be they college or faculty, where they do not currently exist, as well as the teaching of all other disciplines in an ecumenical spirit, free of all prejudices that tend to accumulate over time;

– the teaching of religious classes in the public schools, be they gymnasiums or licentiate, in an ecumenical spirit, placing the accent on common cultural and spiritual values;

– the creation of an ecumenical atmosphere, including at the parish level, through the organization of gatherings at various commemorative occasions, and especially during the week of Prayer for Christian Unity.

IV. Ecumenical Cooperation in Romania: Prospects for the Future

With respect to prospects for future ecumenical cooperation in Romania, it was proposed that an Ecumenical Council of Churches of Romania be founded, with the participation of the Roman Catholic Church as a full member. It would have the following principle objectives:

– the revival of inter-confessional theological conferences, which would be held at regular intervals (one or two times a year);

– the working out of a Romanian ecumenical theology, keeping in mind the problematics of international theology and the specific locale of the churches;

– the compilation of an ecumenical memorial of the martyrs and confessors of the faith during the communist period;

– the preparation of delegates for international ecumenical events; the discussion and deliberation beforehand of these themes at ecumenical gatherings at the national level in Romania;

– the taking on of a mediating and reconciling role between churches in Romania when conflictual situations might arise;

– the effort to celebrate Pascha (Easter) on a common date;

– the expansion of the Week of Prayer for Christian Unity to the parish level;

– pastoral guidelines for cases of mixed marriages, or various religious occasions in the family or society;

– the organization of ecumenical youth camps;

– the exchange of professors and students;

– inter-parish events, choirs, art exhibits, etc.;

– the discussion of problems of common interest between the churches (the restoration of properties, mutual recognition, etc.).

In place of a conclusion, we recall the advice of a holy martyr of the undivided Church, St Cyprian of Carthage:

> God does not receive the sacrifice of a person living in discord. He orders us to leave the altar and first to reconcile ourselves with our brother or sister, and in this way God may receive our prayers offered up in peace. The greatest sacrifice that we can offer God is our peace, our goodwill toward one another, a people gathered together in the unity that exists between the Father, the Son, and the Holy Spirit (*De Dominica oratione*, 23).

Evaluation of New Facts in the Relations of Orthodoxy and the Ecumenical Movement
Thessaloniki, Greece, 29 April – 2 May 1998

1. We delegates of all the canonical Orthodox Churches, by the power of the Risen Christ, gathered at the historical city of Thessaloniki, Greece from 29 April to 2 May 1998, after an invitation of His All Holiness Ecumenical Patriarch Bartholomew, responding to the initiative of the Russian and Serbian Churches and because of the withdrawal of the Georgian Church from the World Council of Churches. The meeting was hosted by the Organization of "Thessaloniki – Cultural Capital of Europe 97" and under the generous hospitality of His Eminence Metropolitan Panteleimon of Thessaloniki.

2. The meeting was presided over by Chrysostomos, the Senior Metropolitan of the See of Ephesus (Ecumenical Patriarchate) and the sessions were held in a spirit of Christian love, fraternal fellowship and common understanding (Cf. List of delegate). The delegates expressed and asked the prayers and blessings of His All Holiness Ecumenical Patriarch Bartholomew and all other Venerable Primates of the Orthodox. The participants received telegrams of congratulations from all the Primates. They expressed also their best wishes to His Beatitude Chrystodoulos, new Archbishop of Athens and of all Greece for his election.

3. Metropolitan Chrysostomos of Ephesus presented an introductory paper on the theme of the meeting, followed by a presentation from all the delegates on the one hand describing their relations to the ecumenical movement and to the WCC in particular and on the other hand evaluating the critical problems they are facing. The discussions analyzed the participation of the Orthodox Churches in the decision-making bodies of the WCC.

4. The delegates unanimously denounced those groups of schismatics, as well as certain extremist groups within the local Orthodox Churches themselves, that are using the theme of ecumenism in order to criticize the Church leadership and undermine its authority, thus attempting to create divisions and schisms within the Church. They also use non-factual material and misinformation in order to support their unjust criticism.

5. The delegates also emphasized that Orthodox participation in the ecumenical movement has always been based on Orthodox Tradition, on the decisions of the Holy Synods of the local Orthodox Churches, and on Pan-Orthodox meetings, such as the Third Pre-Conciliar Conference of 1986 and the meeting of the Primates of the Local Orthodox Churches in 1992.

6. The participants are unanimous in their understanding of the necessity for continuing their participation in various forms of Inter-Christian activity.

7. We have no right to withdraw from the mission laid upon us by our Lord Jesus Christ, the mission of witnessing the Truth before the non-Orthodox world. We must not interrupt relations with Christians of other Confessions who are preapred to work together with us.

8. Indeed the WCC has been a forum where the faith of the Orthodox Church, its mission and its views on a number of issues such as peace, justice, development, and ecology were made more widely known to the non-Orthodox world. A fruitful collaboration was established with the other members of the Council in response to the challenges of modern civilization. Proselytism has been denounced and help extended to Orthodox Churches in difficult situations to enable them to carry forward their mission. Orthodox interests were often defended, especially where the Orthodox minorities were discriminated against. Orthodox views in the process of political, economic and cultural integration were expressed and Orthodox contributions were made in the relations with other faiths. Schismatic groups and so-called renewal groups within Protestantism were not admitted to membership of the Council at Orthodox request.

9. However at the same time there are certain developments within some Protestant members of the Council that are reflected in the debates of the WCC and are regarded as unacceptable by the Orthodox. At many WCC meetings the Orthodox were obliged to be involved in the discussion of questions entirely alien to their tradition. At the Seventh Assembly of the WCC in Canberrra in 1991, and during the Central Committee meetings from 1992 onwards, the Orthodox delegates have take a vigorous stand against intercommunion with non-Orthodox, against inclusive language, ordination of women, the rights of sexual minorities and certain tendencies relating to religious syncretism. Their statements on these subjects were always considered as minority statements and as such could not influence the general trend and ethos of the WCC.

10. After a century of Orthodox participation in the ecumenical movement, and fifty years in the WCC in particular, we do not perceive sufficient progress in the multilateral theological discussions between Christians. On the contrary, the gap between the Orthodox and the Protestants is becoming wider as the aforementioned tendencies within certain Protestant denominations are becoming stronger.

11. During the Orthodox participation of many decades in the ecumenical movement, Orthodoxy has never been betrayed by any representative of a local Orthodox Church. On the contrary, these representatives have always been completely

faithful and obedient to their respective Church authorities, acted in complete agreement with the canonical rules, the Teaching of the Ecumenical Councils, the Church Fathers and the Holy Tradition of the Orthodox Church.

12. We therefore come to the suggestion that the WCC must be radically restructured in order to allow more adequate Orthodox participation. Many Orthodox Churches raise questions as to what are the final criteria of the inclusion of a Church in a wider organization such as the WCC. The same questions exist for the inclusion of the Orthodox Church in the Council. Nevertheless, the theme of the criteria for the inclusion is and will remain a fundamental request of Orthodoxy.

13. All the Orthodox Churches are requested to send official delegates to the Eighth Assembly of the WCC in Harare, December 1998, with the aim of expressing their concerns as follows:

A. Orthodox delegates participating at Harare will present in common this Statement of the Thessaloniki Inter-Orthodox Meeting.

B. Orthodox delegates will not participate in ecumenical services, common prayers, worship and other religious ceremonies at the Assembly.

C. Orthodox delegates generally will not take part in the voting procedure except in certain cases that concern the Orthodox and by unanimous agreement. If it is needed, in the plenary and group discussions, they will present the Orthodox views and positions.

D. These mandates will be maintained until a radical restructuring of the WCC is accomplished to allow adequate Orthodox participation.

14. Thus we state that we are no longer satisfied with the present forms of Orthodox membership in the WCC. If the structures of the WCC are not radically changed, other Orthodox Church will also withdraw from the WCC, as has the church of Georgia. In addition the Orthodox delegates at the Eighth Assembly will be forced to protest if the representatives of sexual minorities are admitted to participation structurally in the Assembly.

15. Finally, the delegates underline that the major decisions concerning the participation of the Orthodox Churches in the ecumenical movement must be in accordance with the pan-Orthodox decisions and must be taken by each local Orthodox Church in consultation with all the other local Orthodox Churches.

16. The delegates also strongly suggested that a Mixed Theological Commission be created with Orthodox members appointed by their own respective Churches and from WCC nominees. The Mixed Commission will being its work after the Harare Assembly by discussing the acceptable forms of Orthodox participation in the ecumenical movement and the radical restructuring of the WCC.

17. May the Risen Lord guide our steps towards the accomplishment of His will and the glory of His divine name.

At Thessaloniki, 1 May 1998

Orthodox Liturgical Renewal and Visible Unity

New Skete Monastery, Cambridge, New York, USA,
26 May – 1 June 1998

Sponsored by the Society for Ecumenical Studies and Inter-Orthodox Relations
and World Council of Churches, Programme Unit I, Unity and Renewal

Introduction

1. "All on earth fall in worship before you; they sing of you, sing of your name!"
(Ps. 66:4 NAB). Every human being is created with the capacity to praise God.
Worship therefore is universal. It lies at the very heart of human existence. But at
the same time, worship is extraordinarily particular. It finds different expression in
each human situation. For this reason worship sometimes has been compared to
language. Through worship we communicate with God. But just as languages have
their own peculiarities of syntax, grammar, and vocabulary and change through time,
so also our ways of worship vary and change. Consequently, the gestures, symbols
and style of a given time or place may not be immediately understandable in another
context.

2. Within Christianity, variety in the "language" of worship is evident from the
beginnings of the Church, as local communities developed their own forms for
expressing and celebrating their faith. Through the centuries, in order to carry out
its mission of spreading the Gospel to all nations and all peoples, the Church has
continued to adapt its ways of worshiping to new contexts. Among the Orthodox
this concern for enculturation is most evident in the use of the vernacular, but it has
been expressed in many other ways as well - in musical idiom, in iconography, and in
order of services.

3. Generally speaking, our Orthodox churches have not confused unity in faith
with uniformity in liturgical practice. They have recognized not only the pastoral
utility but also the inherent value of this rich diversity. But sometimes diversity and
change - however natural and salutary - can cause anxiety and confusion. For a
variety of reasons, this is the case in many parts of the Orthodox world today. For
example, during the decades of communist domination in Eastern Europe, the
Church's mission was effectively limited to maintenance of the inherited forms of
worship within the church building. The post-communist era has brought new
opportunities for mission, but this in turn has raised new questions concerning

adaptation of worship in response to these new circumstances. In other regions, Orthodox worship has developed in very different circumstances and has faced very different challenges, ranging from fundamentalism to secularism and pluralism both religious and cultural. Throughout the world, our churches are now being called upon to address unprecedented challenges to Orthodox unity arising from both internal and external circumstances. And central to discussion of virtually all these challenges is the issue of liturgical worship.

This consultation

4. The present consultation on "Orthodox Liturgical Renewal and Visible Unity" was organized by the World Council of Churches Unit I (Unity and Renewal), in collaboration with the Society for Ecumenical Studies and Inter-Orthodox Relations (Thessaloniki), in order to discuss some of these challenges. Held at New Skete Monastery, near Cambridge, New York, a notable center for Orthodox liturgical study and renewal, the consultation enjoyed true monastic hospitality and experienced the joy of monastic worship. The Ascension cycle of worship was an integral aspect of the consultation's program.

5. The work of this consultation benefited from and built upon the work of previous consultations and inter-Orthodox meetings, such as those organized by the former WCC subunit on Renewal and Congregational Life, whose work has been continued by the Stream on Worship and Spirituality of Unit I. We took special note of the consultation on Christian Spirituality for our Times held at Iasi, Romania in April/May 1994, the consultation Toward a Common Date of Easter held at Aleppo, Syria in March, 1997, and the two consultations on Women in the Life of the Orthodox Church held at Damascus, Syria in October 1996, and Istanbul, Turkey in May 1997. Our work at New Skete built directly on the Inter-Orthodox Consultation on Renewal in Orthodox Worship held at Bucharest, Romania in October 1991. It also took into consideration the contributions on worship made at the Fourth International Conference of Orthodox Theological Schools, held at Bucharest, Romania in August 1996. As all these consultations and conferences have demonstrated, worship must play a significant role both in the internal renewal of church life and in the search for Christian unity.

6. This consultation took place at a time when many Orthodox are reevaluating the ecumenical movement in general and participation in the World Council of Churches in particular. We discussed the report of the Inter-Orthodox Meeting on "Evaluation of New Facts in the Relations of Orthodoxy and the Ecumenical Movement" held at Thessaloniki, Greece in April/May 1998, as well as the Report of the Orthodox Pre-Assembly meeting held at Damascus, Syria in May 1998. These reports had an impact especially on our discussion of the problematics of ecumenical worship.

7. Presentations, papers and discussions in the course of the consultation were marked by a sense of urgency. They addressed a wide range of issues, including the

present state of Orthodox worship in various regions, liturgical language, anthropological and sociological perspectives, the role of liturgy in Christian formation, the ecclesiological significance of baptism and eucharist, and prayer in ecumenical contexts. Participants took note of a host of specific challenges and problems related to liturgical renewal and reform. They also repeatedly called attention to the need to identify basic principles of worship that can serve as criteria both for liturgical renewal in the Orthodox Churches and for Orthodox participation in ecumenical worship. What, in an Orthodox understanding, is the nature of worship itself?

Fundamental Principles

8. In the estimation of the consultation, the following principles are fundamental for Christian worship:
– Worship, to be truly worship, is at once theocentric and dialogical. It includes both God's word to us and our own praise, thanksgiving, supplication, and intercession offered to Him. In worship, God is present to us, and we are present to Him in a unique way.
– Worship is eschatological. It points to the ultimate unity of all in Christ.
– Worship is instrumental. It cannot be an end in itself. Its primary purpose is to bring Christians into communion with the Triune God and, in God, with one another and with all creation.
– Worship is formative. It is the primary way in which the Church's faith – the Church's theology and praxis – is passed on from one generation to the next. It builds faith and forms identity, both individual and corporate.
– Worship is transformative. It invites us to discover, experience and realize our true and eternal mode of being through the illumination of the intellect, the transformation of the passions and the purification of the heart.
– Worship is evangelical, and in this sense it is informative. It tells the story of Jesus Christ and indeed recounts the whole economy of salvation. Worship points beyond the local assembly to God's wider plan for the renewal of human community. Thus it has a direct relationship to mission.
– Worship is ecclesial. Through its worship, the Church finds its fullest expression and realization.
– Worship is inclusive. It is the work of the whole people of God.
– Worship is holistic. God's word is addressed to the entire person, and we praise and thank God not merely with our minds but also with our hearts and bodies.
– Worship is cosmic. It sees the entire creation as sacrament.

Implications for Orthodox renewal

9. These general principles concerning the nature of worship have a number of implications for Orthodox worship in our time. First of all, if the principles enunciated above are to be fully realized, our worship normally should be conducted in the

vernacular, in the language of the people. For centuries the Orthodox have appealed to the example of Sts. Cyril and Methodius. In recent practice, however, this principle often has been violated. Our churches must consider whether the language of their worship in fact conveys its real meaning to the faithful and to the world.

10. Liturgical worship is carried out by the entire assembly, not just by the clergy. For this reason, liturgical prayer generally employs the first person plural. This is clear, for example, in the anaphora, the central prayer of the eucharistic liturgy: "Remembering this saving commandment…, offering you your own of your own…, *we* praise you, *we* bless you, *we* give thanks to you…" The central action here is our corporate offering of praise and thanks, our *eucharistia*. It is appropriate, therefore, for liturgical prayer, the prayer of the assembly, to be recited aloud, for all to hear.

11. Our churches should examine critically the ways in which full participation of the *laos tou Theou* (people of God) in worship is hindered. The corporate nature of liturgical worship demands that we consider how we utilize the power of sacred space. We must be aware of legitimate alternatives for church architecture and furnishings. For example, would not the iconostasis in a more open form serve to keep the people connected to the priestly function that is performed in their name? Where is the appropriate place to proclaim the reading of the Scriptures, and how may this be adapted in particular circumstances? Do choirs and cantors facilitate the congregation's involvement? Does the music adequately convey the meaning of the text? Are certain classes and groups of persons systematically excluded from full participation (e.g., women, as a result of erroneous application of Old Testamental laws on ritual purity; children, as a result of being sent away to Sunday school during the Divine Liturgy)?

12. While the entire people of God are to participate fully in the Church's worship, they do so in different ways, through a diversity of ministries. Recent pan-Orthodox consultations, including the Inter-Orthodox Conference on Rhodes in 1988, have repeatedly called for the restoration of the diaconate for women, but as yet no concrete steps for implementation have been made. We believe that a deeper and more extensive exploration into the role of the diaconate, both male and female, is now long overdue. Reconsideration of the role of other ministries in the Church is also needed.

13. In some Orthodox churches, frequent reception of communion has become the norm, while in others the faithful come only rarely. In both cases, however, the reception of communion is often seen as an act of private devotion. Our churches need to rediscover the communal and corporate dimensions of the eucharist. They also need to reevaluate their various practices related to confession, fasting, and other forms of preparation for communion. This is necessary particularly when these practices not only obscure the ecclesial significance of the eucharist but also discourage frequent communion, thus inhibiting the spiritual growth and nourishment of the faithful.

14. In the Divine Liturgy, we receive spiritual nourishment not only through reception of communion but also through the hearing of God's word in the Scripture

readings. But given the fact that few people regularly attend more than the Sunday morning Liturgy, the lectionary itself needs to be reexamined. In our present usage, only a very small portion of the New Testament is ever heard by the faithful, and the Old Testament is virtually absent. The faithful hear about the miracles of Jesus with great frequency, but they are not exposed to His ethical and moral teaching (e.g., the Sermon on the Mount).

15. The word of God is also made present through the sermon, which is an integral part of liturgical worship. But all too often the sermon is of poor quality or simply omitted. Our churches should devote special attention to this critical need.

16. Other aspects of liturgical worship should not be overlooked. In 20th century Orthodox parish life, the daily office as a communal activity has been virtually abandoned. A Sunday-only church is a church deprived of much of the power of Scripture and most of the treasures of Orthodox hymnography. Our churches must explore new ways in which the discipline of daily prayer can be restored.

17. Our churches must be willing to support and advance a timely, orderly, and informed process of liturgical renewal and reform, in order to recover the essentials of our liturgical tradition. A careful study of worship will help free us from ritual formalism and help us discover and articulate the meaning of our liturgical patrimony. Among other things, such study will help to determine whether our worship today inspires the faithful, young and old, to carry the message of the Gospel into all areas of life and society, and to bear witness (*martyria*) to the compassion, justice, mercy, and wisdom of God.

Implications for Ecumenical Worship

18. The participation of the Orthodox Church in the quest for Christian reconciliation and the restoration of the visible unity of the churches is rooted in the saving words and actions of our Lord as expressed through Scripture and Tradition. In following her Lord, the Church has always sought to proclaim the apostolic faith and to heal the wounds of division through prayer and dialogue. As the Third Pan-Orthodox Pre-Conciliar Conference in 1986 said, "the Orthodox participation in ecumenical movement does not run counter to the nature and history of the Orthodox Church: It constitutes the consistent expression of the Apostolic faith within new historical conditions, in order to respond to new existential demands."

19. From the beginnings of the ecumenical movement, the Orthodox have participated in services of common prayer with Christians of other traditions. Prayer in common with other Christians, especially prayer for the unity of the Church and the healing of divisions, is not only possible but even required because of our shared baptism in the name of the Holy Trinity and our common belief in Jesus Christ our Savior. We affirm this in full awareness that the issue of baptism is highly contentious in the Orthodox world today. Some would claim that it is meaningless to speak of baptism as a spiritual reality outside the Orthodox Church. After careful consideration

of this issue, we find that arguments in support of such claims have no sound historical or theological basis.

20. The present divisions between Christians did not happen overnight or in a single solemn act. Divisions occurred – and continue to occur – over the course of time. Divisions often became evident long after the process of estrangement had begun. In the wake of divisions, different liturgical practices often became symbolic of the sad divisions. Indeed, some liturgical differences, which existed prior to a division and caused no problems whatsoever, were subsequently used to justify schisms.

21. The decision of the Orthodox Church to enter into ecumenical dialogue and prayer with other churches was a decision to begin to reverse the tendency towards greater and deeper divisions. This was a conscious decision, consistent with the Church's ecumenical vocation and with her ways of dealing with past challenges, such as Donatism and separations over christological issues.

22. Within the ecumenical movement, the Orthodox have placed a high priority not only upon the importance of affirming the apostolic faith but also upon the value of prayer for reconciliation and unity among Christian people. Reconciliation will not result simply from formal doctrinal agreements, necessary though these are. These agreements must first be prepared for and then be received at the grassroots level by believers whose hearts have been opened to each other through prayer.

23. The divisions which afflict Christianity today are not simply the result of doctrinal differences and misunderstandings compounded by cultural and political factors. These divisions are also the result of a form of spiritual blindness that manifests itself in pride, arrogance, triumphalism, self-righteousness, and lack of love. We affirm that prayer for the unity of the churches is the necessary foundation for all decisions of doctrine and for the resolution of differences. Our divisions will be healed if we truly approach them with the "mind of Christ" (1 Cor. 2:16). We must always be sensitive to the fact that we are called to speak about the reality of the Triune God with an honesty and humility reflecting the presence of Christ in our midst.

24. The practice of common prayer with other Christians contributes to the process of reconciliation. It is the necessary foundation for the restoration of the visible unity of the churches. We have not, however, reached the point where full communion has been restored between the Orthodox and other churches. Serious differences still need to be examined and resolved. Because of this, the Orthodox continue to affirm that participation in the eucharist is the expression of unity, and we avoid the acceptance of so-called "intercommunion" or "eucharistic hospitality." This painful separation before the Lord's Table is a constant reminder that we have yet to be fully reconciled with each other in the apostolic faith. It is also a challenge to persevere in our prayer for reconciliation and in theological dialogue, which has as its goal the restoration of the visible unity of the churches.

25. In this regard we took note of the special relationship which has developed between the Orthodox Church and the Oriental Orthodox (pre-Chalcedonian) Churches. Nurtured by prayer, our churches have been engaged in theological dialogue

for over thirty years, at first on an informal basis 1964 and since 1985 at the level of an official Joint Theological Commission. As the Anba Bishoi 1989 and Chambésy 1990 statements of the Theological Commission clearly show, our churches have come to see that we share the same Orthodox faith despite centuries of formal alienation. As the Anba Bishoi statement says: "We have inherited from our fathers in Christ the one Apostolic faith and tradition, though as Churches we have been separated from each other for centuries. As two families of Orthodox Churches, long out of communion with each other, we now pray and trust in God to restore that communion on the basis of the common Apostolic faith of the undivided Church of the first centuries which we confess in our common creed." With this joyous recognition in mind, the participants in this consultation look forward to the restoration of full communion between the Orthodox Church and the Oriental Orthodox Churches in the near future. This would be the obvious and indeed necessary consequence of our full agreement in questions of faith.

26. The consultation recognized that in recent times some Orthodox have questioned whether praying with other Christians is in fact contributing to the restoration of the kind of Christian unity willed by Christ. On the one hand, Orthodox in Eastern Europe, who have become the object of western proselytism, feel under siege and have experienced the breakdown of previous ecumenical relationships. On the other hand, many Orthodox argue that some Christian churches in dialogue with us have experienced radical changes in ethos, priorities, and moral stance which have come to be reflected in patterns of prayer and worship.

27. In order for ecumenical services of prayer to contribute to reconciliation and unity, they should reflect the kinds of fundamental principles of Christian worship sketched above. Unfortunately, rather than being theocentric and dialogical, ecumenical worship sometimes has been dominated and driven by issues which not only deflect from the concern for Christian unity and reconciliation but also themselves become the focus of attention. Rather than having communion with the Triune God as its focus, ecumenical worship sometimes has become the platform for particular social and political agendas and causes incompatible with the Gospel. Of course, in worship it is appropriate to lift up our living concerns in prayer. But when these concerns become the dominant element, Christian worship is deformed. Here we must acknowledge that we Orthodox have not always been blameless in this regard.

28. Orthodox participation in ecumenical prayer has been predicated upon the fact that the fundamental convictions of the apostolic faith continue to be expressed through the Scripture readings, prayers, and hymns of the worshipping community. When these fundamental convictions of the apostolic faith are lacking or intentionally distorted, it becomes difficult if not impossible for the Orthodox to participate. When, however, these convictions are embodied in ecumenical worship and do reflect the fundamental principles presented above, we should rejoice in joining our brothers and sisters in Christ in praise of God.

29. Mindful of the prayer of the Lord "that they all may be one," we remain committed to the search for Christian reconciliation and visible unity. We remain convinced that common prayer and common life will, by the grace of the Holy Spirit, lead to the healing of our divisions and disunity, so that God will be glorified and the world will believe.

On the Relationship of the Orthodox Church to the WCC

Statement of the Orthodox Theological Society in America
Boston, USA, 4 – 5 June 1998

1. The Orthodox Theological Society in America, at its annual meeting held at Holy Cross Greek Orthodox School of Theology in Brookline Massachusetts on 4-5 June 1998, chose to focus its entire attention on the current crisis within the ecumenical movement and especially on the question of Orthodox participation in the World Council of Churches. The Society studied the report of the Inter-Orthodox Meeting on "Evaluation of New Facts in the Relations of Orthodoxy and the Ecumenical Movement" held at Thessaloniki, Greece in April/May 1998, the Report of the Orthodox Pre-Assembly meeting held at Damascus, Syria in May 1998, The Report of the WCC Orthodox Task Force on "Orthodox-WCC Relations" dated 29 January 1998, and the Final Statement of the Consultation held in Iasi, Romania in April 1998 on "The Ecumenical Movement in the Twentieth Century: The Role of Theology in Ecumenical Thought and Life in Romania", as well as the WCC Policy Statement: "Towards a Common Understanding and Vision of the World Council of Churches" (CUV) dated September 1997, listened to papers and presentations made by members of the Society involved in the World Council of Churches, and weighed the issue at hand with sobriety and deep concern.

2. The Orthodox Church has been engaged in the ecumenical movement from the outset. The unity of the Church is for us not an option but an imperative, in fact a divine command. The prayer of the Lord to the Father for us: "that they may be one, even as we are one, so that the world might believe," is not simply a pious desire but reflects an ultimate truth. When Christians are divided, the world is denied that sign that is a witness to the healing offered by God to a world afflicted by the sin of separation and alienation. Thus we cannot repudiate this work for Christian unity but must affirm and embrace it.

3. Moreover, we affirm the progress made toward Christian unity especially since the early years of this century, both in the context of the World Council of Churches and in other fora. This progress is due in no small measure to the courage of Christians from every tradition to step outside of themselves and greet the other as a brother or

sister in Christ, to take up the cross of Christ in the quest for Christian unity and to engage the other in a dialogue of love. Differences, schisms and heresies that caused the divisions among Christians were the result of a long process of growing alienation. These divisions will not be healed without effort and even some pain. We all owe much to the ecumenical movement for expressing this process of reconciliation of Christians and the visible unity of the churches.

4. The expectations of the Orthodox Church in this regard were always modest and realistic. While the hope of visible unity was and remains the goal, the practical methodology was simply to lay the groundwork for this through theological dialogue, common life, prayer and working together. We remained patient as long as we were convinced that we shared this common vision with our Christian partners. But this common vision has increasingly been replaced in some ecumenical settings by particular social and political agendas derived solely from human experience and divorced from the Gospel. This has provoked dissatisfaction among us, thus precipitating the current crisis.

5. Criticism of the World Council of Churches (WCC) by the Orthodox has fallen into roughly two categories. On the one hand there are those who spread untruths about the WCC. Either through being misinformed themselves, or in the deliberate intention to misinform others, some extremist groups within or on the fringes of the Orthodox Church, hold that membership in the Council is a heresy in itself. On the other hand, however, there are critics of the WCC who, on the basis of their intense commitment to and involvement with the Council, are deeply disappointed with the directions that it is taking. Just as much as the propaganda of the former groups is to be repudiated or ignored, the criticism of the latter needs to be listened to with care.

6. From our perspective there are two equally important aspects to the relationship between the Orthodox Church and the WCC. One concerns structure or constitution. The current constitutional framework of the WCC mitigates against equitable participation in the governing bodies, advisory councils, and staff by the Orthodox Church because there are two opposite ecclesiologies operative. The number of member churches in the WCC continues to grow, but according to Orthodox ecclesiological principles the number of Orthodox churches will not grow significantly beyond their present number. For the churches of the Reformation, the impulse has been to multiply the number of churches. For the Orthodox, the ecclesiological approach does not easily or quickly allow the creation of new self-governing churches. Simply put, given the constitutional framework of the WCC, the Orthodox churches are not represented commensurate with their place within world Christianity. A number of proposals have been advanced to address this imbalance. None is as yet satisfactory to all parties. But we are convinced that the present structure must be modified.

7. The other concern relates to ethos, to mindset and ways of proceeding. Even more important than the constitutional question is the question of the manner in

which priorities for the Council are set. While the "language" of the WCC sometimes has reflected the Orthodox vision and Orthodox concerns, we believe there is a growing tendency towards ecumenical and theological "language" and "ethos" reflecting priorities and directions foreign to the Orthodox, and alienating the Orthodox. Even the classic struggle within the Council between the Faith and Order movement and the Life and Work movement frames the question of unity in such a way that the Orthodox must convolute their tradition – and, we might add, their understanding of the Gospel itself – in order to enter into the discussion.

8. While as part of its general restructuring the Council needs to address questions of church representation, the Council also needs to be held to its foundational principles. This is particularly appropriate as the Council celebrates its fiftieth anniversary and examines itself in the Common Understanding and Vision process – an eight-year study mandated in 1989 by the Central Committee of the World Council in preparation for the Eighth Assembly in Harare. The Council needs to be more accountable to its *Basis*: "a fellowship of churches which confess the Lord Jesus Christ as God and Saviour according to the scriptures and therefore seek to fulfil together their common calling to the glory of the one God, Father, Son, and Holy Spirit." The Council needs to be continuously accountable to the 1950 Toronto Statement, where among other things it is stated that "the WCC is not and must never become a Super-Church," by refraining from formulations or liturgical rites which suggest an ecclesial identity which the Council in fact does not possess. Finally, the Council needs to be true to its identity as a council of *churches* and not of movements or communities of goodwill

9. The value of theological reflection cannot be underestimated. In our ecumenical discussions, it is not enough simply to identify historical reasons for divisions and points of similarity. More than this, the doctrinal differences which contribute to divisions must be identified and, with the grace of the Holy Spirit, overcome. The ecumenical movement in general and the World Council of Churches in particular must provide the opportunities for theological reflection which is rooted in the Scripture and Tradition of the Church. This theological reflection should respond to the critical issues facing the churches today, especially issues related to the reconciliation of Christians and the restoration of the visible unity of the churches. We affirm that the visible unity of the churches requires that we come to a common confession of the Apostolic faith

10. We must also admit that the weakness of the Orthodox voice is not due simply to the WCC's constitutional framework. Often, it is due to internal problems and disagreements, which hinder our effectiveness. We have not enlisted the number of church people ready, willing and able to participate in ecumenical meetings. We often decline to send delegates to meetings when invited. There are times when we Orthodox are unable to form a common mind, because we ourselves have not settled certain ecclesiological questions. We must adhere to an internal self-discipline that does justice to our own ecclesiology.

11. In recent times some Orthodox have questioned whether praying with other Christians is in fact contributing to the restoration of the kind of Christian unity willed by Christ. We affirm the need for common prayer in order to heal our ancient divisions. Unfortunately, ecumenical worship sometimes has been dominated and driven by issues which not only deflect from the concern for Christian reconciliation and unity but also themselves become the focus of attention. Rather than having communion with the Triune God as its focus, ecumenical worship sometimes has become the platform for particular social and political agendas and causes incompatible with the Gospel. Of course, in worship it is appropriate to lift up our living concerns in prayer. But when these concerns become the dominant element, Christian worship is deformed.

12. Orthodox participation in ecumenical services of prayer has been predicated upon the fact that the fundamental tenets of the apostolic faith continue to be expressed through the Scripture readings, prayers, and hymns of the worshipping community. When these fundamental tenets of the apostolic faith are lacking or intentionally distorted, it becomes difficult if not impossible for the Orthodox to participate. When, however, these convictions are embodied in ecumenical prayer services, that do not have a eucharistic character, and do reflect these fundamental principles, we should rejoice in joining our brothers and sisters in Christ in praise of God.

13. We offer as an illustration of the way in which the unity of the churches can be restored the special relationship that has developed between the Eastern Orthodox and the Oriental Orthodox Churches. Nurtured by prayer, our churches have been engaged in theological dialogue for over thirty years. Through this dialogue our churches have come to see that we share the same Orthodox faith despite centuries of formal alienation. We have grown closer through cooperation in all aspects of ecclesial life. This Society has for many years included as full members theologians from the Oriental Orthodox Churches. We look forward to the restoration of full communion among the Eastern Orthodox and the Oriental Orthodox Churches in the near future. In order to further the quest for restored communion, we urge the hierarchs of the both the Eastern and Oriental Orthodox Churches in America to establish a bilateral dialogue to address the practical questions necessary to attain this goal. We believe this restored communion to be the obvious and indeed necessary consequence and testimony of our full agreement in matters of faith. This final act will provide an example of the manner in which deep divisions lasting hundreds of years can be healed in the dialogue of love.

14. Finally, we wish to affirm our basic and profound commitment to the struggle for Christian reconciliation and the visible unity of the churches. We call upon people of goodwill within every Christian church to join with us in the call of the Lord, so that the world might believe and God might be glorified.

From Canberra to Harare (1991-1998)

Activity Report Reflecting Orthodox Contributions to the WCC
and the WCC's Responses to Orthodox Concerns
Compiled by Georges Lemopoulos, WCC/OCER

The present report, prepared with the contribution of all members of the Orthodox Task Force, gives a sense of the variety of work undertaken by the World Council of Churches at the service of or in cooperation with its Orthodox member churches. Its intention is neither to cover all the programmatic activities of the WCC, nor to affirm that everything possible has been done. It rather constitutes an invitation to assess the work, and to reflect on unaccomplished tasks or activities which could be undertaken in a completely different way for the sake of better responding to the needs and demands of the churches.

It is hoped that as a background information document the present report will help both the staff of the WCC and representatives of Orthodox churches in the governing and consultative bodies of the WCC to give further thought to ways of achieving more sustained, constructive and fruitful cooperation.

1. Visits-Relationships

Relationships with member churches are extremely important for the WCC as they confirm and strengthen its identity as both a fellowship of churches and an instrument in the service of the member churches and the ecumenical movement. Relationships are strengthened particularly through visits in which the WCC is the host rather than the guest. Among these visits, those of Primates of Orthodox Churches have been of major importance. One could argue that the very spirit of these visits constitutes a real challenge both to the Orthodox Churches and to the WCC. They manifest the commitment of Orthodox leadership to the WCC and to the ecumenical movement. Yet they remind us at the same time that much has still to be done in terms of communicating this commitment to larger circles within the Orthodox Churches. The General Secretary has also made visits to most of the Orthodox member churches in order to hear first-hand about the situation of the churches, their understanding of and engagement in the ecumenical movement, and their expectations from the WCC.

- ***Visits of Orthodox Primates to the Ecumenical Centre***
  Patriarch Alexy of Moscow and all Russia (1995), the Ecumenical Patriarch Bartholomaios (1995), Catholicos Ilia of Georgia (1996), the Supreme Catholicos

of all Armenians Karekin I (1996), and Patriarch Ignatius of Antioch (1996) were the heads of Eastern and Oriental Orthodox Churches who visited the Ecumenical Centre in Geneva and had discussions with the General Secretary and senior staff of the WCC.

H.H. Catholicos Aram I of Cilicia, Moderator of the Central Committee, the late Patriarch Parthenios and H.H. Pope Shenouda, WCC Presidents, have frequently visited Geneva within their roles in the leadership of the Council and had opportunities to meet several times with the General Secretary and senior staff of the WCC.

- *Visits of the General Secretary to Orthodox Churches*

The General Secretary has visited the Ecumenical Patriarchate (1993, 1994, 1995), the Moscow Patriarchate (1993, 1998), the Church of Cyprus (1993, 1997), the Serbian Orthodox Church, the Church of Greece, the Orthodox Church in America (1993), the Churches of Romania (1994), Jerusalem (1995), Alexandria, Antioch, and Poland (1996), the Catholicosate of Cilicia (1995), the Malankara Orthodox Church (1995, 1997), the Coptic Orthodox Church, the Syrian Orthodox Church, the Catholicosate of Etchmiadzine (1996), and the Ethiopian Orthodox Church (1997).

Two meetings of the Executive Committee were hosted by Orthodox Churches: in 1994 by the Romanian Orthodox Church, and in 1996 by the Church of Cyprus. In both cases members of the Executive Committee and Staff of the WCC were given the opportunity to visit the local churches and meet with their leadership.

2. Team-Visits

"Living Letters": this is an image that is now widely used in order to qualify the nature and character of ecumenical visits to churches. Indeed, face to face contacts strengthen the fellowship, display the joy of meeting with sisters and brothers, facilitate communication. Thus, in addition to official visits, there are team-visits intending to strengthen regular working relationships, or to offer the opportunity of discovering the life and witness, the liturgical, theological, spiritual and cultural riches of a member church. The WCC also sends ecumenical delegations to regions or churches experiencing particular tensions. Such visits are effective in drawing attention to the sufferings and needs of people and churches, offering support, and collecting information for ecumenical interpretation and advocacy.

- *Albania (1991)*

Immediately after the recent major socio-political changes, a delegation visited Albania on behalf of WCC and CEC in order to make contact with the Albanian authorities, to express concern for and desire to assist the people of Albania, and in particular to renew fellowship with the Orthodox Church which, at that time, had just started reorganizing herself and affirming her role within the new Albanian society. Following this visit, the WCC shipped some twenty-three tons of food and other goods to the country, and an Albanian Orthodox Church group visiting Geneva requested ecumenical support for the training of clergy.

- *Former Yugoslavia (1992)*

The first WCC visit to the country since the beginning of the civil war in 1991. In earlier actions of the WCC there had been messages to the churches, a debate during the Central Committee, interventions with political authorities and support of the efforts deployed by CEC in full cooperation with the LWF, WARC and WCC to bring about dialogue between the churches in Yugoslavia. The purpose of the visit was to express the solidarity of the WCC with its member churches, in particular the Serbian Orthodox Church, to learn more about the situation, and to discuss with church leaders ways in which the WCC could be of help.

- *Armenia-Azerbaijan (1992)*

A joint WCC/CEC staff delegation visited the area and met with political and community leaders as well as with refugees and others suffering from the effects of the conflict. On behalf of the WCC and CEC, they invited the religious leaders to meet on neutral territory.

- *Bulgaria (1992)*

Visit of WCC staff for a national meeting of Bulgarian humanitarian organizations. Close cooperation with the Orthodox Church on issues of mission, diakonia and education. The meeting was followed-up in 1993 by a consultant working with the churches in the country.

- *Albania (1992)*

A follow-up to the first visit of an ecumenical delegation to Albania, this visit included meetings and discussions with the Orthodox Church, the Helsinki Committee, and the Secretariat for Religion. The visiting team paved the way for the membership of the Albanian Orthodox Church in the WCC, explored the possibilities for inaugurating a Round Table for Albania, and discussed the ecumenical contribution to the Theological Seminary of the Orthodox Church.

- *Georgia (1993)*

In January 1993 a joint WCC-CEC delegation visited Georgia at the request of the Georgian Orthodox Church. The aim was to manifest the solidarity of the ecumenical organizations with the Georgian Orthodox Church in the very difficult situation of conflicts in Abkhazia and Ossetia, and of economic and social hardship caused by the civil war and the disintegration of the Soviet Union. The delegation was able to collect and provide extensive background and factual information on the situation which was reported to the WCC and CEC, and to related agencies and organizations.

- *Armenia (1994)*

Team Visit to Armenia and Nagorno-Karabagh. WCC representatives traveled in the region on the invitation of the Armenian Apostolic Church to gather information as a basis for further planning and ecumenical and international support for the people and churches there.

- *Chechnya, Russian Federation (1995)*

On the invitation and with the assistance of the Russian Orthodox Church, WCC representatives visited the region to assess immediate needs of displaced people in the conflict, and to develop relief work with the Russian Orthodox Church in the region.

• *Egypt (1995)*

An exposure visit to the Coptic Orthodox Church in Egypt for people from Bulgaria, Poland, Romania, and Russia engaged in church activities. The visit offered the opportunity to learn about the activities and experiences of the Coptic Church in the field of diakonia.

• *Bulgaria (1997)*

Concern for Bulgaria remained very much on the agendas of the WCC and of CEC in spite of internal ecclesial and socio-political difficulties. In March 1997, WCC/ACT launched an appeal to assist humanitarian relief undertaken by some of the churches and church related organizations. Within this context it was decided that an ecumenical study visit with the participation of some of the support agencies would be an appropriate step to take at this point in time, both with regard to diaconal work and the question of relationships between and within the churches.

• *Georgia (1997)*

An informal visit to H.H. Catholicos Ilia following the decision of the Georgian Orthodox Church to withdraw from the WCC and from CEC.

• *Ecumenical Decade of the Churches in Solidarity with Women*

Team-visits within the framework of the Ecumenical Decade offered the possibility of visiting Orthodox churches in the following countries: India, Japan, Poland, USA (1994), Albania, Ethiopia, Finland, Russia (1995), Czech Republic, Egypt, Jerusalem, Romania, Slovak Republic, and Syria (1996).

• *Jerusalem and the year 2000*

A visit to the Greek Orthodox Patriarchate of Jerusalem and other member churches in the Holy City (August 1996) in order to consider possibilities of a common celebration of the year 2000 in Jerusalem or Bethlehem.

3. Inter-Orthodox Meetings

It has become a policy of the WCC to emphasize the distinctive role of Orthodox theological thought in its life and activities. For this purpose, inter-orthodox meetings are organized prior to major ecumenical events, or in order to offer an Orthodox contribution to specific programmatic concerns. Such meetings are also organized at times of underlying uncertainty in the ecumenical movement or in the relationships between the Orthodox churches and the WCC. During the period under review, marked on the one hand by a growing critical attitude of many Orthodox towards the ecumenical movement, and on the other by the reflection process on the "Common Understanding and Vision of the WCC", most of the inter-orthodox consultations focused on Orthodox participation in the WCC and in the ecumenical movement. Together with the findings of inter-Orthodox meetings, one should recall here the formal contributions of Orthodox Churches to the reflection process on the "Common Understanding and Vision of the WCC" (Ecumenical Patriarchate, Patriarchate of Antioch, Moscow Patriarchate, Romanian Orthodox Church, and the Church of Greece), as well as the opportunities offered to the General Secretary to discuss with Heads and officers of Orthodox Churches issues related to Orthodox participation in the ecumenical movement.

- *"The Orthodox Churches and the World Council of Churches" (Chambésy, 1991)*
Participants in this meeting reflected on Orthodox relations with the WCC after the Canberra Assembly, addressing theological, ecclesiological and organizational aspects concerning the involvement of the Orthodox Churches in the ecumenical movement and in the WCC. The Report of the consultation was presented to the 1992 Central Committee meeting and was fully discussed during a plenary session.

- *"The Ecumenical Movement, the Churches, and the WCC" (Chambésy, 1995)*
This consultation was convened in relation to the reflection process on the "Common Understanding and Vision of the WCC", with the aim of pointing the way forward, reviewing the ecumenical commitment of the Orthodox Churches, and attempting to clarify underlying uncertainties in their relations to the WCC. The report of the consultation was submitted to the Orthodox Churches in order to facilitate their task in stating their views about the ecumenical movement, as well as to the leadership of the WCC as a contribution to the ongoing common reflection process.

- *"Inter-Orthodox Consultation on Gospel and Cultures" (Addis Ababa, Ethiopia, 1996)*
The aim of this meeting was to initiate a reflection within the Orthodox Churches on the theme of the Conference on World Mission and Evangelism in Salvador, Bahia, Brazil (1996).

- *An informal encounter in Antélias (1996)*
At the invitation of H.H. Catholicos Aram I of Cilicia, Moderator of the Central Committee of the WCC, Orthodox and Protestant members of the Central Committee explored together perspectives for Orthodox participation in the ecumenical movement of the future, focusing mainly on questions such as "Where are we in the ecumenical movement as Orthodox?" and "What is expected from the Orthodox in the ecumenical movement?" An Aide-Memoire summarizing the discussions and suggestions of the encounter was shared with the heads of Orthodox churches for their information and further action.

- *"Discerning the Signs of the Times: Women in the Life of the Orthodox Church"*
Two gatherings involving women representing Eastern and Oriental Orthodox Churches. The first was hosted by H.B. Ignatius IV, Patriarch of Antioch (Syria, 1997), involving especially women from the Middle East, Asia and Africa, with a few women from other regions of the world. The second was hosted by H.H. Bartholomaios, Ecumenical Patriarch (Istanbul, 1997), and drew participants from Europe as well as North and South America, with a few women from the Middle East. These meetings strongly affirmed the many gifts that Orthodox women bring to the ecumenical movement and established their commitment to the WCC Decade of Churches in Solidarity with Women.

- *"Gospel and Cultures: Pan-African Inter-Orthodox Consultation" (Kampala, Uganda, 1997)*
The first meeting of its kind, it brought together representatives of local communities, as well as church workers in missionary and educational institutions throughout Africa, offering them the opportunity to reflect together about the present and future of Orthodox life and witness in Africa.
- *Orthodox Pre-Assembly Meeting (Ma'arat Saydnaya, Syria, May 1998)*
The aim of this meeting was to prepare delegates to the Harare Assembly and help them to make a fuller contribution to the Assembly. Its goals were: (a) to deepen theological reflection on the Assembly theme as an Orthodox contribution to the ecumenical vision; (b) to introduce the Assembly agenda and its process, and discuss Orthodox participation in and contributions to the life and activities of the WCC; (c) to discuss the relations between the Orthodox Churches and the WCC.
- *"Orthodox Liturgical Renewal and Visible Unity" (Cambridge, New York, May 1998)*
This consultation helped set out principles of worship in the Orthodox understanding, examining implications for renewal in Orthodox church life, for the ecumenical endeavor, and for prayer in ecumenical settings.

4. Multilateral Theological Dialogue

The dominant feature of practically all the programmatic activities and studies within the framework of the multilateral theological dialogue has been the ecclesiology of koinonia, with the deep awareness that this is the most promising theme of contemporary ecumenical theology, resonating with contemplative experience and the experience of close relationships between churches. Orthodox theologians have contributed to the discussions bringing the self-understanding of their tradition and their experience from the work of the bilateral theological dialogues. They have also reminded us constantly that one of the areas in which the concept of koinonia appears to have considerable potential for ecumenical progress is that of tackling questions of church structure, ministry, authority and, especially, Tradition.

- *Faith and Order Apostolic Faith Study*
At the urging and with the continued support of the Orthodox (and other) churches, Faith and Order took up an extensive study of the Apostolic Faith, focusing in particular on the Nicene-Constantinopolitan Creed. This study produced several publications, the major ones being *Confessing the One Faith* (1991) and the study guide *Towards Sharing the One Faith* (1996).
- *"Christian Spirituality for our Times" (Iasi, Romania, 1994)*
Participants in this meeting urged further study of movements of spiritual renewal in the churches, new work on a common celebration of Easter and special attention to spirituality in the life of the Eighth Assembly, including the formulation of new guidelines on eucharistic sharing.

- *"Towards a Common Date for Easter"* (Aleppo, 1997)

This consultation was sponsored in cooperation with the Middle East Council of Churches, and hosted by the Syrian Orthodox Archdiocese of Aleppo. It brought together official representatives of Christian World Communions, the Orthodox Churches and the Roman Catholic Church. It produced a statement containing recommendations on the common observance of the Date of Easter in the new millennium, with the recognition that the two present methods of calculation will agree in 2001. The report has been sent to the churches represented at the consultation and to the member churches of the WCC.

- *"The Role of Theology in Ecumenical Thought and Life in Romania"* (Iasi, Romania, 1998)

This meeting sought to "take the pulse" of ecumenical life within Romania as well as assess the relationships of local churches with the WCC, past and present.

5. Mission, Evangelism, Proselytism

Over the years, the Orthodox made a substantial contribution in the field of mission and evangelism in unity. They have brought to the process of ecumenical theological reflection the ethos, praxis and experience of witnessing to the Gospel in different circumstances which Orthodox have accumulated during the almost two millennia of ecclesial history and tradition. In the period since the last Assembly in Canberra, the Orthodox contribution concentrated mainly on (a) the way to common witness which implies adopting responsible relationships in mission and renouncing proselytism, and (b) reflection on the close interrelationship between Gospel and cultures. It is understandable that, especially because of the changes in Central and Eastern Europe, the period between the two assemblies was deeply marked by ecumenical reflection on proselytism, and ecumenical action seeking to prevent competitive missionary activities which negatively affect relationships between churches and Christian communities.

- *"Uniatism: An Ecumenical Response towards the healing of Memories"*

Team visits, arranged at the request of Orthodox members of the Central Committee, to Romania, the Slovak Republic, Belarus and Ukraine, followed by a Consultation (Geneva, 1992), drawing the attention of Protestant member churches around the world to the reality of Uniatism, challenging it as a model claiming to lead to unity. Having studied and discussed the reports of the team visits and of the consultation, the Central Committee of the WCC adopted and widely circulated a document entitled: *"Uniatism: An Ecumenical Response towards the healing of Memories"*.

- *"Proclaiming Christ Today"* (Alexandria, 1995)

An Orthodox-Evangelical Consultation which offered the opportunity for frank and fruitful discussion on evangelization and proselytism, especially in contexts where in many local situations the Orthodox and Evangelical constituencies experience tension and conflict.

- *"Mission, evangelism and proselytism"* (St Sergius Lavra, 1995)
  Consultation organized in cooperation with the Department on Mission of the Russian Orthodox Church. The findings of this meeting were presented to the World Conference on Mission and Evangelism and served as background material for the drafting of a WCC Statement on Mission, Evangelism, and Proselytism.
- *World Conference on Mission and Evangelism* (Salvador Bahia, Brazil, 1996)
  An Orthodox hierarch and theologian – H.E. Metropolitan Kyrill of Smolensk and Kalliningrad – invited to be the main speaker in the World Conference thus ensuring that Orthodox concerns about the present mission situation and the challenge of proselytism were placed at the very heart of this important gathering as well as on the future agenda of the WCC.
- *"The Challenge of Proselytism and the Call to Common Witness"* (1996)
  Publication of a Study Document prepared by the Joint Working Group between the World Council of Churches and the Roman Catholic Church.
- *"Towards Common Witness – A call to adopt responsible relationships in mission and to renounce proselytism"*
  A document/statement adopted by the Central Committee of the WCC and recommended to the member churches. Drawing largely from the Study Document of the JWG, this statement was prepared after a broad consultative process involving mission agencies, churches, missiologists, theologians, local congregations, and monastic orders. Special efforts were made to bring together in dialogue the "proselytizers" and the "proselytized" and to involve not only WCC member churches but also members of the Evangelical, Pentecostal and Charismatic constituencies.

6. Theological Education – Ecumenical Formation

The WCC has always been supportive of efforts by Orthodox Churches to build, maintain, and develop their theological schools. Especially during the period under review, when new opportunities were given to Orthodox Churches in Central and Eastern Europe to increase the number of their theological schools and seminaries, the programme on Ecumenical Theological Education has positively responded to a considerable number of requests, supporting many initiatives and covering many needs. Meanwhile, there has been a conscious effort to increase the number of workshops, meetings and consultations involving young Orthodox theologians in order to share experiences and information about the ecumenical movement. Taking also into consideration the critical questions being raised about the ecumenical movement and the WCC, working with and for the younger generation has been one of the most sustained and systematic activities during this period. The areas of theological education and ecumenical formation has also provided opportunity for increased collaboration with Orthodox theological schools (e.g. Balamand, Thessaloniki), and with Syndesmos (the World Fellowship of Orthodox Youth).

- *"Orthodox Theology and Spirituality"*
  Seminars organized by the Ecumenical Institute, Bossey, to promote Orthodox theology and spirituality. Participants in these seminars are usually interested persons

from other churches and confessions who are also given the opportunity to discover Orthodox liturgical life (Bossey, 1991; Thessaloniki 1992; Bossey, 1993; Iasi, 1994; Bossey, 1995; Orthodox Academy, Crete, 1996; Bossey 1997; Inter-Orthodox Center, Penteli-Athens, 1998).

• *"Theological Education for Witness and Service Today"*

Seminars for students and young professors of theology from Central and Eastern Europe (Bossey, 1991; Potsdam, 1992; Thessaloniki, 1993; Düsseldorf, 1995; Chambésy, 1996). These seminars offered a number of young students, professors and priests the opportunity of meeting with their colleagues from other countries and churches, and discussing with them the needs and priorities of theological education after the socio-political changes in the former socialist world.

• *"Classic and Contextual Theology"* (Thessaloniki, 1992)

Seminar organized by the Ecumenical Institute, Bossey, together with the Theological Faculty of Thessaloniki, to initiate the study on Gospel and cultures, in order to encourage younger theologians to participate in the study process and to reflect as faculty members of both academic institutions on how the issue could be presented as a common concern of the churches in the coming years.

• *"Ecumenism in Search of a New Vision"* (Thessaloniki, 1993)

Public lecture by the WCC General Secretary at the University of Thessaloniki. Meeting with the Faculty and discussion with students. Cooperation with the Association for Ecumenical Studies and Inter-Orthodox Information.

• *"Women and Orthodox Spirituality"*

Three Seminars in Bossey (1992-1997) for intensive theological dialogue, introducing the participants to Orthodox spirituality and its potential for ecumenical dialogue. The aim of the seminars was to study with women and men spirituality in Christian life, inspired by feminine images and symbols in the Bible, in respective ecclesiologies and theological traditions, and especially in the Orthodox tradition.

• *"Orthodox Youth and the Ecumenical Movement"*

The first of the two seminars (Värska, Estonia, 1994), organized jointly with Syndesmos and the World Student Christian Federation (WSCF) Europe Region, gathered together young Orthodox people who were involved in one way or another in the ecumenical movement to review the situation in terms of participation and to modify plans and strategies. Again organized jointly with Syndesmos, the second seminar (Chambésy, 1995) was a powerful awareness-raising experience as it enabled young Orthodox people to share their experiences and information about the ecumenical movement and Orthodox involvement in it.

• *"Missionary and Ecumenical Formation of Orthodox Youth"* (Romania, 1995)

Young Orthodox from the churches of Bulgaria, Constantinople, and Romania met for this workshop in the St Maria Monastery in Techirghiol. In attendance also were resource persons, Orthodox and Protestant, from Ghana, Switzerland, and Romania. Participants discussed and shared with each other the problems and concerns of young people regarding the mission of the Church and the ecumenical situations in their various contexts.

- *Ecumenical Formation of parish priests and ministers in the Middle East*

In collaboration with the Middle East Council of Churches, an ecumenical initiative was begun at the local level in 1995 and still continues. The main objective of this long-term process is the ecumenical formation of parish priests and ministers at the local (national) level. The programme is addressing priests and pastors from the Orthodox, Protestant and Catholic churches in the region.

- *"The Church as Inclusive Community: The place and role of the differently-abled in its life, education, and mission" (Sibiu, Romania, 1996)*

Orthodox teachers and church leadership were given the opportunity of studying together an important human and pastoral concern from an educational and missiological perspective.

- *Ecumenical Scholarships*

In assisting Orthodox Churches to prepare their workers and future leadership, 170 scholarships were granted for one academic year to priests and laypersons, young women and men, from practically all Orthodox member churches. A second year extension was ensured for sixty of these students. In addition, there has been cooperation between the Scholarships Office of the WCC and the Orthodox Programme of the Diakonisches Werk which grants scholarships to Orthodox students. To these numbers and facts should be added the fact that fifty-five Orthodox students were given the opportunity to participate in the Graduate School of the Ecumenical Institute, Bossey.

- *Stewards' Programme*

Intentional Leadership training programmes on the occasion of WCC governing body meetings and other major events. Orthodox young people have participated in every such programme in the period since Canberra.

7. Religious Education

In 1991, following the debate on the future of WCC programmes focusing on education, and at the request of its Orthodox members, the Central Committee agreed to consider religious education as a priority item to be followed up by the WCC Education staff. Its minutes cdocument the commitment "...that religious education in Eastern Europe be considered a key concern". Together with what has been reported above about theological education and ecumenical formation, the activities related to religious education listed below highlight the fact that a number of programmatic activities of the WCC have tried to respond to an urgent Orthodox concern. It is also important to underline here the fact that WCC activities in this area have been substantially assisted by many Orthodox Churches who were glad to be included in the process, e.g. the Orthodox Church in Japan and the Coptic Orthodox Church, or to contribute to the process by hosting meetings, e.g. the Moscow Patriarchate, the Church of Cyprus, the Orthodox Church in America, the Orthodox Church in Finland, and the Catholicosate of Cilicia (Antelias).

- Monitoring and supporting the work of Orthodox churches in Central and Eastern Europe in the field of religious education. The main emphasis was on strengthening local churches to compete with missionary activities in their countries, as well as to build up the faith of recently baptized persons. In view of these challenges the programme included: (a) curriculum development; (b) leadership/teacher training programmes with on-site experience; and (c) training in course writing and presentation. Some of the more important stages of this programme were the following:

• Consultation in Moscow (1992), hosted by the Russian Orthodox Church, to identify the needs of the churches in Central and Eastern Europe in religious education in the post-communist period of their history. Symposium on Orthodox Curriculum in Cyprus (1994), Leadership Training Programme through exposure and exchange in the USA (1994), and a workshop on skills training for curriculum development for teachers of religion and persons responsible for curriculum writing in Finland (1995). There were also activities in Albania, Armenia, Bulgaria, the Czech Republic, Poland, Romania, Russia, and Slovakia. Although it was not possible to organize an activity in each country, the presence of Orthodox educators from practically all countries concerned was assured.

• Cooperation with the Religious Education Department as well as the Department of External Church Relations of the Moscow Patriarchate and contribution towards the publication of two manuals for catechism entitled *"The Good Tree"* and *"First Steps to God"*, prepared by religious educators.

• Extension of the educational cooperation with the Russian Orthodox Church to the Central Asian Republics and the Southern Caucasus. The emphasis was on Christian Religious Education in Pluralist Societies. In 1995, a meeting was held in Tashkent for Christian and Muslim educators from the five Central Asian Republics with the title *"Living together under one sky."*

Several local leadership training seminars were organized in addition to the major Orthodox events.

8. Justice, Peace, Creation

Since the Canberra Assembly the churches have moved together in new and powerful ways to confront the causes of injustice and death, articulating together a theology of life, opposing together various forms of violence, and assisting each other in their struggles within their respective contexts. The work of the WCC shows that the ecumenical movement is strengthened by common endeavours in the areas of justice, peace, and care for the creation. Churches with serious theological differences are often able to work together in formulating an ecumenical strategy on issues of justice, or in serving together the immediate needs of refugees, or in confronting emerging conflicts in their own countries. The activities listed here are some examples from among the many efforts made to respond to the broken world in its pain and suffering, but also to the broken church in her need for reconciliation and unity.

- *Promoting Peace in the Caucasus*

    In February 1993, the WCC and CEC invited religious leaders from Armenia and Azerbaijan to meet on neutral territory. The meeting took place under WCC auspices in Switzerland between H.H. Vasken I, Patriarch Catholicos of All Armenians, and Sheikh-ul-Islam Pasha-zadeh, Chairman of the Muslim religious Board for Causasia. The two leaders signed a joint communiqué calling for a peaceful resolution of the problems dividing them, for the unconditional release of hostages, and for the humane treatment of prisoners of war. Furthermore, they gave their support to efforts being made by the UN and the CSCE to find a peaceful resolution to the conflict. They also announced the establishment of a United Humanitarian Relief Fund "to render assistance without distinction of nationality or faith to all those who suffer".

- *"Christian Faith and Human Enmity" (Moscow, 1994; Minsk, 1996)*

    In cooperation with the Department of External Church Relations, the WCC encouraged, accompanied and assisted the Russian Orthodox Church in her efforts to organize two important inter-confessional consultations, bringing together representatives of Christian churches in the former Soviet Union to discuss their concern for peace and for creating an appropriate infrastructure for continuing Christian cooperation in Russia.

- *"Christian Faith and Economy" (Moscow, 1994).*

    Consultation organized in cooperation with the Department of External Church Relations of the Russian Orthodox Church, bringing together theologians and experts from academic and financial circles and encouraging them to discuss the implications of present economic trends on the life and witness of the churches and what could be the genuine contribution of theological reflection to the development of a humane and just economic model.

- *Promoting peace in the former Yugoslavia (Geneva, 1994).*

    At the invitation of the General Secretaries of the WCC and CEC, representatives of the Serbian Orthodox Church, the Ecumenical Patriarchate, the Moscow Patriarchate, the Church of Greece, the Evangelical Church in Germany, the Swiss Protestant Church Federation, the Church of Sweden, the Council of Churches for Britain and Ireland, the Church of England, and the NCCCUSA met in Geneva for dialogue on the role of the ecumenical movement in promoting peace in the territory of the former Yugoslavia.

- *Refugee and Migration Service*

    There has been close collaboration between the WCC and the MECC Service to Refugees, Displaced and Migrants. A main emphasis of this work has been capacity building in the area of church ministry to uprooted people in which the Orthodox churches in the region are active participants. Between 1995-1998, for example, five training workshops for refugee ministry have been held in Lebanon, Jordan, Egypt and Syria. The MECC/WCC Working Group on Refugees, Displaced and Migrants meets annually to review concerns related to uprooted people in the region, to set priorities and recommend actions; Orthodox churches are represented in the membership the Working Group. The Coptic Church in Egypt is also an active member of the Ecumenical Coordinating Committee for Uprooted People in Egypt and offers income generating training opportunities for refugees in Egypt. A concrete example of this cooperation is the Consultation on refugees, displaced persons and migrants co-sponsored by the WCC and the MECC in Abbasia, Egypt, in 1995. The aim of this encounter was to raise awareness among Egyptian churches on the situation of Sudanese refugees. Forty-two people attended, mostly from the Coptic Orthodox Church.

• *Churches' concern for creation*

A number of Orthodox initiatives (e.g. summer Seminars on Halki Island organized by the Ecumenical Patriarchate in 1994, 1995, 1997; Syndesmos Seminars and Publications) were encouraged, accompanied and supported.

9. Resource sharing – Diakonia

From the start, diakonia and Christian service have been central to the meaning of the ecumenical movement, and the Orthodox churches have been actively involved in shaping the theology and practice of this dimension of the WCC's mandate. Churches in the WCC are encouraged to explore and develop more just ways of sharing resources and power and better forms of development. The WCC unit on Sharing and Service has worked closely with Orthodox churches throughout the world, but mainly in Europe and the Middle East, to accompany and support the revival of Orthodox church activity in response to human suffering and need. Some of the main initiatives taken with Orthodox churches for the benefit of their churches and societies are listed below:

• *Albania Round Table programme*

The WCC has played an active role in support of the revival of the Albanian Orthodox Church. In 1992, a specialized diaconal arm of this church was established to channel medicines and relief supplies to the Albanian population. Since 1993, annual meetings of international partners have been convened in the framework of a Round Table to provide resources for a range of social, educational and "inner-church" projects in the country. In 1997, over US $500,000 was channelled to church programmes in the country.

• *Armenia Round Table programme*

Round Table meetings involving the Armenian Apostolic Church were held in 1993 and 1996. As a result, programmes have been initiated with church and international partners in the following priority areas: (a) Social diakonia and development work, including agricultural and medical work, (b) Religious and theological education, including teaching and publications, (c) Church reconstruction. A WCC Round Table office was established in Holy Etchmiadzine in 1997 to coordinate the work in the country with the blessing of the Apostolic Church.

• *Russia Round Table programme*

Since 1992, WCC has worked closely with the Russian Orthodox Church and related partners. The Round Table programme "Education for Change" (1992-1996) focused on support for Orthodox diaconal initiatives, including training for social workers and actions for the most vulnerable in society. The programme also gave priority to education, and with the support of international partners, over a million essential theological and catechetical books were published for use in Orthodox theological schools and churches. In addition, Orthodox TV and radio projects were implemented and new printing facilities were established for the Russian Orthodox Church. WCC has also worked closely with the Russian Orthodox Church in the area of emergencies, and significant support was channelled through the church to vulnerable parts of Russian society.

- *WCC/CEC Priority Project Fund*

The WCC/CEC Priority Project Fund has allowed ecumenical funds to be channelled to church initiatives in areas of crucial need in Europe. The St Sergius Institute of Orthodox Theology in Paris, the French-language Orthodox Press Service, and Syndesmos, (the World Fellowship of Orthodox Youth), are just some of the Orthodox beneficiaries of this ecumenical support.

- *WCC Unit IV Eastern Europe Office*

In 1995, the WCC established an office located in Poland to support the revival of diaconal service of the churches in the region. The office is headed by a member of the Polish Orthodox Church, and works closely with Orthodox churches in several countries, including Belarus, Russia and Ukraine.

- *Round Table with the MECC's Department of Service to Palestinian Refugees*

This Round Table brings together international partners (donor agencies) and local churches to respond to the needs of Palestinian Refugees in five areas: West Bank and Jerusalem, Gaza, Galilee, Jordan and Lebanon. It was established in 1971 in its most recent form. In fact the Council had started giving help to Palestinian Refugees from the very beginning of the Palestinian problem. The Orthodox churches along with other churches are part of this diaconal service.

- *Round Table with MECC's Emergency, Rehabilitation and Reconstruction Programme in Lebanon*

Established in 1988 to respond to the plight of the people of Lebanon during and after the civil war, this Round Table also brings together international partners and local churches in Lebanon (Orthodox, Protestant and also Catholic) to design, follow up and evaluate a programme which is implemented by the staff who are closely accompanied by committees composed of representatives from all the churches.

- *Round Table for the Coptic Orthodox Church*

This Round Table was established in 1985 mainly to help the Coptic Church in its diakonia, development and social work. It brings together international partners and the Coptic Orthodox Church to accompany, follow up and evaluate the programme which was designed together.

- *Operational Budget of the MECC*

The WCC acts as coordinator between the international partners and the MECC concerning their programmes. Orthodox, Protestant and Catholic churches are all members of MECC.

- *Programme for churches in Turkey*

Coordinating assistance from international partners to programmes of the Syrian Orthodox Church in Turabdin, South-East Turkey (especially to support the Mor Gabriel Monastery), the Syrian Orthodox parishes in Istanbul, and the Armenian Apostolic church (mainly parishes and institutions in Istanbul).

- *Priority Fund*

This Fund was set up to support yearly Priority Projects from the churches in the Middle East. It is mainly addressed to Orthodox and Protestant churches and to a much lesser extent to the Catholic churches.

10. Inter-religious Dialogue

At their meeting in Chambésy immediately after the Canberra Assembly, Orthodox representatives raised fundamental questions about the dialogue with other religious traditions. This, however, did not prevent them from stating that "the Orthodox have a long and living experience with members of other religions. Respect for the humanity of others and their sincerely held convictions calls for increased efforts at understanding and peaceful relations, and, whenever possible and appropriate, cooperation in areas of mutual concern." The few activities listed below show that efforts focused on promoting dialogue on issues of mutual interest, a dialogue which could facilitate coexistence and cooperation at the local level.

- *"The Spiritual Significance of Jerusalem for Jews, Christians and Muslims"*

Two colloquia (Glion, Switzerland, 1993; Thessaloniki, Greece, 1996) aiming at facilitating dialogue on an issue that is permeated with a singular religious attention by all three religious communities.

- *"Christian-Muslim Conference on Religion in Central Asia" (Tashkent, 1995)*

Religious leaders of Orthodox and Muslim communities in the five Central Asian Republics were given the opportunity to describe their local situation. Affirming their determination to combat fanaticism and sectarianism, they appealed to the WCC for help in dealing with the threat to interreligious harmony posed by an influx of foreign missionary groups into Central Asia.

11. Consultations with specific interest for or hosted by Orthodox Churches

As a tangible sign of their commitment to the ecumenical movement, Orthodox churches and institutions have often hosted meetings and consultations organized by the WCC. This has been a long term practice, allowing a financial contribution to the Council and offering at the same time an ecclesial, theological, liturgical, and spiritual milieu which is extremely important for the work undertaken by the Council. Thus, most of the activities listed below highlight the significance of the "relational" character of many programmatic activities, which not only respond to concrete needs but also constitute unique opportunities for strengthening the fellowship.

• *"Missionary Congregations in Secularized Europe"*. A long-range programme (1989-1993), including a series of small consultations in various places and exposure visits for parish priests and active members of parishes especially from Orthodox Churches in Eastern European countries.

Meeting of the Advisory Group on Inter-religious dialogue in Istanbul, Turkey (1994).

Meeting of the Unit IV Commission: Sharing and Service, in Alexandria, Egypt (1995).

• *"Christian-Muslim Studies" (1995)*. Consultation jointly organized by WCC/ OIRR leading to the establishment of the Center for Christian-Muslim Studies of the Orthodox University of Balamand, Lebanon.

• *"The Prophetic Mission of Churches in Response to Forced Displacement of People" (Addis Ababa, 1995)*. Global Consultation hosted by the Ethiopian Orthodox Church, in cooperation with the Mekane Yesus Lutheran Church and the Roman Catholic Church. Responding to an urgent human situation for which churches' response and action is extremely important, the consultation has also encouraged ecumenical relationship among the three churches through a joint project.

• *Plenary of the Joint Working Group* between the WCC and the Roman Catholic Church (Orthodox Academy, Crete, 1994; Orthodox Centre, Chambésy, Switzerland, 1996).

• *Theological Consultation at the Ecumenical Institute of Bossey* (1996) in memory of the late Prof. Nikos Nissiotis, former director of the Institute.

• *"Mutual Views and Changing Relations between Christians and Muslims" (Balamand, 1997)*. Colloquium organized in cooperation with the Orthodox University of Balamand.

• *Consultation of Christian and Muslim Centres* specialized in the Study of Islam and Christian-Muslim Relations, hosted by the Orthodox University of Balamand.

• *Meeting of the Faith and Order Board* (Istanbul, Turkey, 1998).

12. International Affairs – Public Issues

This has been a period marked by the most radical political transformation in the world since the end of the Second World War. Many of these changes have especially affected those parts of the world with Orthodox Christian majorities, or where the Orthodox churches have special historical attachments. It has also been a time when the notion of a "clash of cultures" has tended to assign attitudes and motives to the Orthodox churches which are detrimental to their witness for peace and democracy. The WCC has sought to accompany and assist these member churches in a time of transition. The actions listed here are only the public or diplomatic manifestations of this cooperation and accompaniment. Behind them lie multiple efforts to assist these churches with material aid in situations of grave natural and man-made disasters, to interpret the witness of these churches to an often doubting West, and to offer the solidarity of the ecumenical movement with them in times of need. Listed below are only a few representative examples.

- **Former Yugoslavia** (November 1992). Letter from the General Secretaries of the WCC and the CEC to the European governments expressing concern at the plight of thousands of human beings caught up in the civil war and offering services to help the victims.
- **Bosnia-Herzegovina** (December 1992). Letter from General Secretaries of WCC and CEC to the U.N. Secretary-General expressing growing concern about the war and calling upon the U.N. to intensify the search within the international community for a negotiated solution.
- **Armenia/Azerbaijan** (February 1993). Joint appeal by both religious leaders calling on their governments for peaceful resolution of the conflict and for the unconditional release of all hostages and the humane treatment of prisoners of war in the conflict over Nagorno-Karabagh, and announcing the establishment of a United International Humanitarian Fund to give assistance to the victims regardless of faith and nationality.
- **Jerusalem** (May 1993). Statement by participants at the meeting on "The Spiritual Significance of Jerusalem for Jews, Christians and Muslims", agreeing that religious organizations should foster rather than hamper efforts to achieve peace in the city, committing themselves to work to guarantee its sanctity, maintaining its delicate historical, architectural and demographic balance, and condemning all violence and violations of human and national rights.
- **Azerbaijan** (August 1993). Press release condemning the capture of Armenian forces on Azerbaijan territory as a flagrant violation of international law, and calling for an immediate cease-fire to end the escalating war.
- **Georgia** (September 1993). Letter to H.H. Ilia II expressing distress about the conflict in Abkhazia, assuring him of our thoughts and prayers for a speedy end to the conflict.
- **Former Yugoslavia** (October 1993). Letter from the General Secretaries of WCC and CEC to the UN Secretary-General drawing attention to the devastating effects of the current sanctions, urging him to review the policy and enforcement of sanctions.
- **Turkey** (November 1993). Letter to the Prime Minister expressing concern for the status of minorities in Turkey, and in particular the Greek community and its religious expression.
- **Albania** (October 1994). Letter to the Permanent Representative to the UN expressing concern about provisions affecting church-state relations contained in the new draft Constitution submitted for approval by referendum.
- **Chechnya** (December 1994). Letter to H.H. Alexy II encouraging him and Mufti Alsabekov in their joint appeal to those who have the power to refrain from the use of weapons as a means of resolving this dispute and calling for renewed negotiations between the Chechen leadership and the Federal authorities of Russia.
- **Armenia** (April 1995). Letter to the Catholicos of all Armenians and the Catholicosate of Cilicia on the occasion of the 80th anniversary of the Armenian Genocide, expressing concern and solidarity; affirming the WCC's commitment for justice, and praying that the memory of the Armenian martyrs become a source of renewed hope, faith and vision.
- **Middle East** (April 1996). Statement expressing deep concern about Israeli attacks on Lebanon, appealing to the international community to stand firm in its commitment against the use of violence and terror as a means to resolve conflicts, and assuring the churches and people of Lebanon of the WCC's solidarity and continuing prayers.
- • **Ukraine** (April 1996). Statement calling to mind the continuing nature of the Chernobyl disaster, expressing the Council's continued support for existing work with church-related initiatives, especially those to alleviate the suffering of children.
- **Cyprus** (August 1996). Statement expressing concern at the ethnic clashes, and appealing to the leadership of the Greek and Turkish communities to ensure the sanctity of the buffer zone established by the UN to achieve a just and peaceful solution of the conflict.
- **Turkey** (October 1996). Letter to H.H. Patriarch Bartholomew expressing concern over the bomb attack on the Ecumenical Patriarchate; letter to Prime Minister Erbakan expressing gratitude for the

rapid response by the authorities, and giving assurance of the WCC's full cooperation for the protection of the premises of the Patriarchate from any further act of intolerance and aggression.

• **Cyprus** (February 1997). Statement on the situation in Cyprus, issued by the Executive Committee of the WCC meeting at the Kykko Monastery.

• **Albania** (March 1997). Statement by the General Secretaries of the WCC and CEC expressing concern at this time of crisis, welcoming the repeated appeals of the religious leaders to end violence in finding a just and negotiated solution, and urging churches and agencies to assist in the task of meeting human needs and strengthening church ministries to the people.

13. Publications

Orthodox churches have always considered their participation in the ecumenical movement as an opportunity to witness to their faith and share with sisters and brothers of other traditions their theological convictions, liturgical resources and spiritual experiences. Orthodox theologians have manifested their readiness to reconsider through dialogue centuries-old theological issues, to take on contemporary challenges arising from the encounter of distinct traditions and cultures, or to face new sources of tension. The fruits of such a commitment form a rich collection of essays, articles, studies and books which are an integral part of the contemporary ecumenical bibliography. Some of the books published by, or with the contribution of, the WCC during the period under review are listed below:

Belopopsky, Alexander, and Oikonomou, Dimitri (ed.),
> *Orthodoxy and Ecology: Resource Book*, Syndesmos, 1996.

Bria, Ion (ed.)
> *The Sense of Ecumenical Tradition. The ecumenical vision and the witness of the Orthodox*, Geneva: WCC, 1991.

Bria, Ion,
> "Romania: Orthodox identity at a crossroads of Europe", Geneva: WCC, Gospel and Culture Pamphlet No 3, 1995.

Bria Ion,
> *The Liturgy after the Liturgy: Mission and Witness from an Orthodox Perspective*, Geneva: WCC, 1996.

FitzGerald, Thomas,
> *The Orthodox Church*, Westport, Conn.: Greenwood Press, 1995.

FitzGerald, Thomas,
> *The Ecumenical Patriarchate and Christian Unity*, Brookline, Mass.: Holy Cross Orthodox Press, 1997.

George, K.M.,
> *The Silent Roots: Orthodox perspectives on Christian spirituality*, Geneva: WCC, 1994.

George, K.M.,
> "The Early Church. Defending the Faith, Witness and Proclamation: Patristic Perspectives", Geneva: WCC, Gospel and Culture Pamphlet 15, 1996.

Keshishian, Aram,
> *Conciliar Fellowship: A common goal*, Geneva: WCC, 1992.

Lemopoulos, Georges (ed.),
> *You Shall be my Witnesses! Mission Stories from the Eastern and Oriental Orthodox Churches*, Katerini: Tertios, 1992.

Lemopoulos, Georges (ed.),
>   *The Seventh Assembly of the World Council of Churches, Canberra, February 1991: The Assembly, Documents and Evaluations,* Katerini: Tertios, 1992 (in Greek).

Lemopoulos, Georges (transl.),
>   *The Churches' Mission in a post-Communist Society: Common Witness and Diakonia in Romania* (original title: "Window on AIDRom"), Katerini:Tertios, 1993 (in Greek)

Lemopoulos, Georges (ed.),
>   *Let Us Pray to the Lord. A collection of prayers from Eastern and Oriental Orthodox traditions,* Geneva: WCC, 1996.

Lemopoulos, Georges (ed.),
>   *The Ecumenical Movement, the Churches and the World Council of Churches.An Orthodox contribution to the reflection process on "The Common Understanding and Vision of the WCC",* Geneva: WCC, Syndesmos: Bialystok, 1996.

Limouris, Gennadios (ed.),
>   *The Place of the Woman in the Orthodox Church and the Question of the Ordination of Women.* Inter-orthodoxSymposium,Rhodes,Greece, 30 October-7 November 1988, Katerini: Tertios, 1992.

Limouris, Gennadios (ed.),
>   *Orthodox Visions of Ecumenism: Statements, Messages, and Reports on the Ecumenical Movement,* Geneva: WCC, 1994.

Sabev, Todor,
>   *The Orthodox Churches in the WCC: Towards the Future,* Geneva: WCC, Bialystok: Syndesmos, 1996.

Sauca, Ioan (ed.),
>   *Orthodoxy and Cultures: Inter-Orthodox Consultation on Gospel and Cultures, Addis Ababa, Ethiopia, 19-27 January 1996,* Geneva: WCC, 1996.

Van Beek, Huibert, and Lemopoulos, Georges (ed.),
>   *Proclaiming Christ Today: Orthodox-Evangelical Consultation, Alexandria, July 1995,* Geneva: WCC – Bialystok: Syndesmos, 1996.

>   "Lenten Liturgical Bible Studies", in: *Turn to God: Rejoice in Hope, Bible Studies-Meditations-Liturgical Aids,* Geneva: WCC, 1996.

In preparation:

Belopopsky, Alexander, and Talvivaara, Anu (ed.),
>   *Orthodox Youth and Ecumenism: Resource Book,* Geneva: WCC – Bialystok: Syndesmos.

FitzGerald, Kyriaki,
>   Papers from the two meetings with Orthodox women (Damascus and Istanbul).

Pirri-Simonian, Teny,
>   Reports of the Religious Education Programme.

Pirri-Simonian, Teny,
>   Papers of Bossey Seminars on Women and Orthodox Spirituality.

14. Looking Ahead

The period under review began with many hopes and expectations. Indeed, the wind of change and freedom in Central and Eastern Europe offered the churches possibilities for renewed ecumenical commitment. There was tremendous potential for strengthened cooperation in offering a common witness, in enabling the local churches to rebuild and organize their parish life, their diaconal services and their religious and theological education. In this atmosphere of joy and promising possibilities, the only canonical Orthodox Church which was not member of the fellowship of the WCC, the Autocephalous Orthodox Church of Albania, joined her sisters in membership of the WCC. Yet only a few years later many Orthodox Churches have witnessed the increase of an extremely critical and even hostile attitude towards the ecumenical movement and the WCC. Competitive relations in mission, uneasiness with parts of the ecumenical agenda, internal sociopolitical and economic uncertainties, new possibilities for clergy and laity to participate in reflection and decision-making processes are only some of the reasons which might explain the new reality. Whatever the causes of the emerging difficulties were, one of their consequences has been the withdrawal of the Georgian Orthodox Church from the membership of the WCC and of CEC, while in some other churches Orthodox participation in the ecumenical movement is being extensively discussed.

It is difficult to draw any conclusion at this point. Orthodox Churches will have to go through this painful and yet necessary experience, as was the case with many other churches in the past and in many other contexts. Orthodox Churches will have to continue to review together the fundamental principles of their participation in the ecumenical movement and, in the light of new ecclesial, pastoral, missionary, and ecumenical realities, formulate anew their positions and their expectations. The ecumenical movement itself, and particularly the WCC will have to pay more attention to this new situation and to listen more carefully to those voices coming from Orthodox sisters and brothers who may have a different understanding of or different expectations from the movement.

It is hoped therefore that the contents of the present report shall constitute a factual and objective basis for future discussions, common reflection, and attempts to assess the past, in order to face together the challenges of the present, and to anticipate together the future.

Geneva, February 1998

Orthodox-WCC Relations
A Contribution from the Orthodox Task Force
28 January 1998

The WCC Orthodox Task Force has prepared these observations for the Staff Executive Group at the request of the General Secretary, Dr Konrad Raiser. His request follows upon a discussion at the 1997 Central Committee meeting and its recommendation that the Executive Committee "design and implement a procedure for conducting a dialogue on the Orthodox Churches' participation in and contribution to the life of the WCC."

The discussions of the Orthodox Task Force which led to this paper took note of the serious concern and alarm which many of our colleagues and others associated with the Council have expressed with regard to the issue of Orthodox participation in the WCC. The Church of Georgia has withdrawn from membership in the Council. The Council of Bishops of the Russian Orthodox Church and the Holy Synod of Bishops of the Serbian Orthodox Church have requested a pan-Orthodox discussion of Orthodox participation in the WCC. In many other places, including North America and Western Europe, the involvement of the Orthodox in the WCC is a topic of serious discussion. In our own visits to Orthodox churches, the members of the Orthodox Task Force are frequently questioned about the purpose and the direction of the Council, and of Orthodox participation in it.

Such statements of alarm and concern, while real and pressing, need to be taken in the context of the growing popular antiecumenical sentiment within the Orthodox churches, but also in the context of what has been since the beginning a serious and heartfelt commitment to the ecumenical movement on the part of the Orthodox. This commitment has been expressed powerfully through the Third Pre-conciliar Pan-Orthodox Conference (1986), the active participation of many Eastern and Oriental Orthodox heads of churches and hierarchs, and the continuous constructive Orthodox contribution to ecumenical thought.

1. Orthodox Concerns: Recent Statements

Orthodox participants have expressed their concerns regarding the WCC within the context of a number of recent consultations as well as at the Canberra Assembly and in inter-Orthodox consultations which followed it. The following examples should be noted.

The Sofia Consultation (1981) mainly – although not exclusively – focused on procedural, structural and institutional concerns: Orthodox representation in governing and consultative bodies; Orthodox representation on all levels of WCC staff; nomination of Orthodox representatives; voting procedures especially with regard to issues of faith. Almost twenty years later, it could be said that most of these concerns received a response at some level. The proposal for a "family model" was also made in Sofia, though in a preliminary way and mainly with reference to decision-making procedures.

During the *World Conference on Mission and Evangelism* (San Antonio, 1989) the Orthodox expressed their concern with regard to the agenda of the WCC in connection to its Basis, i.e., about the centrality of Christ, inclusive language and the ordination of women to the priesthood.

The *Reflection of Orthodox Participants* at the Canberra Assembly (1991), and that of the *Inter-Orthodox Consultation* at Chambésy (1991) took the WCC *agenda* as their entry point. Both statements stressed the imperative of working for visible unity, expressed concern about increasing departure form the Basis (in the nature and scope of some programmes as well as in language), and criticized the way in which priorities for the WCC are defined. In Canberra there was reference to the decision-making processes, while in Chambésy vital activities for the life and witness of the Orthodox churches were highlighted (Christian education; ecumenical formation).

The *Orthodox Consultation on the CUV* at Chambésy (1996) for the first time classified the difficulties ("dilemmas," according to the document itself) faced by the Orthodox under three headings: **theological**, **cultural**, and **procedural**. Even if the contents of each heading often repeated previous concerns, the methodology implied was new and may prove helpful in future reflections on the tensions and uncertainties which underlie the relationship between the WCC and the Orthodox churches.

A number of significant questions emerge here which need to be taken into serious consideration in future discussions:

(a)   Why do the Orthodox feel that their concerns have not been or are not being heard? Why did the Orthodox feel the need to go back to the practice of "separate statements" in spite of the fact that preparatory Orthodox consultations were organized before every major ecumenical meeting?

(b)   If the Orthodox concerns were recognized by the senior staff and the leadership of the WCC, why did these concerns not have a clear and visible impact on the WCC's activities as a whole?

(c)   What is the significance of the fact that many of the concerns expressed by the Orthodox, and thus labeled as "Orthodox," are in fact held in common with many other partners within the fellowship?

2. New Challenges

We recognize that many of the concerns identified by the Orthodox in recent years have been affected by a number of new challenges which face both the Orthodox Church and the Council.

(a) *New developments in the ecumenical community.*

Paragraph 1.4 of the CUV document recalls the changes in the Council and in the ecumenical movement during the last fifty years: the increase in member churches; the increase in membership from the South; greater cooperation with national and regional ecumenical organizations; evolving Roman Catholic participation in the ecumenical movement; greater participation of women in the life of the WCC; an emerging common tradition of shared convictions on faith, life and witness. The way in which these developments influence the life of the Council has to be taken seriously into consideration in terms of its ecumenical, theological, relational, and institutional consequences. Each of these factors influence in one way or another, positively or negatively, the degree of Orthodox participation in the ecumenical movement and the WCC.

(b) *New developments in the Protestant churches.*

There is an Orthodox perception that present-day Protestant partners have undergone radical changes in ethos and priorities compared to those with which dialogue and cooperation had started before and during the creation of the WCC. Among the perceived factors which led to changes within the mainline Protestant churches one could mention: an internal crisis with deep theological and ecclesiological and ethical roots, leading to tensions or even divisions within the same Communion; an inability to challenge the world agenda stemming partly from an over identification with that agenda. Another element to be kept in mind is the fact that Evangelical and Pentecostal churches are growing rapidly, and that there are signs that some are open to the ecumenical movement. The following questions arise: To what extent do internal developments in the Protestant world affect Orthodox participation in the ecumenical movement? To what extent is "evangelical ecumenism" a challenge both to Orthodox and mainline Protestants within the WCC? To what extent would a fuller appreciation of the life and witness of Evangelical and Pentecostal communities contribute to further divisions within the "Protestant" family?

(c) *New developments in the Roman Catholic Church.*

Roman Catholic commitment to ecumenism has radically changed since the Second Vatican Council. The RCC is involved in bilateral dialogues with the Orthodox Church and many other churches and confessional families. The RCC is also a full partner in "conciliar ecumenism" and has accepted full membership in a great number of National Councils of Churches and some Regional Ecumenical Organizations. At the same time it is apparent that the RCC is involved in renewed mission activity in predominantly Orthodox contexts. What does all of this mean for Orthodox participation in the ecumenical movement? What does it mean in terms of the "Protestant-Orthodox" dialogue within the WCC? And, what does it mean for the

WCC itself at a time when there is a search for a more inclusive and appropriate "ethos?"

(d) *New developments in the Orthodox churches.*

Especially after political changes in Central and Eastern Europe, it is clear that both the WCC and Orthodox churches should direct greater attention towards the theological and ecclesiological issues which the Orthodox have identified with regard to their participation in the ecumenical movement. Likewise, both the WCC and the Orthodox churches must also pay greater attention to the new sociological and cultural realities and dynamics — including both new opportunities as well as new tendencies towards nationalism and isolationism — which are shaping peoples' lives and the churches' witness in their respective societies. Internal tensions (theological, ecclesial, socio-political, personal) are important factors which need to be identified in order to understand the present situation. What is the relationship between these new internal challenges and the difficulties within the ecumenical movement? What was the real impact of WCC documents and statements on Common Witness and Proselytism both within the member churches and within particular difficult contexts? How is the fellowship experienced and manifested in such sensitive contexts?

3. Fundamental Orthodox questions

Looking more carefully at previous Orthodox documents, as well as to the few Orthodox responses to the CUV draft, certain fundamental Orthodox questions and concerns emerge. These could form the main points of an agenda for future encounters and discussions:

– *the nature of the unity we seek*

Orthodox have opposed what some call "a confessional or denominational adjustment" and repeatedly have called for unity in the faith, tradition, and life of the undivided Church, the *Una Sancta*. Uncertainties around this question lead to inevitable unclarities in WCC statements, as well as in the positions taken by staff and in the programmes they administer, not to mention debates and criticism surrounding "Branch" ecclesiologies, unity and diversity, the understanding of visible unity, and so on.

– *membership and ecclesiology*

The meaning of membership in the WCC is well set out in the CUV, but issues arise from certain realities apparent from the list of WCC member churches. The Council has expressed its joy at new developments and convergences within the Protestant world, especially in Europe (Porvoo, Leuenberg, Meissen). However, the fact that many churches of the same ecclesial and theological tradition are accepted as members of the WCC from the same region or country raises a number of questions from the Orthodox perspective. What does local ecumenism mean for Protestant churches of the same historical tradition? What is the understanding of a local (Protestant) church "truly united?"

– the nature and character of WCC documents and decisions

In spite of the official, institutional position of the WCC, representatives of member churches and active ecumenists, as well as some WCC staff, nurture uncertainties about the character of the documents prepared or the decisions taken by the WCC (even some Orthodox would speak of "agreed documents" similar to the ones of the bi-laterals). The Antelias meeting has initiated a discussion on this subject and offered some clarifications. The CUV document provides some hints in its Preface. But much still needs to be done. WCC documents often remain unclear on certain basic levels: who is speaking – "the WCC", "the churches", a (or the) "Universal Church?"

– ambiguity of terminology

The Orthodox have consistently held that the "ecumenical movement" refers specifically to the quest for Christian reconciliation and unity. In the discussions related to the CUV, it was clear that there is growing ambiguity regarding the meaning of the phrase. The CUV has tried to bring some clarification regarding the understanding of the word "ecumenical." Yet, Orthodox feel that the phrase "ecumenical movement" receives various interpretations. Sometimes the phrase is used to describe inter-Protestant activities. At other times, it is used to refer to a wide range of associations devoted to particular causes and often involving non-Christians. It can also be taken to refer to a vague post-denominational reality. The different meanings of the word "ecumenical" and the phrase "ecumenical movement" are creating serious misunderstandings and are leading to considerable frustration.

– the ecclesiological problem

The problems cited in the two above paragraphs points to a more basic issue. The WCC by its nature embraces churches which have different ecclesiologies and self-understandings. Somewhat simplistically put, some (i.e., Orthodox, Roman Catholics) identify their church or church family with the *Una Sancta*, while acknowledging ecclesial reality outside their ecclesial borders. Others (i.e., many Protestants) see the *Una Sancta* in "universalist" terms as constituted by the sum of the different Christian churches in the form they exist now. But a clear accounting for these ecclesiologies and their implications, such as can happily be found in CUV chapter 3, is the exception rather than the rule in WCC documents. The WCC's commitment to embrace the churches' different self-understandings is more often addressed through vague phraseology, or through statements which imply rather the Protestant understanding as expressed above, speaking of the member churches as the universal church of Christ.

– the WCC agenda and priorities

One may accept the reality that the WCC follows its member churches' requests and needs in defining its agenda. At the same time, the Council is quite rightly obliged to play a prophetic role and suggest to the churches issues of wider concern (racism, the dignity of women and concern for the creation would be three examples). However, the Orthodox Churches are concerned about the genesis and content of some of the WCC agenda. Sometimes the agenda is fixed at the staff level, sometimes at the level of a governing body. The process of decision-making, the relationship between the priorities of member churches, of the governing bodies, and the final forms of programmes and actions of staff is often inconsistent and is sometimes contradictory. How can the Orthodox introduce more effectively their priorities and concerns into the agenda of the WCC?

– representation and participation

Aside from the fact that the "25% rule" of Orthodox participation is a current "working hypothesis" and not a constitutional provision, it should be clear that the nature of "ecclesial/confessional" representation and participation needs to be approached differently from any other categories which are grounded in sociological and geographical criteria. The Orthodox find it perplexing to be seen and dealt within "quota" terms alongside "women", "youth", or people from certain geographical regions. The 25% rule was instituted in recognition of the fact that there are very different ecclesiologies operating in the Orthodox Church and the various Protestant churches. These different ecclesiologies are the basis for the wide discrepancy between the number of regional Orthodox churches and the number of Protestant churches. Related to this is the issue of adequate Orthodox representation on WCC staff, in programmatic and senior management positions.

In this context the Orthodox need also to ask themselves why they find it difficult to produce qualified Orthodox participants in ecumenical activities, and financial resources to support ecumenical organizations. This question involves both internal Orthodox problems as well as all the ambiguities of Orthodox relations with the WCC which are being addressed in this paper. The two clearly feed into each other, which points to the need to address both poles: intra-Orthodox dynamics and WCC dynamics.

– worship

The Orthodox recognize that greater attention is being given to the importance of worship at WCC Assemblies, consultations and meetings. At the same time however, Orthodox are troubled at many aspects of these worship services. More often that not, these services reflect a distinctively Protestant ethos while often referred to as being "ecumenical." Moreover, as has been stated before, Orthodox are deeply troubled when these services include so-called "inclusive language." Given that our existence as a fellowship is grounded in the first article of the WCC constitution, declaring the glorification of God, Father, Son and Holy Spirit, should not all worship services, at every level of WCC life, use the language which we have adopted in our Basis?

– The question of intercommunion or "eucharistic hospitality"

Having their own particular understanding of what the Eucharist is and means, the Orthodox have consistently emphasized that participation in the Eucharist is an expression of unity, and have therefore avoided formally any acceptance of "intercommunion" or "eucharistic hospitality." While the position of the Orthodox is constantly reaffirmed, there is a reluctance among some Protestants to honor this perspective. The theological reasons are by-and-large disregarded in favor of interpreting the Orthodox stance as "backward", "closed-minded" or even "arrogant". Recent discussions with regard to the Eucharistic celebrations at the coming Assembly have reflected the above. It is also in this regard that the Orthodox have noted that the so-called "Lima Liturgy" cannot be properly be viewed as an "ecumenical" liturgy in which all can participate. Likewise, the Orthodox would also be unable to endorse or to participate fully in any gathering which gives the impression of being an "ecumenical Eucharist."

– *Orthodox "culture"*

While the Orthodox come from many different regions with their own cultures, there can be said to exist as well an Orthodox culture. The structures, styles and protocols emanating from this culture are often difficult for non-Orthodox to understand and appreciate. In particular, Orthodox relationship to clergy and hierarchy, including forms of address for them and attitude towards them, can for some be alienating. Related to this, Orthodox protocols can have the effect of slowing down processes which would otherwise operate in a more "well-oiled" Western way. It is to be regretted, however, when these kinds of situations are viewed with intolerance, or worse, a sense of moral condescension.

4. Towards a new ethos

Konrad Raiser's reflections in his book *To Be the Church* and those of H.H. Catholicos Aram I of Cilicia in his report to the CC of September 1997 offer valuable insights into the direction of a new ethos for the Council. Raiser points toward developments and new challenges. Catholicos Aram introduces preliminary thoughts about the "consensus" model. To what extent could the awareness of a deadlock on the one hand, and some concrete suggestions on the other, inform and enrich the future debate about a "new ethos" in terms of experiencing and manifesting the fellowship (representation, decision-making, etc.)? To what extent could the search for a "new ethos" be related to the concern for a "new model" of organization such as the "family model" suggested by the Orthodox and others?

Discussions on the "family model" should certainly take into consideration the experiences of the REOs and the NCCs who have adopted some form of this model or who are considering its adoption. Is it possible that the "family model" could provide a way out of the present polarizations between "Orthodox" and "Protestants" within the WCC? Is it also possible that this model could provide a basis for full participation in the membership of the Council of other churches? If the latter is the case, the other potential partners should be included in the discussions right from the beginning. Finally, it might be necessary to find a new vocabulary to address the dynamic we have been up until now calling the "family model." For example, it might be helpful to raise the question of the relationship between "church family" and "church ethos."

5. Concrete steps towards a genuine dialogue

The following are suggestions which could help keep us oriented towards a genuine and fruitful dialogue:

– Keep the issue of an "Orthodox-Protestant dialogue" within the WCC continuously on the agenda of the Central and Executive Committees as a major concern. The aim here is to facilitate an ever clearer understanding of the various Orthodox concerns and positions. As we have said, these concerns may result from different factors. Yet they often reflect real pastoral and theological dynamics or orientations which are either radically or subtly different from the Protestant ones.

– Continue with to organize meetings similar to the one held in Antelias. This entails (a) an emphasis on the *sharing* rather than the *decision-making* character of the encounter, (b) a *de facto* expression of the 50/50 reality of Orthodox and Protestant participation in the Council, and (c) relating WCC activities and vision to the highest level of authority in the Orthodox churches.

– Listen more carefully, especially during high-level visits, to Orthodox concerns, particularly in the places where there are internal difficulties. This should be done with attention to Orthodox sensitivities and protocol for such contacts.

– Provide better visibility, in the form of information about and interpretation, of WCC activities and projects related to the Orthodox churches (especially theological and Christian education; ecumenical formation; missiological preparation).

– Encourage and assist, through both human and material resources, Orthodox Institutions which are ready to facilitate and carry on ecumenical relationships and dialogues at various levels, and in particular those which take up the task of the ecumenical formation of the younger generation (e.g., Balamand, Holy Cross, St. Vladimir's, the Orthodox Academy in Crete, the Ecumenical Society in Thessaloniki, etc.)

Conclusion

These are particularly critical times for the WCC and its relationship with the Orthodox churches. The Harare Assembly is perceived by some member churches as a decisive opportunity to develop or end their participation in the WCC. The Orthodox Task Force offers these observations with the hope that they will contribute to further reflection within the WCC with the goal of enhancing Orthodox participation. The concerns which have been identified here are not the result only of internal difficulties within certain Orthodox churches, nor are they to be seen as a purely sociopolitical phenomenon. They are being raised throughout the Orthodox churches in all parts of the world, and some are shared as well by many other ecumenical partners. It is our view that the issues and concerns noted in this paper must become the topic of serious and continuous exchange within the various governing bodies of the WCC, as well as among staff colleagues.

We offer these reflections in the hope that they will facilitate this discussion, and with the conviction that genuine dialogue at all levels can contribute in strengthening the fellowship.